FORTUNE'S ALWAYS HIDING?

FORTUNE'S ALWAYS HIDING?

West Ham United from the Inside

KIRK BLOWS

MAINSTREAM
PUBLISHING

EDINBURGH AND LONDON

First published in Great Britain in 1999 by
MAINSTREAM PUBLISHING COMPANY (EDINBURGH) LTD
7 Albany Street
Edinburgh EH1 3UG

ISBN 1 84018 250 4

A catalogue record for this book is available from the British Library

Typeset in Garamond
Printed and bound in Great Britain by Creative Print Design

Acknowledgements

Dedicated to my mother Pat and sister Karen for their continued support.

With thanks to: Miss Jo Davies, Miss Terry Lewis and Miss Cathy Howes for their encouragement, to Penny Ganz and Helen Casey, and to my fellow Eastsiders, Gerry Levey, John Raven, Spencer Banks and Robert Banks for putting up with me.

Also to: Martin Allen, Rachel Anderson, Richard Austin, Steve Bacon, Robert Banks, Julian Baskcomb, Ian Bishop, Steve Blowers, John and Rob Bolle, Billy Bonds, Tim Breacker, Nick Callow, Tony Cottee, Gerry Cox, Trevor Davies, Julian and Kay Dicks and family, Paolo Di Canio, Darren at the Skiddaw, Andy Dillon, Iain Dowie, Pandora D'Souza, Philip Evans, Samantha Finn, Gary Firmager, Marc-Vivien Foe, Danny Francis, Paulo Futre, Eddie Gillam, John Green, Richard Hall, Steve Harris, John Hartson, John Hellier, Shaka Hislop, Tony and Chris Hogg, Mattie Holmes, Tina Huggett, Michael Hughes, Don Hutchison, Marc Isaacs, John at the Carlton Bridge, Frank Lampard Jnr, Frank Lampard Snr, Alan Lewis, Lily's Bar, Steve Lomas, John Lyall, Lou Macari, Javier Margas, Marquis of Granby, Alvin Martin, Tony McDonald, Ludek Miklosko, Sally Miller, John Moncur, Cliff Moulder, Jeremy Nicholas, Niall O'Mara, Hamant Patel, Steve Potts, Frank Praverman, Tony Prince, Chris Raistrick, Harry Redknapp, Antonia Rodwell, Kevin Rolfe, Keith Rowland, Neil Ruddock, Joe Sach, Les Sealey, Ben Sharratt, John Smith, Damian Smyth, Russell Stander, Jack Steggles, Peter Stewart, Peter Storrie, Mitchell Sutton, Tennents Extra, Adam Velasco, Geoff Weston, Marney Whyte, Gwyn Williams, Danny Williamson, West Ham Utd Supporters Club, Ian Wright and Kathy Zerouk, without whom . . .

Chapter One

'RUSHIE, YOU'RE A F***ING C***!!!'

His face was a deep claret and the air around him blue as an exasperated Harry Redknapp tore his hair out in frustration from the touchline. Matthew Rush was having what's commonly known as a nightmare as the Hammers struggled against TSV Munich 1860 in a friendly game to commemorate the thirtieth anniversary of that famous European Cup-Winners' Cup final win over the Germans. But Harry was hardly in friendly mood as the erratic winger fired balls into space, outer space and all over the place.

'You're a c***, Rush! Frank, is he a c*** or what?'

Assistant boss Frank Lampard turned to his appropriately fury-faced friend and in typically relaxed manner replied, 'Yeah, he's a c***, Harry.'

The date was 29 July 1995 and it was a sunny Saturday evening in Munich. The West Ham management had kindly allowed the representatives of West Ham's official club magazine to sit alongside them on the bench inside the Grünwalder stadium and we loved every minute of it, even if Harry didn't.

He had good reason to complain, of course – his team had gone 2–0 down to a mediocre side and were playing like 11 strangers. While Rush was having a terrible time on the right flank, Northern Ireland international Keith Rowland was trying nervously to operate on the left side of defence as substitute goalie Les Sealey – operating in an unofficial coaching capacity – virtually played the Irishman's game for him from the sidelines. 'Touch, Keith . . . Man on, Rowlie . . . Knock it long, Keith . . . Wide, wide, WIDE!!!'

All this made for tremendous entertainment, though, to the extent that we hardly noticed the Hammers scoring twice in the last five minutes of the half to pull things back to 2–2. A comical collision between Rowland and midfielder Danny Williamson, however, allowed the Germans to regain the advantage as Manfred Schwabl ran on to grab his second goal, before birthday boy Alvin Martin – a sprightly 37 – quickly got *his* second of the match to set up an exciting final 20 minutes.

A penalty award five minutes from time surely meant the Hammers had the game in the bag, but Martin Allen's tame shot was saved and, with time running out, a quick free kick was played back to Rowland. The defender was caught napping, however, and before you could say 'lousy leiderhose' Winkler had intercepted and smacked the ball past goalkeeper Ludek Miklosko into the back of the net. 4–3 to TSV.

'We've got the draw, one of our players is down injured and what do we do? Take a f***king quick free kick to somebody who's not looking! Ridiculous!' exclaimed Redknapp in disbelief as he trudged away in disgust, leaving us first-timers on the bench wondering what the West Ham boss was like when his team was in serious competition. To make matters worse, Dutch striker Marco Boogers had been making his début following his £800,000 arrival from Sparta Rotterdam and, despite winning that penalty, he had been guilty of three glaring misses during the game.

'Finishing is apparently his strong point!' quipped the ever-affable Frank Lampard as we reflected on the match over dinner back at the team's hotel later that evening. Harry was sitting beside me and, thankfully, was in a rather more restrained frame of mind by then. 'The thing is, you just can't buy a player for less than a million nowadays,' he said, somewhat resignedly.

'Er, why have you just bought one then?' I asked.

'That's all we could afford,' he admitted, well aware that some more wheeler-dealing was going to have to take place for the club to build on its successful battle against relegation a few months earlier. Despite an impressive run which had seen just one defeat in the final 11 games, culminating in the 1–1 draw with Manchester United that denied Alex Ferguson's men the Premiership trophy, the bookies had made the Hammers joint favourites – alongside Coventry – for the big drop the following year. If the performance against TSV was anything to go by, it was gonna be another long hard season, just like the last one . . .

Chapter Two

West Ham may have survived their first year back in the top flight, finishing a comfortable thirteenth in a season which had seen much-worshipped left-back Julian Dicks swapped for Liverpool's David Burrows, Mike Marsh and the cash to buy striker Lee Chapman from Portsmouth, but it was the summer of 1994 (rather than the promotion celebrations of 1993) that I feel represents the most significant watershed in recent Hammers history.

Harry Redknapp replaced Billy Bonds as manager on 10 August, just ten days before the new campaign's kick-off, and the controversy is still being discussed to this day as a direct result of the icy silence which has formed a frozen wall between the two men.

Billy and Harry had been great mates, of course. They played together in West Ham's colours for a period of five years after Bonds's arrival from Charlton Athletic in 1967 and, such was the instant rapport between them, Redknapp was best man at Billy's wedding that year. While Bonzo established himself as a living legend at Upton Park over the next 21 seasons as a player, putting on his boots of battle a remarkable 793 times and captaining the Hammers to two FA Cup wins (eventually moving into the manager's chair in 1990), Harry left for Bournemouth in 1972 and, following spells in different capacities at Brentford, Oxford and Seattle, returned to the south coast to establish himself as a manager who knew how to play his cards right when dealt a tough hand.

After a nine-year tenure at Dean Court, 'H' (as the popular Cockney was known) was invited back to West Ham as Billy's assistant following the club's traumatic relegation from Division One in 1992 amid the controversy of the Bond Scheme. With opposition to the fund-raising concept reaching intense levels and matches being repeatedly disrupted by public protests, it seemed as if Billy was on the verge of losing patience, especially when we heard that a fan had shown aggression towards him at the end of the final game of the season.

With Redknapp at Bonzo's side, however, things stabilised and, despite a mere £215,000 being spent on three new players during the close season, the Hammers enjoyed a successful campaign to bounce straight back (to what was now known as the Premiership). Nevertheless, many got the feeling that it was Harry who was pulling the strings within the management partnership, assuming control on the training field and becoming increasingly active in the transfer market.

The departure of the controversial Dicks shortly into the season, as the Hammers struggled to acclimatise to top-flight football again, was an early example of Redknapp's gambling instincts. The tough-tackling defender had already had a bust-up with a frustrated Bonds during the half-time break at Coventry in August ('He smashed a fella in the face with his elbow and when we told him he was being irresponsible he wanted to have a fight with Bill!' revealed Harry when I later spoke to him about the incident) and with relationships as flawed as the early campaign's results, the sale of the club's best player was seen as a necessary sacrifice.

'It was *me* who sold Julian to Liverpool,' declared Redknapp when I interviewed him for the player's *Terminator* biography in 1996. 'I thought a change of club might just sort him out and I knew Bill wasn't happy with Dicksy being here.' Both management partners acknowledged the gamble they were taking by letting Dicks go, but the three-for-the-price-of-one deal has since become something of a Redknapp trademark and it was no surprise to hear that it was he who negotiated the terms with Anfield boss Graeme Souness.

The shifting balance of power between the two men – in terms of their roles – would not have gone unnoticed by the West Ham board of directors and when Redknapp advised them of an offer he'd received to return to Bournemouth in a senior capacity, they were understandably reluctant to see him go.

Discussions between the various parties then ensued, during which it was suggested that a change of responsibilities take place, with Billy perhaps becoming a paid director. His nose put out of joint, however, Bonds announced his intention to leave and, although needing a couple of days to consider how things might be perceived, Redknapp formally accepted the post as first-team manager while agreeing a five-year contract.

Hence it was Harry's mugshot which adorned the inaugural issue of the revamped *Hammers News*, with the word *Magazine* attached to the monthly publication's name to reflect its new-look format (following seven years as a tabloid newspaper). The management shake-up had clearly taken place in the later stages of the August '94 issue's production, but there was still time to dedicate the opening news pages to the story while editor Tony McDonald also paid tribute to Bonds, mourning 'the departure of a great club servant'.

The magazine's policy of addressing all the key topics of debate was reflected in its detailing of how Redknapp had threatened to quit the club too, so concerned was he by suggestions that he'd cynically manipulated the situation. 'I couldn't have lived with the thought that people might be thinking I'd stabbed my mate in the back,' he said. Billy's comment that the club had looked to 'shuffle the pack' and move him upstairs was also aired.

Managing director Peter Storrie stressed that the club had been 'in a very difficult position' with Bonds apparently intimating that he might not want to continue on his own should Harry have taken Bournemouth's offer. 'We were faced with the possibility of not only losing one part of the management duo but two! And where would that have left us?' added Storrie, as the magazine attempted to deal with the question of whether some kind of stitch-up had taken place, as had been suggested by some.

There was certainly a feeling that Bonds was becoming increasingly disenchanted with things, especially after £1 million-new-signing Joey Beauchamp had complained of feeling homesick just a day after leaving Oxford United. Billy would hardly have been in the best of temperaments as the club broached the issue of his position at Upton Park. Needless to say, Redknapp's immediate duty – aside from appointing brother-in-law Frank Lampard as his assistant – was to bounce Beauchamp out of the club.

Bonds headed through the exit gates with a cheque paying up the remaining three years of his contract, reported to be in the region of £500,000, and while it is standard for clubs to attach confidentiality agreements to pay-offs, those who know Billy well understand that the man has far too much dignity to complain publicly about his treatment or start pointing accusatory fingers. Immediately, at least. At the time of this upheaval I was just a freelance contributor to *Hammers News Magazine* (*HNM*), but having moved into the editor's chair in December 1994 I've since come into contact with several people who know exactly how Bonds feels about the circumstances of his departure and Redknapp's role in it.

The matter entered the public domain again in 1998 when Harry confirmed in his autobiography that the pair had not spoken for four years, attributing the deterioration of their relationship as much to people stirring up trouble by communicating erroneous information between them as to his assuming Billy's position. I interviewed Redknapp about his book when it hit the shelves and couldn't resist the opportunity of asking him if the matter was something he'd particularly wanted to clarify. 'I knew that people would want to know about what happened when I took over at West Ham, so it was just a case of telling it how it was. It was a very difficult time,' he confided, 'probably the most difficult period I've ever been through in football. I came back to my home in Bournemouth after Billy had said he was leaving and I really had no intention of going back to West Ham. It was only after talking to Frank Lampard and Peter Storrie that I decided to take the job, because I didn't want anybody to think I had done anything to Bill that wasn't right.'

When asked about the four-year silence, he admitted that he 'hadn't really spoken to Billy for ten years before going back to West Ham anyway. Bill's not the type of bloke who picks up the phone, he's a very private person.'

That may well be the case – Bonds was renowned for being first out of the showers and heading off home during his playing days, putting his family ahead of socialising, but he clearly continues to feel he has good reason to maintain his stance. I interviewed Billy when writing *Terminator* and was grateful for his honesty and time, but with Julian already having gone to Liverpool by the time of the management mix-up, there was no reason to bring the subject up. But that wasn't the case in April 1999 when I was asked if I'd be interested in running an exclusive interview with Bonzo in *HNM*.

Given the man's 27 years at Upton Park, as player, captain, youth-team manager and first-team boss, I thought he was certainly entitled to his place in the magazine for the very first time since leaving the club. I therefore awarded the feature five pages and, although knowing it was the piece that readers would want to turn to first, I resisted the temptation to make it the lead story and placed it second to a conversation with Italian hitman Paolo Di Canio. Don't want to be seen gratuitously digging dirt now, do we?

We therefore focused the conversation on what Bonds will be remembered most for – what he achieved as player and manager – but it was still fair to ask if he could foresee the day when he and Harry might see eye to eye and be friends again. 'No, I've got no time for the man,' he replied, although he denied that any bitterness still remained regarding his departure. 'Life's too short to worry about things like that – it's all water under the bridge.'

While never attempting to rid his veins of claret-and-blue blood ('I'm still a West Ham man,' he insisted) Billy has also managed Millwall and coached at Queens Park Rangers, while in more recent times he's been seen in various press boxes as a match analyst for Capital Gold Sport. I found myself sitting next to him during the game at Derby County in December 1997 (nope, didn't raise the subject of his leaving then either!), but the first time I can recall Bonds actually attending a press conference in the presence of Redknapp was at Leicester's Filbert Street ground towards the end of the 1998–99 season.

Bill sat at the back of the room, with apparently no eye contact taking place between the two men. And following the publication of the Bonds interview in *HNM*, I subsequently heard that Harry was less than pleased to see the piece, something which surprised me somewhat given its balanced approach and also the fact that, according to his own book, he 'still loves him to bits'.

Whatever Redknapp's intentions when talking to the West Ham board in 1994, it's understandable that Billy should feel victimised and under-appreciated as a manager, especially after presiding over two promotions. Yet the directors made the right decision in offering Harry control of first-team affairs. It's easy to say that now, of course, with the squad having established itself in the Premiership and secured the second-best league placing in the club's history (fifth, in 1999). I've also spoken to several men – Dicks and Jimmy Quinn, among them – who've played under Bonzo and question how much he really was cut out to be a manager.

The Hammers hierarchy should be credited with recognising Redknapp's growing influence on the team's fortunes during his two years as Billy's assistant and fans should at least be reassured to see the directors making brave decisions if that's what they feel is in the best interests of the club. Such actions might seem ruthless but previous West Ham boards may not have had the foresight to initiate the change – unless, of course, it was too late. In view of Bonds's apparent reluctance as boss (being thrust into the hotseat after the controversial exit of Lou Macari in February 1990), Harry's cardsharp character and 24-hours-a-day enthusiasm for all things football made him the ideal man to further the club's potential under relatively limited resources.

Ironically, despite the successful 1998–99 campaign that opened the door to Europe, there were some whispering doubts about Redknapp's own long-term future at Upton Park. But that's running ahead of ourselves . . .

Chapter Three

'Er, there's a bit of a problem, mate. Gazza's eaten your questions!'

John Moncur was apologetic as he explained why he wasn't in a position to run through the 'Profile on . . .' questionnaire for the September '94 issue of *Hammers News Magazine*. 'Paul's been around for a few days and, you know what he's like, he saw your sheet and stuffed it into his mouth. D'ya wanna send it through to me again?'

Needless to say, when we did get the papers returned the still-lingering Gascoigne had offered some of his own responses on John's behalf . . . But then that's what that particular feature was always about – entertainment. As well as presenting an ideal reason to phone around the first-team squad in my early days as a contributor to *HNM*, it allowed me the opportunity to ask more interesting and offbeat questions. I could delve into players' record collections, find out when they last got drunk ('Hey, I'm *still* drunk!' quipped Dutch striker Jeroen Boere) and ask them about brushes with the law ('I brush with the law every day,' confessed Mattie Holmes, 'my next door neighbour's a police officer!').

And we certainly needed some entertaining in the early part of the 1994–95 season: the team failed to score in its first three games, won just one out of its first eight league matches and lost 2–1 at Third-Division Walsall in the first leg of the Coca-Cola Cup second round.

Mile End-born midfielder Moncur had been an £850,000 close-season buy from Swindon, while defender Adrian Whitbread – another London lad with the recently relegated Wiltshire outfit – had arrived at Upton Park as part of the deal that sent Joey Beauchamp back into obscurity. But Harry's first major investment as boss came with the purchase of attacking midfielder Don Hutchison who'd developed something of a bad-boy reputation at Liverpool for drunkenly sticking beer bottle labels on his private parts (whatever takes your fancy). Not surprisingly, he struggled to shake off his 'Budweiser' tag after signing for a club-record £1.5 million a handful of games into the campaign.

'We're only a couple of players away from being a half-decent side,' insisted Redknapp (for the first time but not for the last) and within a couple of months he'd thrown down the welcome-home mat to two former Hammers favourites exiled on Merseyside – Tony Cottee and Julian Dicks.

TC had spent a difficult six seasons with Everton after moving for a British record fee of £2.2 million in 1988 and was delighted to head south in exchange for left-back David Burrows, while Dicksy had fallen out with new Liverpool boss Roy Evans and had been forced to train with the kids after being told he was overweight. With his newly shaven head it's not quite true that he resembled Buster Bloodvessel of Bad Manners when returning for a bargain bin down-payment of £100,000, but the big, bad, bald one was clearly some way short of full fitness. 'Julian wasn't in the best of shape when he left West Ham and he wasn't in the best of shape when he came back,' acknowledged Harry when I later spoke to him about the defender's return. True to form, the Terminator picked up a booking on his début, in the 2–0 win against Southampton in October, while Cottee's first match was even more eventful: the little striker was sent off in the 0–0 draw at Liverpool for an uncharacteristic lunge on Rob Jones.

While Cottee's name rarely found itself being scribbled into referees' notebooks, the likes of Dicks and Hutchison made regular appearances in the bad-boys pages. Despite getting carded just once in his 14-month spell at Anfield, Julian succeeded in getting booked no less than six times before the end of December and winning himself a suspension. Hutch, meanwhile, had also picked up his first ban after being sent off on 5 November for two wild tackles on Leicester's Lee Philpott.

With the 1–0 home victory seemingly failing to fan the flames of his anger, Redknapp scorched into the Geordie boy at the press conference afterwards: 'It's personal with me and Hutchison. If he's gonna let me down, he'll let anyone down.' As if the red card wasn't bad enough, Harry had also discovered via a phone call that Don and Julian had broken club rules two days before the match. It was kept under wraps at the time but Dicksy told me all about it 18 months later while working on *Terminator* together.

'Hutch, Kenny Brown and I went out drinking on the Thursday before the Leicester game,' he revealed. 'We went to Romford straight after training and got absolutely bladdered, carrying on into the night. But somebody rang up Harry and told him that the three of us were out on the town.'

Redknapp duly hauled a red-faced and red-carded Hutchison over the coals in his office the following Tuesday, fining him two weeks' wages, while Dicks – who'd scored his first penalty since returning to win the game – was let off after apologising for his indiscretion. Hutch wasn't too convinced by the mystery caller who'd supposedly tipped Harry off, however. When being interviewed for Julian's book, he told me: 'Harry's a bit shifty like that. He tried that with me once before when he said he'd had a call saying I was out on the piss. I knew for a fact I hadn't, but it's something that Harry does. On that occasion he caught us out, though.'

Redknapp later admitted to me that alarm bells had started to ring at that time, having brought the two Liverpool outcasts – drinking buddies in their final days at Anfield – to Upton Park. 'There was just that little spell when I thought I may have made a ricket in bringing Hutchison and Dicks back together,' he confessed. Whatever Harry's reservations, results had started to improve and, as well as eventually squeezing past Walsall and blowing bubbles against Chelsea in the Coca-Cola Cup, the team had moved into a comfortable mid-table position.

The most significant development from a personal point of view came in December when *HNM* chief Tony McDonald invited me to take on the day-to-day editorial responsibilities (at Independent UK Sports Publications, who produced the magazine on a contractual basis). I'd already started to spend time in the office occasionally and, having edited magazines in men's lifestyle and rock music environments during the previous 10 years, I knew I'd never get a better opportunity to move into football full-time. Just as Who guitarist Pete Townshend had frequently expressed anxieties over windmilling his right arm through six strings while losing his youth, I'd begun to question the dignity of reviewing Black Sabbath albums when you're in your thirties.

One of my first opportunities to rub shoulders with football's famous faces came with the *West Ham United Who's Who* book launch at Upton Park on 7 December. More than 40 Hammers heroes from the past and present were in attendance, including Alan Sealey, Alan Taylor, Ernie Gregory, Ray Stewart and Julian Dicks, but the man who made the biggest impression on me was Malcolm Allison, who founded the West Ham academy during the '50s. Holding a glass of champagne and puffing on his trademark cigar, he exuded charisma, character and charm as he held court and entertained us with amusing anecdotes of his days in the game. He was such brilliant company, in fact, that his signature in my copy of the book didn't seem quite enough. Then I spotted it. Malcolm had finished puffing away and had stuck the remains of his cigar in an ashtray. What better way to commemorate the moment? I therefore wrapped it in a serviette and stuffed into my pocket. Sad but true . . .

I rang Tony Cottee for the first time just before Christmas and was immediately warmed by his friendly nature. We had a chat for the 'It's

Unusual' page – in which a player reflects on his bizarre experiences – and TC wasn't short on stories. Aside from talking about eating crocodiles and complaining about the state of Albania, he revealed that his former boss at Everton, Howard Kendall, used to 'encourage us to have a drink on Friday nights'. Continued Tone: 'Most managers discourage that but if we were in a hotel he'd openly say that if we wanted a drink or a few glasses of wine then that was no problem. But you'd have one glass, then want another and then another . . . It could get a bit out of hand.' Maybe, just maybe, it helped Howard feel a touch less guilty about his own indulgences . . .

Cottee celebrated Christmas early with a hat-trick which crushed Manchester City, but generally there was little cheer in the air as prospects started to go back down the pan. First-Division Bolton had turned up at Upton Park to win a Coca-Cola Cup tie 3–1, while a run of just 2 wins in 11 league games left the team slumped in twentieth position come February (and with 4 of the 22 clubs going down that season, it was hardly the most advisable of places to be). TC had every reason to be delighted on 4 February, though, when he scored his hundredth league goal (from 232 starts) in Hammers colours up at Leicester. I was pretty happy, too: we'd delayed production of the next issue to acknowledge Tony's feat and if he'd failed at Filbert Street I'd have had bugger all to stick on the cover.

The other main talking point in the magazine was Alvin Martin being sent off during the home game with Sheffield Wednesday. The veteran defender had lost his balance and gone sprawling in front of Wednesday's Mark Bright in midfield, and referee Paul Danson – known as Dirty Danson by some – brandished the red card for a so-called professional foul. The incident became a national talking point for days, as papers (one of which described it as 'the worst refereeing decision of the season') whipped up the campaign for video replays to be used to help officials in their decision-making processes.

As editor, I could at least channel my frustration over the whole shenanigans into the pages of the magazine. First I generated an 'editorial comment' piece, in which I castigated Danson for his 'complete misinterpretation of events' while acknowledging that he at least had the decency to later amend the red card to a yellow one. 'Honest mistakes are being penalised as much as calculated foul play, because some officials can't tell the difference,' I complained. I also telephoned Harry Redknapp to get his thoughts on the debate. 'I think the FA had a lot to do with Danson changing his verdict,' he told me. 'I think they looked at it and realised it was the wrong decision. I still feel aggrieved because it was an important game and it cost us dearly. Maybe there's a case for the game being replayed,' he added, joking that if he was Alan Sugar (the Spurs supremo who'd just won a battle with the FA) he'd probably have a good chance of succeeding.

We dedicated two pages to the affair and after revealing the views of Alvin, his anguished boss and the press, I realised that nothing had been heard from the man in black himself. I couldn't see there being much chance of getting Danson's phone number, until somebody in the office suddenly chucked me a little book containing various officials' details. 'This could be dangerous information if it fell into the wrong hands,' I laughed, as I tapped out his number. Sadly, only the missus was at home and, although I left a message emphasising that we weren't looking to attack Paul but simply wanted to gauge his thoughts on the pressures of being a ref and whether he felt video technology should be used, Mr Danson decided not to call us back. At least I could title the panel 'It's all gone quiet over there . . .', even if there wasn't much to say in it.

After one error of judgement too many, Danson did eventually lose his place in the Premiership (and was demoted to the lower divisions), but of immediate concern at that time was West Ham's own status. I didn't want to end the season as editor of a magazine in the Endsleigh League!

Talking to the players generally brought a smile to my face, however, as I gradually started to get to know them. I rang former Manchester City winger Michael Hughes (signed on loan from Strasbourg midway through the season) and he told me about the strangest piece of advice he'd ever received. 'When I first arrived at City I was finding it hard to fit in and manager Tony Book told me, "Look, why don't you go down to the pub and have a few Guinnesses!"' (Not *another* player being force-fed alcohol!) Whether Hughesy was listening to a half-time team-talk or not wasn't disclosed.

The amiable Irishman also revealed his love of country-and-western music. 'I like Kenny Rogers best,' he declared, without the faintest hint of embarrassment. I'd just introduced a new feature called 'Sounds Good?' to the magazine, based on the idea of blagging a few copies of a CD I fancied and getting one of the players to give it their verdict. Convivial midfielder Ian Bishop kicked the series off by giving the thumbs up to Simple Minds, while a depressed Danny Williamson turned Supergrass (giving 'I Should Coco' the thumbs down), Alvin Martin got Strangled with the 'About Time' album and Mattie Holmes simply wanted to strangle me after being sent the new Duran Duran CD. Martin Allen revealed that one of his favourite groups was Haircut One Hundred (yuk!) and went so far as to explain what happened every time he played one of his compilation tapes on the team bus: 'These tapes have been known to be stamped on and smashed with the studs spanner. Julian Dicks picks up my tapes and crushes them. It hurts me very much . . .' whined the 'Mad Dog' with dripping tongue firmly in cheek.

I'd chosen Bish first because he was always happy to talk. A Scouser with an appealing sense of humour, he willingly co-operated whenever I rang him with ideas, and he was never afraid to speak his mind. I can remember the Hammers losing 4–2 at Blackburn towards the end of 1994 and seeing Ian getting booked immediately after Alan Shearer had won and converted a penalty (some things never change). I gave him a call to find out what the yellow card was all about. 'I felt that Shearer had dived and the referee had been conned, so I held my nose and pulled an imaginary toilet chain, just to indicate that the whole thing stank,' he said, still flush-faced at finishing up a loo-ser.

Another real character is Les Sealey, who'd recently arrived at the club and now (play) acts as goalkeeping coach. 'I've done plenty of mad things, but some of them you can't print – I'd get nicked!' declared the much-travelled madcap while driving up to a game in the north in one of his classic cars. Amid talk of fishing for hammerhead sharks and eating sheep's eyes (as you do), he revealed the long sought-after secret of Sir Alex Ferguson's success. 'When I was at United we had a meeting before a cup game against Leeds. Alex had all the players out on a board and said, "Right, this is my team talk." He then got hold of all the players in white, swept them off the board and said, "Don't lose!" And we didn't.'

I'm glad the Hammers have had somebody like Sealey at the club, even though some view him as a big mouth with far too much influence. From my experience of sitting on the bench during that friendly in Munich, I can imagine what a pain in the arse he must be for some players at times, acting in his self-appointed role as chief coach and cheerleader, but it's refreshing to see people at the club showing such passion. There's been more than one game when Les has been the first to leap on to the pitch at the final whistle in jubilation over a hard-earned victory. A real Eastender, he's always supported the Hammers, even if he did upset a few people when he turned round to us sufferers on Upton Park's North Bank in 1982 and raised both fists in joy as his Coventry side romped to a 3–0 win. I've forgiven you, Les, honest I have.

Somehow, Harry Redknapp managed to turn things around towards the end of the 1994–95 campaign. Defender Marc Rieper was another loan-signing during the season and, after a wobbly start, he came into the side at the expense of the injured Martin, while Jeroen Boere re-emerged up front and scored a couple of times – most notably an equaliser four minutes into injury time at Ipswich (who'd lost their last eight games).

Don Hutchison scored the only goal in a memorable win at Arsenal in March, and was duly rewarded by my sending him a copy of the new Terence Trent D'Arby album. 'Couldn't you have sent me something decent?' he moaned, listing a couple of CDs he wanted to save money on. 'I tell you what, I'll give it a go in the bath and see if something stands out,' he said, leaving me wondering just quite what he meant.

Cottee struck twice in the last eight minutes against Norwich at Upton Park to bring the Hammers back from the dead in a match that saw Andy Johnson sent off for the Canaries after Spencer Prior upended TC – and from there the team lost just one more match, at Palace in May. Moncur and Hutchison scored the goals at Villa Park to leave the other claret-and-blues in relegation trouble, while Hutch got the second in a 2–0 home win over championship-chasing Blackburn Rovers which had rival Manchester United fans leaping up and down. David Batty should have been sent off for a typically nasty challenge on Bishop and the West Ham midfielder got even more abuse after dragging the ball away from Batty and slipping it through the legs of Stuart Ripley. 'Tim Sherwood came across and snapped, "Don't take the piss or he'll kick you again!" I know Tim and don't expect that kind of thing from him,' complained Bish afterwards.

The resurgence in form came without any assistance from transfer-deadline-day-signing Dieter Eckstein. The striker on loan from Schalke 04 became the first German to join the Hammers. He had apparently spent three days on trial and played a reserve match before agreeing to stay until the end of the season. Considering the possibility of putting our super saviour-to-be on the cover of *HNM* after hearing of his arrival, I gave manager Redknapp a call to find out more about the star hitman. 'So, Harry, is there a chance you could sign Eckstein permanently?' I asked.

'Mmm . . . too early to say,' he said rather cautiously.

'Well, just so that I can gauge his true status, how much would he be worth if you wanted to buy him?' I enquired.

'Well, from what I've seen so far, Kirk, about tuppence ha'penny.'

'Er . . . does that mean he's unlikely to start at Forest on Saturday?'

'The way he's going, he'll be lucky to make it on to the team bus!'

Needless to say, deadline-beater Dieter never made a single appearance for West Ham.

With just two games of the season left, the Hammers were still vulnerable to the threat of relegation and needed points. There was just one problem, however . . . the final two games were against Liverpool and Manchester United. Oops! Actually, we needn't have worried, what with emergency forward Hutchison (filling in for the sidelined Cottee and Boere) having a right laugh against his former team-mates and scoring twice to help secure a 3–0 midweek win that guaranteed Premiership survival. At least we could relax against United on Sunday . . .

Chapter Four

For many, Ludek Miklosko's heroics against Manchester United on 14 May 1995 rate as the greatest individual performance from any West Ham player in recent years. United went into the game needing a victory and hoped that Blackburn would be denied a win at Liverpool, in which case the title would be theirs. With both games taking place simultaneously, it was up to Alex Ferguson's men to complete, at least, their part of the equation . . . and then hope for good news from Anfield. Thank God and all His friends and family that the Hammers didn't need anything from the game themselves to be safe. I don't think I could have survived the tension.

Despite my new position on *Hammers News Magazine*, I was determined to continue watching games at Upton Park in the same way I always had – as a fan with my mates. As a teenager I'd started off in the lower West Stand, two of us regularly squeezing through the turnstiles together as one and splitting the profit with the gateman. Memories include my mate Joe catching the ball and waiting for Tottenham's Danny Thomas to retrieve it, before chucking it as hard as he could at the player's groin. Ouch! Joe also once abused Scottish international midfielder Don Masson something rotten the year after his country's embarrassing performances in the 1978 World Cup. 'Remember Argentina, Masson!' he bellowed during the home game with Notts County (which we lost), only to be silenced when the player came and sat on the wall in front of us during a break in play. 'How's it going then, lads?' said Don, as my mate's face went a deeper crimson than the West Ham shirts.

Then there was sweet little Johnny, sitting on the West Stand wall with his mum. 'Ah, it's probably one of his first games,' we thought, as he took in the events of the day with wide-eyed glee. Predictably, the Hammers were crap (against a 10-man Wrexham after keeper Dai Davies had manhandled the referee for failing to spot a blatant bit of basketball from Pop Robson who literally placed the ball on Bonzo's head to score). Suddenly, the silence was pierced by the sound of a little atom bomb exploding. 'West Ham, I've seen more life in a gangrenous c***!' screamed little Johnny, leaving us so appalled at his shocking words that they're still ringing around in our heads 20 years later. And mummy didn't even smack him!

Hoping to mix with a better class of punter, we moved into the North Bank at the beginning of the '80s. That was in the days when coppers chucked people out but didn't seem to mind if they paid to get back in again. I remember a bloke in front of us giving the referee a right mouthful during one match before the long arm of the law stretched across and pointed him towards the exit gates. Five minutes later, the guy was back again, still giving it the big one but with a rather revised vocabulary. 'Ooh, you cad, ref! You bounder!' The cops just laughed.

I've had a couple of minor experiences at the hands of the law myself, both at away games. In the '80s there was a group of about six or seven of us who would travel around the country by coach. We'd sit at the back and usually leave the bus via the rear door. We'd just reversed into our bay outside Villa Park and I opened the door, only to see the heavy thing slammed shut again by the copper outside and me nearly losing my hand in the process. Relieved that I still had any fingers left, I decided to put them to good use, producing some colourful sign language that even the most ignorant of police officers would understand. Our man clearly did because, by the time I'd made my way to the front of the bus, he was waiting for me at the steps. Needless to say, my feet never touched the ground. I was slung up against the side of the vehicle and, in my shock, lost control of my bowels and unleashed a noise (and smell) that left half of Birmingham shaking. 'Your shit stinks!' roared the officer, before ordering me to sit on the tarmac and take my Doctor Martens off. He laughed as he pulled the laces out of the boots and chuckled again when he slung the leather back at me. 'Now put 'em on again,' he demanded. Now I know what Richard Gere felt like in *An Officer and a Gentleman*. It didn't get any better inside the ground, where a policeman spent the entire first half tapping my ankles with his toes to try and force a response. 'Go on, lad, just say something . . .' was the expression he wore, as the law – weary of hooliganism – decided to get the upper hand by intimidating the supporters first.

The other occasion coincided with the shortest football match I've ever witnessed – about 90 seconds. Well, that was all I got to see. It was a midweek match at Southampton in 1985 and right-back Ray Stewart couldn't have been playing too well of late because, as the game kicked off, a pal of mine said, 'I see Ray Stewart's f***ing playing again.' I nodded and thought no more of it until I began to sense a kerfuffle in the crowd behind me. I turned around and saw two policeman carving their way through the throng and heading our way. Just above there was a steward directing them down the terrace: 'Yeah, that's him, the one in the leather jacket.' Then I realised he was pointing at me. As I stuttered and stammered my innocence, I was turfed out of The Dell and taken to a little hut, where my details were taken and I was warned not to gain access to the ground again. With the local pub closed, I therefore had little choice but to roam the streets and listen to the crowd as the Hammers played out a 1–1 draw.

With other friends having season tickets in the Chicken Run we subsequently moved again and when the standing terrace was replaced with seating we moved upstairs into the East Stand upper tier where I remain to this very day. It wouldn't have been the same in the Upton Park press box. I've occasionally watched games from there (in the West Stand) and, even though many of the reporters have a real affection for the club, it's still not considered cool to reveal one's allegiances too much. Professional protocol does not allow for jumping up and down, shouting at the top of your voice and abusing the referee.

In truth, I wanted the best of both worlds. Of course, I relished the idea of editing my own club's official magazine, but I was determined not to lose the feeling we all get from being with our fellow supporters. Sure, I had to observe events through professional eyes, but I wanted to continue enjoying myself on a Saturday afternoon as well. If anything, my new position consolidated my passion for the club and when you feel that way about something it's natural to want to reveal your emotions. Football had been a social activity, too. With my friends living in Essex and in different parts of London, it was only West Ham's playing that brought us all back together every week. Hence we continued to meet for home games in the ground-floor bar of the West Ham United Supporters' Club adjacent to the Bobby Moore Stand in Castle Street.

It's special games such as that famous one against Manchester United in 1995 which are so much more rewarding when your fervour and fanaticism is allowed full rein. The Hammers were safe but the next best thing, given that we were unlikely ever to be contesting the title ourselves, was to have a direct say in who was going to win it. Even better if we had a chance of denying United, with whom there was little love lost, particularly after Paul Ince had revealed his (wrong) colours a full month before heading to Old Trafford in 1989. West Ham had buggered up the Reds once before – just three years earlier when Kenny Brown scored the only goal of the game and Alex Ferguson famously complained that the level of effort from the already-relegated Hammers was obscene – but could they do it again? Lightning never strikes twice, does it?

Man. Utd had won the championship in the two intervening seasons but realised a third successive triumph was not going to come easily when Michael Hughes sidefooted a ball from Mattie Holmes past a stunned Peter Schmeichel on the half-hour mark. As if things weren't dark enough, with United wearing their all-black strip, their misery was compounded when they discovered at half-time that Alan Shearer had put Rovers ahead at Anfield. Brian McClair threw his side a lifeline, though, when he headed home Gary Neville's free kick just seven minutes into the second period and moments later it became apparent that Liverpool had pegged Blackburn back. Now all United needed was a winner. But they reckoned *without* the super-human efforts of Miklosko in goal. The bouncing Czech denied Mark Hughes, Andy Cole (thrice) and the much berated Ince, while defenders Steve Potts and Marc Rieper mopped up time and time again during the never-ending series of goalmouth scrambles.

It was an incredible climax: nobody present will ever forget those frantic final 15 minutes. The Hammers held on, leaving Blackburn as champions despite falling to Jamie Redknapp's last-minute goal on Merseyside. United therefore trudged out of Upton Park empty-handed, without so much as a quick drink afterwards, and the least we could do was commemorate the event in the pages of *Hammers News Magazine*. We devoted extra space to the match report, running a lovely little shot of the Carling Premiership podium which would have been used for the presentation, if needed, along with the caption: '*What, no trophy?!*' Then I was told that the advertising team had failed to sell the back page of the issue. With United also losing the FA Cup final to Everton before we went to press, the least we could do was run a full-page photograph of happy Hammers celebrating next to an aggrieved Ince waiting for the ground to open up and swallow him. We needed a headline, of course, and in a flash of inspiration it duly arrived: 'FOREVER BLOWING DOUBLES!'

Chapter Five

Within 24 hours of their exhausting efforts against Manchester United, the West Ham squad found itself being herded up for a gruelling 12-hour flight to Singapore, on their way to Australia where four games in various locations had been arranged. 'It was just stupid,' complained Julian Dicks to me afterwards. 'Four games in eight days was ridiculous after the season we'd just had. The lads had no break. We were playing, getting pissed during the evening, flying off next morning, staying in that night, playing again the next day, getting pissed in the evening, then flying off again . . .'

As it was, Dicksy had far less reason to groan as he wasn't even playing, – he had chipped an ankle bone in the match against his former Liverpool team-mates the previous week. In fact, he shouldn't have been on the trip at all. 'The surgeon said, "You're not going", telling me that the ankle would swell up too much inside the plaster on the plane. But I rang up Harry and told him I wanted to go to Australia and he said, "Fair enough, it's up to you." On the flight it was so painful I said to the doctor, "Get this thing off, it's throbbing!" So he went and got a kitchen knife and started to saw it off (the plaster, not the foot). It must have taken him about forty minutes.'

Julian certainly wasn't bothered about missing a few 'mickey mouse friendlies' – which saw weakened Hammers teams draw 2–2 with Western Australia, 1–1 with Victoria and play two games against Australia Under-23, winning 1–0 and losing 4–0, for which they received some local criticism. He wasn't particularly impressed by with some of the places they visited either. 'Sydney was a shit-hole,' he told me. 'Kings Cross was filthy and full of prostitutes, although Surfer's Paradise was nice when we got there.'

Dicksy certainly seemed happy enough in the photograph we ran of him (with cigar sticking out of mouth), along with Hutch and Adrian Whitbread heading off to the beach, with buckets and spades probably just out of shot. Steve Blowers, my chief contributor to *HNM*, had made the trip to Oz and was accompanying the team on their travels, while Tony Cottee had agreed to supply an exclusive 'Down Under Diary' for the magazine. It was a great gesture by Tony, as most players would have baulked at the idea of working during what they would consider to be a holiday, and he did a fantastic job. He clearly enjoyed putting pen to paper and, over the following years, I'd see plenty of evidence to suggest that, failing to make the break into management he'd always welcome, he'd certainly have the potential to be successful in the media. The June '95 issue therefore had TC on the cover, complete with hat, Sydney T-shirt and boomerang, and the event was given a six-page special.

We followed it up in July with another seven pages of coverage, with Martin Allen delivering his own 'Postcard from Australia'. The midfielder clearly appreciated the opportunity of experiencing a new country and enjoyed visiting the sights. 'He was buzzing,' said Dicksy. 'We went to see the Sydney Opera House and he loved it, while Hutch, Moncs and me were like, "Yeah, so what?"'

In some respects that little tale says much about the character of the man with the tail, Martin who carries around the 'Mad Dog' label on his little coat. I got to know him better when working on Julian's biography and he clearly has more substance than many give him credit for. It was something that disturbed him a little and, as he opened up enough, he revealed to me: 'I used to have a bit of a hang-up about people knowing me as Mad Dog. I thought they might see me as just a thug with no brain who used to go round shouting at referees and arguing with people, when I was bringing up two children, had my own company, ran my own soccer schools and did lots of charity work. I must admit, though, I did play along with it at times.'

Martin needed great support from Dicks during the Australian venture, with his father Dennis unwell and causing him great concern. 'Julian was good to me when my dad was ill,' he confided. 'Being on the other side of the world when my dad had a short time to live wasn't easy and I'll always remember his kindness on that trip. I was also hanging out with Hutch and Moncs and, even though people see them as rogues, they're quality blokes.' When Dennis finally succumbed to cancer in July, Martin realised he couldn't keep playing at Upton Park knowing his dad was no longer in his usual seat and he soon joined Portsmouth in a loan move that was made permanent in February 1996.

Also through the exit gates before the new season got into gear were Trevor Morley (to Reading), Mattie Holmes (who went to champions Blackburn Rovers in exchange for Robbie Slater plus £600,000 and was so lonely in his new hotel that he gave me his telephone number and told me to ring any time I fancied a chat) and Matthew Rush (who headed to Norwich in a £330,000 deal with Harry's words probably still ringing in his ears). Although loanee Michael Hughes temporarily returned to France (before making another short-term agreement in the autumn), Superman lookalike Marc Rieper had signed permanently in a £1.1 million deal prior to the United game in May, while warhorse Alvin Martin was given a new one-year deal.

There were also changes taking place at *Hammers News Magazine*, with design being brought in-house for the first time. I'd complained to the hierarchy at Independent Magazines (UK) Ltd that it was impossible to influence the look and feel of the publication if I wasn't working directly with an art editor and, once they'd calculated that we'd actually be saving money in the process, I was duly allowed to appoint one. So who was going to appear on the first cover of the new-look *HNM*? Marco Boogers, come on down . . .

OK, he'd failed to impress on his début in Munich but you can't judge a player on one game – or can you? Certainly, the club had been pleased to land the Dutch striker in June, when my fax machine gave birth to a statement which read: 'West Ham United are delighted to announce the signing of Sparta Rotterdam centre-forward for a fee of around £1 million. Marco, who is 28 years of age, has played for Sparta since October 1994 and played 25 games, scoring 11 goals. He was named the third best player in Holland last season. Despite starting his career as a winger and not switching to centre-forward until 1990, he has a career record of 103 goals in 278 league games.' The press release also included a statement from MD Peter Storrie, who declared: 'The club are pleased to buy a quality striker for such a reasonable fee and it proves that value for money can still be found.'

For some reason I decided to keep that sheet of paper and it continues to amuse me to this day. At the time, however, despite his less than convincing outing in Munich, I still considered it worth my while sticking Marco on the cover of the August/September issue. There was not much else going on and, except for those who'd made the trip out to Germany, nobody had seen him play yet. In fact, we'd started to have doubts over how many times Harry Redknapp himself had actually seen him play. I made sure our 'WALKING IN A BOOGIE WONDERLAND?' coverline had a question mark, just in case he did turn out to be a lemon.

The fact that Boogers only made it on to the pitch as a 65th-minute substitute in our opening game against Leeds United didn't exactly suggest a huge amount of confidence in the guy and once again he was only on the bench for the following match at Old Trafford. Tony McDonald (known from now on as Mac), Steve Blowers and I found ourselves sitting in front of former United hero Paddy Crerand and to have to listen to 90 minutes of the most prejudiced commentary ever was enough to make us want to get up and leave. We're glad we didn't, of course, because we'd have missed the only notable achievement of Boogers's short West Ham career – getting sent off. It seemed as if he'd only been on the pitch a few moments when, bang, he took out Gary Neville with all the force of an out-of-control caravan. When red came Marco's way, it wasn't just in the shape of the referee's card, and Andy Cole and Gary Pallister formed a queue to have a pop at the beleaguered Dutchman.

Despite seeing their team lose 2–1 to a below-par United (who'd just sold Ince, Kanchelskis and Hughes), bosses Redknapp and Lampard were in reasonably good spirits. Harry was asked as to the whereabouts of the recently signed (but not yet available to play) Stan Lazaridis, (the Aussie had impressed for Western Australia against the Hammers in the summer), and 'H' duly declared: 'He's probably out shagging sheep somewhere.' Moments later, the ever-friendly Frank Snr was flicking through the pages of the latest *HNM* next to the team bus, philosophical about the evening's events. 'Yep, same old West Ham, isn't it?' he said, as West Ham once again failed to take advantage of a situation where, with a bit more belief, they might actually have won.

As if Marco's 'horror tackle' (according to *The Sun*) didn't raise enough unfortunate headlines, he then Boogered off to Holland to spend some time with his wife who was said to be experiencing pregnancy problems. That may well have been the case, but when the striker failed to return to Upton Park, news then emerged that he was mentally ill and now living in a caravan! (*Clubcall*'s Chris Raistrick proudly claims responsibility for such stories.) The reality, of course, was that he was in no mood to play football – having admitted to *HNM* (when we finally tracked him down) that he was 'very disillusioned' at having to sit out games on the bench – and had taken his family off on holiday. Ultimately Peter Storrie, who many feel had initiated the purchase of Boogers, had to fly out to Holland to resolve the situation. It had all started to get very confusing, though, when Storrie insisted that the player still had a future at Upton Park, while at the same time Redknapp had suggested it would probably be better for all parties if the striker was sold. Harry did a good job in backtracking when I quizzed him on the issue, declaring: 'Peter was only saying what I'd already said – that if Marco does return he'll start off with a clean slate. I won't bear grudges if he comes back and gets on with it but, having said that, if another club came in for him, maybe it would be better if he went back home.'

Redknapp was less than happy when I suggested he got a very different kind of player (one that didn't look remotely like scoring goals) to the one he expected. 'Of course he's the kind of player I expected!' he retorted. 'I knew exactly what I was getting.' (Why d'ya buy him then, Harry?) It had also been rumoured that the manager had never seen the striker live in action, to which he said, 'I don't know who dreamt that one up, that I bought him after just watching a video. What a load of nonsense! I had seen him play – once – but I did watch a video as well. I didn't want a big target man, I wanted somebody who could get into the box and score goals, but he was coming too deep for my liking.'

While we were left scratching our heads as to what game Harry had actually seen Boogers play in, given that the club wasn't linked with the player until after the Dutch season was over, it seemed that he then changed his mind as to what he did want from a striker when it came to bringing a new face in. Or not such a new one, as it turned out. I was on the tube with Mac one evening, chatting about the current situation, when he told me that Harry was on the verge of bringing a former Hammer back to Upton Park. 'Any idea who it is?' he quizzed. I reeled off a couple of names but to no avail. 'Dowie,' he said.

'DOWIE!!!' I stormed. 'You're joking!' Sadly, he was in no mood to jest.

Boogers did come back to England, of course, but he never did get to start a game for West Ham, making just two further appearances as a substitute in heavy defeats by Villa and Blackburn. And after a spell in the reserves ended with a cartilage injury, he eventually returned to his homeland by joining FC Groningen on loan. We never saw him again, despite being tempted to undertake a tour of caravan sights and mental institutions when visiting northern Holland for our Intertoto Cup clash with Heerenveen in 1999.

Likewise, we never thought we'd see Iain Dowie playing for the Hammers again. The Northern Irish striker had left Upton Park in 1991 after just five months in claret and blue, having scored only four times in a dozen appearances. I could recall him scoring on his début, against Barnsley, as the team chased promotion from the Second Division (Dowie's natural habitat), but the game I remembered most was the 1–0 defeat at Brighton. West Ham had all the possession and created chance after chance in a match they needed to win, only for 'Bartman' (in honour of his custard-topped head) to send each opportunity high or wide.

Now Iain was to get a second chance with his boyhood heroes, with Harry negotiating a deal with Crystal Palace which saw Jeroen Boere cross the Thames in the opposite direction. The club had to pay an additional £125,000 in cash and even I had to admit that it was peanuts, especially as the rugged striker had bagged 36 goals in 141 appearances for

Southampton and Palace since his departure. We desperately needed *somebody* up front and maybe Dowie's physical presence would work wonders alongside the diminutive Tony Cottee.

Although reluctant to award Iain *HNM* cover status (that pleasure went to Julian Dicks – rather appropriately, as it would turn out), I was eager to conduct the magazine's interview myself. I'd spent most of the year happily talking to players for our more off-beat features, but on this occasion I had a burning desire to chew the football fat. I arranged for my photographer to get a shot of Iain with his new shirt inside Upton Park prior to the game with Chelsea, and gave him a ring at home that evening. 'I'd heard some things on the grapevine during the summer [funny, I didn't think Harry was looking for a target man?] but when West Ham signed Marco Boogers I thought that was the end of it,' he told me. 'But there was no doubt in my mind that I wanted to come back.'

What struck me about Dowie in conversation was how nice he was. He held former boss Billy Bonds in the 'highest regard', despite having been turfed out of Upton Park prematurely first time around, and although he didn't feel he had anything to prove, he was desperate to do well for the fans he felt he'd struck a good relationship with during his first period. 'They appreciate people who play in a passionate manner and are committed to the club,' he said, acknowledging one of his fundamental strengths. I later attributed to myself the same characteristics as I wrote through the night and wrapped up the issue with my designer at 4 a.m. . . .

Another piece I'd done that month was with Ludek Miklosko. I'd seen from my experience of having shared the team bus with the players to and from the Munich game that summer that Ludo pretty much kept himself to himself. The keeper had been reluctant to take part in our 'Profile On . . .' series, but on this occasion I managed to persuade him that it was only lighthearted fun and wasn't to be taken too seriously. I was subsequently rewarded with a typical piece of Czech humour (or was it logic?) So, Ludo, whose wall would you land on if you were a fly? 'I think, if I was a fly, I would be a very heavy fly . . . and so I'd drop OFF the wall.' Absolutely brilliant!

Finally, I had a strange experience when discussing the new Blur album with Keith Rowland for our 'Sounds Good?' page. I'd sent the Northern Irish defender a copy of 'The Great Escape' and he was happy to give me his verdict ('I'll give it 5¾ out of 10!') during 10 minutes of conversation in which he described the album as 'very varied', while sounding somewhat vague. Days later, the CD came back to me in an unopened package, with the address marked as not recognised by the Post Office. I still haven't worked that one out . . .

Chapter Six

Having not featured Julian Dicks on the cover since his return to the club 11 months earlier, I found a typically aggressive shot of the man screaming at the camera for our October 1995 issue. Looking for a different angle for the feature itself, we spoke to Dicks about his unique preparation for games, knowing his preference for two cans of coke and a bath instead of a traditional warm-up. The article was already written and designed as the Hammers took on Chelsea in a televised game at Upton Park just a couple of days before our final pages were printed. With two draws (at Nottingham Forest and at home to Tottenham) indicating slight improvement following the opening two defeats, the team was looking for its first victory of the campaign – but the Blues took control with goals from Dennis Wise and John Spencer with a two-minute spell around the half-hour mark. Don Hutchison pulled one back in the second half but Spencer wrapped things up in the final minutes to send Chelsea home happy, although it wasn't the brace of goals that put the little Scot's name in the headlines.

An incident had taken place in the 35th minute, in which Dicks and Spencer challenged for the ball and the latter fell to the ground. Julian was seen to jump over his opponent but with his opponent staying down and needing treatment, it was obvious he'd been caught by Dicksy's boot. Little did we realise the kind of impact the story would make as we watched the Chelsea man's head being sponged, especially as he was able to continue playing (albeit bloodied and bandaged).

The 19,228 crowd would also have been unaware of how much of Sky Sports' post-match analysis would focus on the clash, with co-commentator Trevor Francis accusing Dicks of 'retribution' and Andy Gray suggesting he should have been sent off. With such views being beamed into the Upton Park press room via TV monitors, it was perhaps not surprising that the next day's tabloids would explode the incident all over their back pages, with all and sundry claiming that Julian had viciously brought his studs down on Spencer's head with full intent.

Due to such hysteria in the media, I knew the magazine's original

Dicks feature would look silly without some acknowledgement of what had taken place, so I gave Julian a call the following afternoon to get extra material for a side-panel. 'I tried to jump over John and didn't even know I'd landed on him until I saw the blood running down the side of his head,' he told me. 'The referee booked me for the challenge [apparently for shirt-tugging] but didn't see any stamping and neither did Harry Redknapp or [Blues boss] Glenn Hoddle. At half-time John asked me if I'd meant it and I told him I hadn't. But I knew the press would make the most of it. And I thought Andy Gray was bang out of order to say I should have been sent off. It's not nice when you're branded a nutter and a headcase.'

I was prepared to believe Julian, even though the TV pictures did little to support his case. *The Sun* had even gone so far as to run the full sequence of shots, showing Dicks vaulting the grounded Spencer and then bringing his right boot down on the player. With such incriminating evidence in front of them, it was hardly surprising that literally nobody gave him the benefit of the doubt. Even Harry Redknapp pointed an accusatory finger at his player. Julian later told me how, amid the debate over the subsequent couple of days, his boss had confronted him during training. 'I was kicking a ball against a wall and Harry came out and asked, "Did you mean it?" When I told him I hadn't he called me a f***ing liar. It was only when I swore on my kids' lives that he said he believed me.'

It seems that Spencer himself – hardly in the best position to see with his face in the dirt – accepted Julian's reassurances that the contact had been accidental. All of this might have been quickly forgotten, however, if events hadn't taken a turn for the worse the following Saturday when the Hammers visited Highbury. The match itself will be remembered for many things – Ian Wright's two penalties (one missed, one converted to win the points) and goalkeeper Les Sealey (the only Hammer left on the bench) having to make an emergency appearance up front after John Moncur was carried off – but it was Dicksy's fifth red card in West Ham colours that sparked a furore. Coming just five days after the Spencer incident, the sending-off was terrible timing on Julian's part. In fact it was terrible timing in the tackle that resulted in the two cautions (as well as one of the penalties).

All hell subsequently broke loose: Conservative MP-cum-radio presenter David Mellor calling Dicks 'an animal' on air (after which it was reported that legal action was being taken) and front-page headlines announced that Julian's two daughters, Kattie and Jessica, had been attacked at school.

With the next issue of *HNM* going on sale within days of the Arsenal game, we couldn't have chosen a better time to put Julian on the cover, even though hasty coverage had been made of the Chelsea game alone. By getting Dicks to talk generally about his feeling victimised – 'If I do anything wrong people will be straight on to it,' he moaned – the piece still had relevance and it left us scope to address his situation in greater depth the following month. It was no surprise when, in the wake of the sending-off, the FA formally announced that Dicks had been charged with bringing the game into disrepute for his clash with Spencer.

Although unable to talk about the charge itself, Julian was happy to discuss all the other areas of controversy when I rang him for our next issue. 'I thought I was hard-done-by at Arsenal,' he complained. 'They weren't nasty tackles but defenders get sent off for things like that now. I actually thought I got a slight touch of the ball on both occasions.'

As for Mellor's comments, he revealed: 'I've got to see what happens with the FA enquiry before deciding what to do about those. I was sent a tape of what he said and he was bang out of order. I'm not an animal and if he wants to call me things he should meet me somewhere so that we can discuss it there and then.' I knew what he was trying to say but I couldn't help conjuring up visions of Dicksy kicking the shit out of the former cabinet minister in a dark alley somewhere.

But what about those 'children attacked' headlines? 'After it happened, I spoke to my solicitor who put together a press release, stating exactly what had happened – that one of my kids had got tripped up at school. The point was to tell the press that all the stick I was getting was affecting my children, so they should cut it out and leave me alone. Obviously, they thought "sod that" and blew the story up to a ridiculous level. You've got wars going on and kids dying around the world, but they put *me* on the front page! It makes no sense.'

He was right, of course, but I had to question the wisdom of volunteering information to the press. It was obvious they'd exploit the situation even further to keep Dicksy's name in the headlines. That's what sensationalism is all about. My job, however, was to reflect on events in an objective way and encourage Julian to reveal his true thoughts. I fully enjoyed having the opportunity to discuss such matters with him and these conversations went some way towards us establishing some kind of relationship. At this point in time there was no reason for him to particularly trust me but he seemed quite happy to talk openly about the way the game was treating him and the effect it was having.

My own opinion was that Julian rarely received the benefit of the doubt most players got from referees, but that he'd been partly responsible for that situation himself. His temperament had certainly been suspect in previous years – particularly the 1992–93 season in which he'd been sent off three times and where every pitch became a sheet of ice as opponents sought to wind him up – but it was now up to Dicks to recognise the realities of his current environment and learn to avoid confrontation. I could understand him feeling victimised, however, and called for people to stop jumping on the bandwagon to vilify him.

Such views were expressed in a new column entitled 'The Ed Mouths Off!' and I thought the magazine benefited from voicing its own opinion on what was going on, rather than just existing as a medium for Dicks to offer his defence. It was also right that we should provide a platform for the fans to have their say and so we canvassed opinion at the following home game (against Everton, in which Julian held his nerve to score twice from the spot). In view of the fact that most official magazines downplay such controversies (or even ignore them altogether), I like to think our approach helped us win credibility with the fans, some of whom inevitably held the view that we existed purely to pump out club propaganda.

We prided ourselves on venturing into areas where others feared to tread and went even further into the Dicks debate by probing what Harry Redknapp felt about recent events. 'I felt Julian had to go,' said 'H' when I asked if the Arsenal sending-off had been unfortunate. 'He could have gone even earlier, for pulling down Wrighty as he was cutting in on goal, so that was a let-off. What he's got to do now is concentrate on football and play like he did against Everton and in the Coca-Cola Cup game at Bristol Rovers' [where it seemed as if every set of eyes in the ground were focused purely on Dicksy's movements].

Julian was subsequently banned for three matches following his appointment with the FA on 19 October, during which he met referee Robbie Hart who'd previously said he should have issued a red card for the Spencer incident. 'Yet he came up to me and said he hoped I got off!' Julian later told me. 'I felt like smacking him there and then!'

Chapter Seven

'If I think you're a mug I'll tell you. I say what I think and I can't help that.'

Harry Redknapp, as ever, was speaking his mind. And he had plenty on it when I made contact with him to reflect on the opening of the 1995–96 campaign. Despite having rung the manager up for the occasional quote, this was my first in-depth interview with Harry for *HNM*, as previously I'd been happy to allow Tony Mac – who'd had a two-year head start on getting to know him (Redknapp arrived at the club when *Hammers News* was in tabloid form) – to reap the benefits of having already won his trust and confidence. But this time there was lots I wanted to discuss with him myself.

Aside from the Julian Dicks situation, we'd had the Boogers disappearance, Dowie's return, changes in the backroom team (with reserve-team boss Paul Hilton being axed, followed by the departure of long-serving chief scout Ronnie Boyce and colleague Ronnie Gale) and an upturn in results since the Arsenal match, with two Coca-Cola Cup wins over Bristol Rovers alongside a draw at Southampton and victory against Everton.

My first suggestion was that Harry might be feeling the pressure as he commenced his second season in charge in disappointing circumstances. 'Not at all,' he refuted. 'There's been much less pressure than during my first season: Billy had left, everything was in turmoil and I think I performed a miracle to keep the club up. But we've had a difficult start this season.'

The view of many at that time was that Redknapp was starting to throw his weight around a bit more within the club and if that meant ruffling feathers and making himself unpopular with some people then so be it. At first-team level it meant making changes in defence, brushing Alvin Martin free of cobwebs and thrusting him back into action. 'You can't change the way some people are,' said Harry, as he complained about the lack of vocal authority at the back. It was a clear reference to Steve Potts, who may have been ever-dependable as a defender but went about his job with all the presence of a mute lamb.

Up the other end of the field, Don Hutchison was finding himself pushed out of the equation and some felt there had obviously been some kind of falling-out with the boss. Harry denied any such notion and insisted he'd done everything he could to get the Geordie into his side. 'I think he's got terrific ability but I end up messing up systems to try and accommodate him. But I can only pick so many men and if I'm playing with two up front and two wingers there's no place for him. Hutch insists he wants to play in central midfield, but I'm happy with Ian Bishop and John Moncur at the moment. I've tried to shuffle things around, but it wasn't getting us anywhere. It's just down to me picking a team I think will get results so, no, I haven't had a barney with Hutch and I don't have any problems with him. I know Hutchison better than anybody does. I know him better than he knows himself,' he told me.

Rumours of a problem between the two had stemmed from Redknapp's public outburst following Don's being sent off against Leicester the previous year, while another bust-up had occurred at The Dell in March when the manager hurled a tray of sandwiches over Hutchison's head. 'He stood there, wearing all this ham, cheese and tomato, and all I could think was: "Harry, what have you done that for? You're starving!"' joked Redknapp afterwards, as he laughed off the sarney barney.

Further down the tunnel, Hilton had been sacrificed to make way for long-time associate Frank Burrows. 'I've got the greatest respect for Paul Hilton, who's a good lad and did a good job, but as a manager you have to make decisions,' said Harry, when I asked him about the development. 'I've decided that I'm going to make changes to my staff and that's my right to do so. If I don't get the job done I'll get the sack, it's as simple as that. People come and people go – it happens at every other football club so why shouldn't it happen at West Ham? You've got to get the best people in to improve your club.'

Given that Ronnie Boyce had been a loyal servant of the club for 37 years, as a player (scoring the winner in the 1964 FA Cup final against Preston and proving influential as the Hammers gained European Cup-Winners' Cup glory the following year) and later, serving under John Lyall and Billy Bonds, as first-team coach before taking on the role of chief scout in 1991, it was natural that many people should be concerned to see an important part of the club's foundations being replaced. The traditional West Ham way was based on stability and loyalty – Harry was still only the eighth manager in the club's history – and some didn't like the idea of people with the club's interests at heart being shown the door.

I could understand those views, yet I was pleased to see Redknapp making changes, as long as he was making them for the right reasons. For too long the Hammers had played things safe and, while continuity is a vital ingredient to any club's long-term success, I wasn't unhappy to see Harry getting the broom out and moving the furniture around a bit. There were others around me, however, who were a little sceptical and questioned Redknapp's motives, particularly as he needed to go some way to convince some people of his potential as a top-flight manager.

Chapter Eight

There was always a remote possibility that I might at some stage get to wear Tony Cottee's shirt but I never thought I'd see the day when he got to wear one of mine! It was early November, on the day of the launch of TC's *Claret & Blues* autobiography, and the little striker and I were walking across the Upton Park turf discussing ideas for the exclusive photographs we wanted to accompany the book extract that was running in the magazine that month.

Tony had been a West Ham fan all his life and the piece we'd selected was one in which he reflected on his days following the Hammers around the country as a kid. It was therefore imperative to dress him up as a supporter for the photographs, so I dug out an old claret-and-blue striped rugby shirt (that was far too small for me now) and a West Ham scarf with a dubious history, including being used as an impromptu prop by a stripper in an East End boozer after a trip to a game had been postponed many a year ago. I decided this was more information than Tony actually needed, stuck the scarf in his hands and duly positioned him around various parts of the Boleyn Ground to get the shots we wanted.

Cottee had spent the best part of a year working on the book with Tony Mac and we were both impressed with the enthusiasm the player injected into the project. Around the time of its launch, myself and Tony (McDonald, not Cottee) found ourselves buried in drunken conversation about all-things claret and blue in one of Soho's late-night watering holes (working hard at quenching our thirst – or was it quenching our thirst after working so hard?). As the last traces of blood in our alcohol streams began to disappear, I started waffling on about Julian Dicks who was in the process of sitting out his three-match ban for violent conduct, complaining that he was misunderstood and was a far more complex character than anybody ever gave him credit for. 'Y'know, his life makes for a fassschinating ssshhtory. Ssshhomebody ssshhould write a book about it,' I slurred.

'Well, why don't you write one then?' said Mac, igniting a new flame of ambition within me. From that moment on, it was a challenge I had to pursue. Cottee's book had been published by Independent UK Sports, even though the company's core business was in the magazine market, and there would be no problems getting a deal agreed with my employers. But would Julian – and, more importantly, his agent Rachel Anderson – be interested? Of course, anybody could generate an unofficial book but, with my relationship with Dicks and West Ham United to protect, the project would need to be officially endorsed. We'd also require Julian's co-operation and that of his family, friends and playing colleagues, past and present.

A meeting was arranged at Rachel's office in Westcliff and I tabled the proposal. The idea of an official Dicksy biography was not a new one – apparently *The Star*'s chief soccer writer Lee Clayton (a Hammers fan) had discussed the possibility – yet no real progress had been made. But Rachel was keen, feeling the time was right and also recognising that our package had certain strengths. Other companies may have been in a position to make offers that on the surface appeared more financially attractive, but as publishers of the official club magazine I knew we had a few ace cards. We'd be in a position to guarantee full exposure in the pages of *HNM*, through unlimited free advertising, while parent company Independent Newspapers PLC owned a number of regional titles which could be used to promote the book.

I could also promise a sincere approach to the project, while other writers may have seen it as nothing more than an opportunity to exploit Julian's notoriety and make a quick buck. Rachel seemed to like what she heard, so gave me the green light in principle, with the finer points of the agreement to be discussed in the weeks leading up to Christmas.

Then the problems began. Developments were taking place behind the scenes at Independent UK Sports and it was suggested to me that no contract with Julian's representatives should be signed until the new year. When I questioned why, I was told that certain changes were being made and that everything would become clear after Christmas. Great! I'd negotiated a deal to produce Dicksy's official biography and then had to time-waste for a couple of months.

In the meantime, at least things were picking up on the pitch. Wins at Wimbledon and Sheffield Wednesday had seen the team climb to twelfth in the table and, despite a disastrous 4–1 home defeat by Aston Villa in November (where every WHU man played as if his legs were tied together), they bounced back with an impressive 3–0 victory at Bolton Wanderers. With the struggling Premiership new boys waiting to move into a new stadium, Burnden Park represented the last opportunity for fans to stand and watch a top-flight match from the terraces. Time for a special *HNM* report . . .

'Violence returned to the terraces at Burnden Park. Even before a ball had been kicked in earnest on the pitch, the few thousand WHU supporters in the visitors' pen had witnessed murder on the stone steps.'

You'll be relieved to know I was talking about an inflatable Santa Claus that, along with a plastic frog, penguin and giant hammer, was hurled around for a good half hour by fans making up their own entertainment. This outbreak of infantile behaviour was no doubt prompted by the return to a standing terrace, which resembled a giant kiddies play-pen by the time the game kicked off. By half-time, however, our feet were frozen solid, the ever-blackening skies had started to take a mighty great leak and suddenly the idea of coughing up £11 for a square foot of northern terracing seemed less of a good idea – especially as the game was still goalless. Fortunately, things picked up in the second period, with Bishop letting fly from 25 yards, Cottee pouncing from close range and Danny Williamson running from box to box to score the third (amazingly described as a 'tap-in' in one local match report). And just to compound the theory that we were seeing things, the floodlights had illuminated to resemble giant yellow toothbrushes in the sky and an old lady, of at least 70, was seen leading the crowd into a rousing rendition of 'We are those bastards in claret and blue . . .' And to think that people complain about the youth of today.

November also saw fans pay tribute to Alvin Martin, who'd already announced his intention to hang up his boots at the end of the campaign, at his testimonial game against Chelsea at Upton Park. I was surprised by the paltry 8,710 attendance, given Alvin's 20-year career at West Ham, but I knew that he was sincere when he thanked every single one of them through the pages of the magazine. The funny thing about the day itself, though, was that while I'd taken a place in the press box instead of buying a ticket for my usual seat (sorry, Alvin!), various other members of the writing fraternity opted to pay to get in – just so they'd be able to surround Chelsea director Matthew Harding (at that time engaged in battle with chairman Ken Bates) who'd joined his supporters in the Centenary Stand.

Dicksy was back in the news a few weeks later when the Hammers went up to Goodison Park for the televised match against Everton on 11 December. Ludek Miklosko had got completely disorientated when challenging Daniel Amokachi just before half-time and, after mistaking the Nigerian striker's head for the ball, he was duly rewarded with a card that reflected his own blushes when waved in his face. With no keeper on the bench, Julian volunteered his services and his first duty was to pick the ball out of the net after David Unsworth converted the resulting spot-kick to make it 2–0.

'Yeah, I'm coaching Peter Shilton now!' he laughed, in acknow-ledgement of the goalkeeping legend's arrival at Upton Park on an emergency one-month's contract. 'I quite enjoyed taking the gloves, although I got a bit of stick from the Everton fans. "You fat bastard!" and stuff like that.' With Dicks conceding just one more goal, he was, rewarded surprisingly, with the man-of-the-match award and a bottle of bubbly from Sky, although, as he revealed to me, 'It's not the best champagne in the world, to be honest with you.'

Despite Ludo's being sent off proving a key factor in the result, it was the Hammers' second heavy away defeat in succession, having falling 4–2 to Blackburn the week before. And there was no cheer in the next three trips up north either: Middlesbrough also romped to a 4–2 win, Manchester City won 2–1 on New Year's Day and Leeds United claimed the points via two Tomas Brolin goals (the Swedish international's one decent game for the club).

Hammers fans have good reason to remember the City and Leeds games. An injury to the banned Miklosko's replacement, Les Sealey, meant that 17-year-old Neil Finn became the youngest keeper to play in the Premiership in the match at Maine Road, while at Elland Road it was a man just three weeks away from his thirty-seventh birthday who made the headlines – as Lee Chapman, having returned on loan to the team with whom he won the 1992 championship, promptly got sent off against his former Hammers team-mates. He was not a happy Chappy.

With the season having seen Ludo sent off and suspended (bringing his run of 162 consecutive league games to a close), Sealey making his first appearance for West Ham as a striker (!), Dicks playing in goal, fresh-faced Finn making history and veteran Shilton being drafted in, it was no wonder we decided to devote a large chunk of the February issue of *HNM* to a 'Between The Sticks With . . .' special feature, in which we spoke to all five men (or should that be four men and a boy?).

As if six defeats in seven league games during December and January hadn't made my job on the magazine hard enough, I was advised that publisher Philip Evans would be leaving (Tony McDonald assuming the majority of his responsibilities) while the sports division was to become fully integrated with the rest of the company (rather than being viewed as a satellite operation) which would now be known as Independent Magazines (UK) Ltd. A new MD had been appointed and one of his first announcements was that the company would cease to publish books, due to the initial investment being too high and the returns too speculative. We'd put the Tony Cottee book on the market in hardback form and even though it did well initially the company would not see the profits for some time. Hence it was goodbye, Julian . . .

I was therefore left with no alternative but to break the bad news to Rachel Anderson. Obviously there was some embarrassment on my part, having acting on behalf of a company that had done a sudden U-turn (even though nothing had yet been signed) so, to try and offset my embarrasement and her disappointment, I confirmed the news while proposing that I subsequently approach other publishers on her behalf. This would protect my position as the book's author while saving Rachel the hassle of trying to find another deal herself. And, of course, I'd still be in a position to promote the book in the pages of the magazine when it eventually came out.

Fortunately she agreed and I immediately set about generating a detailed synopsis to circulate to publishing houses. One amusing reply I received was from Bloomsbury, whose David Reynolds advised that he wouldn't be pursuing the offer, confessing to being 'a staunch Tottenham fan' (as if that should make a difference). He also revealed that the company was publishing Gerry Francis's autobiography that summer and didn't feel they 'had room for two big football books on their list that year'. I assume their book went the same way as Mr Francis . . .

A number of other publishers were rather more positive in their response and once I had three definite, interested parties I put the prospective deals in front of Rachel to examine, suggesting we go with one particular outfit who shared our vision that the book should be produced in softback, and thus affordable for most of Julian's fans. This was the main concern of Dicksy himself; the advance and royalties were hardly going to make a huge difference to his income given his earnings from West Ham (an estimated £10,000 a week), so he might as well ensure that his fans weren't being asked to shell out around £17 for a hardback. How many other players in today's game would have the same attitude?

A meeting was arranged between Rachel, Julian, the top man from Polar Publishing (also named Julian) and myself at Palms, a lounge bar on the A127 just outside Romford. Dicksy was as quiet as a mouse while Rachel, Julian II (as we'll call him) and I discussed the general approach, possible titles, photograph sources and who I would need access to for interviews and research material. I stressed the point that most authorised biographies suffer from being watered down accounts of the celebrity's life and the biggest fear was that people would think the book was some kind of attempt to rewrite Julian's life or paint him as an angel. Given his image and reputation there would also be a temptation on most author's parts simply to hang the story over the framework of the many incidents of controversy, using huge dollops of tabloid style sensationalism.

I was adamant that the project would represent an alternative. The idea had stemmed initially from a genuine fascination with Julian as a character – his public image was of a brain-dead bonehead wreaking havoc everywhere he threw his (skinhead) moonstomp boots, while my experience of conversing with him for the magazine had suggested his private persona was something very different. I was intrigued by this dichotomy of personalities and, even if I was successful in finding out who the *real* Julian Dicks was, I wanted to discover why he'd turned out that way. The aim was to explore the evolution of his character and I was determined to leave no stone unturned to achieve this quest.

'Do what you like, I don't care,' was Julian's rather minimalist response. In many ways that one sentence summed up his attitude towards the way he's perceived – he genuinely doesn't give a hoot as to what other people think of him. He knows who he is and so do the people around him who matter – his family and friends – and if others want to misunderstand him or jump to conclusions based on what they see when he's in action, then so be it. His answer was music to my ears, for I was getting the best of both worlds. I was to enjoy the benefits of having the book officially endorsed, having access to everyone and anyone associated with Julian's life and playing career, while having licence to present his story exactly as I found it. The world, as Derek Trotter would say, was my lobster!

Chapter Nine

The early part of 1996 was full of change and contrast. As one record signing, Don Hutchison, was on his way out of Upton Park (moving to Sheffield United for an initial £850,000 and completing a spectacular downward spiral – from Liverpool to the First Division in less than 18 months), another was being made in the form of £1.65 million central-defender Slaven Bilic from Karlsruher. The 27-year-old Croatian international may have looked like Doctor Death on the cover of our February issue ('He looks like he's been doing heroin!' said one bloke I overhead on the tube) but his arrival coincided with a spectacular revival on the pitch.

Following a 1–0 home defeat by Manchester United – which saw five Reds booked and Nicky Butt sent off, yet all fingers pointing at Dicks for a 'horror tackle' which, accordingly to Sky's Andy Gray, could have broken Andy Cole's leg (if he'd actually made contact) – the Hammers turned the corner to start an amazing run of five consecutive Premiership wins. A two-goal lead against Coventry at Upton Park looked to have been thrown away until Dowie, with his sixth goal since his return, guaranteed full points in the final five minutes, while Robbie Slater struck to beat Nottingham Forest in a match that was perhaps more memorable for the late appearance of Portuguese loanee Dani. The 19-year-old whizzkid – known in full as Daniel Da Cruz Carvalho – arrived in the East End from Sporting Lisbon amid a blizzard of hope and hype, with rumours of him having made records, appeared in films and strolled along the catwalks of Europe. It was mostly rubbish, of course, but he never lost his playboy image, and Harry Redknapp joked in the press conference at Villa later in the season, 'He's so good looking, my players in training don't know whether to mark him or f*** him!'

West Ham fans certainly took him to their hearts after the twice-capped international headed in a fifth-minute winner at White Hart Lane, in a match that saw Bilic finally cut through the red tape to make his début. Another live Sky game, the Hammers produced a thrilling performance on a disgraceful pitch to leave both punters and pundits

45

purring. 'West Ham staged a TV presentation of Beauty & The Beast as heart-throb Dani and he-man Julian Dicks combined to defeat a stunned and disbelieving Tottenham,' wrote the *Daily Express*. 'Times change at the Academy, but not the good habits on which it was founded. Hammers, playing their attractive passing game, handled a heavy pitch far better than the home side and made Spurs look second best,' said the *Daily Mirror*, while *The Sun* described it as West Ham's 'greatest performance in years'.

As a fan this was just the sort of stuff I wanted to read, but as editor of *HNM* I could use this material to great effect in the pages of the magazine. Under the heading 'Muddy Marvels' I dedicated two pages (aside from the match report) to reflect the views of the press and make an additional comment myself. 'Special mention must go to the travelling fans. Up in the Paxton Road south upper tier, they sang themselves silly in support of a team dredging up every last ounce of energy on a pitch that sapped all resources. It was a brilliant effort on everybody's part,' I wrote, hardly able to contain my delight.

Foam was forming in my mouth for different reasons, however, when the Hammers crashed to an embarrassing 3–0 defeat at Grimsby Town in an FA Cup replay just 48 hours after the Spurs game. Alvin Martin complained about the lack of commitment from the team but, without wanting to make excuses, I had to make a point about the fairness of having to play an important match so soon. To confirm their Jekyll & Hyde character, though, the team bounced back with a great 2–1 win at Chelsea just four days later. With the John Spencer incident still fresh in people's minds, it was no surprise that Dicksy should be subjected to constant abuse from the Stamford Bridge faithful but, as usual, he had the last laugh when he thumped in a header from Dani's corner to equalise. 'I was over the moon to score and ran behind the goal to give it the big one,' he told me, 'knowing there were Chelsea fans there.'

Danny Williamson scored the winner and found the net again to send Hammers on their way to another three points against Premiership leaders Newcastle, with Cottee getting a second. Five league wins in a row for the first time in 10 years: for once we could forget about a relegation battle and look towards finishing in the top half – a rare feeling at the time.

By now the media had started to refer to 'West Ham's United Nations' because of the number of different languages circulating the Hammers' dressing-room. *The Sun* had already acknowledged the increasingly cosmopolitan look of the side in their praise for the win at Spurs – 'Dani, the East End's very own Portu-geezer, was only the half of it. This was a night when nation spoke unto nation. A night when Croats, Czechs, Danes, Englishmen, Irishmen and even a Yank [the on-loan John Harkes] unified under one banner to beat the hell out of Tottenham Hotspur.' Meanwhile a furore had started to develop over Harry Redknapp's attempts to introduce yet another nationality in Romanian Ilie Dumitrescu. The out-of-favour Spurs midfielder had been signed as a replacement for Don Hutchison in January, but by the time the Hammers arrived at White Hart Lane on 12 February, the Department of Employment had already denied him a renewal of his work permit as a result of not having played in 75 per cent of Tottenham's games since arriving in England. 'It would have been easier to have bought him from Steaua Bucharest,' moaned club secretary Richard Skirrow.

The situation dragged on as West Ham appealed against the decision and everybody had an opinion on the matter. PFA chief executive Gordon Taylor, who offered his 'observations' to the DoE, complained about managers not thinking about the 'best long-term interests of the game' when recruiting foreign talent, while Dumitrescu – a member of the PFA – deplored the organisation for failing to support him. England boss Terry Venables, Newcastle manager Kevin Keegan (who had the same problem with Swiss defender Marc Hottiger), MP Tony Banks and Tottenham's Alan Sugar all criticised the verdict, while Hammers MD Peter Storrie and manager Redknapp spoke of the 'devastating' effect this had had on the player. 'I've had him crying his eyes out in my office,' said 'H', although some found this somewhat difficult to imagine.

Given that Ilie had played for his country on 52 occasions there would have been no problem buying him from abroad, but with the British game suddenly being flooded with waves of foreign talent in the wake of the Bosman ruling, this was the authorities' way of trying to stem the tide. I fully understood the logic of the '75 per cent ruling' but it was also an absolute folly; rather than ensuring opportunities for home-grown youngsters, managers would start picking some of the foreigners in their ranks just to ensure that permits were renewed, hence pushing the kids out of the side. I suggested as much to Harry once but he instantly denied that anybody would pick a team on such a basis.

I rang Dumi up during this period to organise a brief photo session before one of the home games and his English left something to be desired, although I got the impression his command of the language fluctuated somewhat depending on who he was talking to (just as his performances varied according to the opposition). I'd also acquired a cutting from *The Sun* (dated 15 January 1995) in which he was exposed for allegedly having had a 'four-in-a-bed sex romp behind his wife's back'.

Under the headline of 'DUMI'S RAT IT AGAIN', a photograph showed the Romanian in bed with two teenage models – on whom he'd supposedly spent £8,000 – and looking happier than a lottery-winner. It made me wonder how Dumitrescu was keeping himself occupied during those long periods on the sidelines . . .

The obstacles were ultimately overcome, of course, as West Ham tried to solve the issue by insisting they were applying for a new permit as opposed to a renewal of the existing one, and Dumi eventually made his début as a substitute against Middlesbrough on 9 March. Typically, he was struck down with hamstring problems after just three appearances and although he returned briefly at the beginning of the following campaign, we were all left wondering what all the fuss had been about as he drifted out of Harry's first-team plans. 'He was an 'orrible bloke,' sniffed Iain Dowie, a man who never has a bad word for *anybody*, during a pre-match chat at Anfield after the Romanian had been flogged to Mexicans Futbal Club de America for just under £1 million. 'Ilie hasn't played the required amount of games to earn an extension to his work permit and we ran the risk of losing him for nothing,' explained Peter Storrie, without the faintest hint of embarrassment as Gordon Taylor could be seen grinning with folded arms through the windows of his office.

The sequence of five Premiership wins ended on 24 February when the Hammers came up against Arsenal at Upton Park. John Hartson scored the only goal of the game in the very first minute, taking full advantage of a horrendous back-pass from the much-booed Harkes and, even though a confident West Ham completely dominated the match, their luck was summed up when Dicksy – still seeing stars from an earlier clash with Ray Parlour – fired a below-par penalty kick straight at David Seaman. 'I realised straight after the game that I couldn't remember any of it,' Julian told me when he'd returned to his senses. 'The club doctor told me I'd been concussed and had put myself on autopilot.' (I wonder what Harkes's excuse was!)

Despite having a firm hold on mid-table respectability, I was impressed by the team's determination to keep going even though a European qualification place was way beyond them. 'It's boring now there's no threat of relegation,' complained one of my colleagues in the East Stand and it was hard to tell if he was joking or not. A thrilling 2–2 draw at Coventry was followed by a 2–0 win over Boro, before the wheels – and one man – fell off at Newcastle in a match beamed live on Sky. Pottsy fell victim to David Ginola's histrionics and referee Stephen Lodge's lack of discretion, leaving a 10-man Hammers (with Les Sealey finally appearing between the sticks for his beloved boyhood heroes at the ripe old age of 38) to try and keep the score down as the Toon Army hit top gear. Somehow we kept them down to three but I was still fuming about the sending-off when a delighted Kevin Keegan appeared for the post-match press conference. I was so tempted to say something like, 'Yeah, but Ginola's a diver and it's easy against 10 men,' when diplomacy got the better of me and I just nodded as KK reflected on their 30-odd goalscoring opportunities. (I think they might have won anyway.)

Other memorable games from the final furlong that season include a 4–2 win over Manchester City (in which Julian scored arguably the team's goal of the season with a 30-yard piledriver) to help the Maine Road men turn into the side alleys of the Endsleigh League, plus a 1–1 draw in the new 'ecru' coloured shirt at Villa Park (thanks in part to Dani who set up the equaliser for Cottee with his first touch after coming on as an 83rd-minute substitute). As Harry made jokes about his pair of good-lookers in the Portuguese starlet and, er, Dowie (!), there were serious doubts developing about Dani's attitude – which began to explain why he wasn't figuring as often as we'd have liked. My personal view was that, while he was still on loan and the club was paying his wages, we should have got as much out of him as we could. Redknapp, meanwhile, had to set examples to the rest of the squad and he later declared, after it became known that Dani had been omitted from the team to face QPR because of his failure to turn up for training the day before, 'I can't run a football club like that. How can I tell Ian Bishop or Danny Williamson, who do turn up for training every day, that they're not playing and that Dani is? The next thing I'll know is that all the players will be playing golf every morning!'

Commitment was a vital factor and if any player personified that as much as Hammer-of-the-Year Dicks, then it would arguably have been Iain Dowie, whose efforts that season were rewarded with the runner-up trophy. I'd been one of the Northern Irish striker's biggest critics but I had to admit that, at the price the club paid (£125,000 plus Jeroen Boere, valued at £150,000), we'd got a bargain. Dowie's tally in WHU colours for the year may have been a modest nine but, writing prior to the season's end and assuming the big man would finish in double figures, I calculated that £8.5 million Stan Collymore, £7.5 million Andy Cole and the £12.7 million pairing of Les Ferdinand and Faustino Asprilla would have to score 309, 273 and 462 goals respectively to justify their transfer fees on a pro-rata basis.

To flip the coin, it could be said that if your man up front isn't getting the 20 goals a year needed to compete at the right end of the table, then it doesn't matter how cheaply he arrived. 'Dowie always gives 100 per cent', was the popular call up in the East Stand, while my response used to be, 'Yeah, but 100 per cent of nothing is nothing!'

With the Hammers finishing tenth in the table after their final-day draw with Sheffield Wednesday nobody could complain about Iain's contribution that season, which shouldn't be judged purely on goals scored anyway. I therefore felt the striker thoroughly deserved his place on the cover of the May issue of *HNM* and rang Iain at home to let him know we wanted to acknowledge his achievements. 'I'm having a new house built at the moment so if you'd like to send your photographer round I'll be happy to pose for pictures,' said the amiable 31-year-old. 'My wife came up with the design of the house along with an architect and we've had a hand in everything really,' he explained, as I wrote of how the ever-industrious striker was cementing his relationship with the fans and getting his hands muddy both on and off the pitch. 'It's been a hell of a job but it'll be worth it,' he added, before turning his thoughts towards his return to Upton Park. 'I've enjoyed my time back here and it's coincided with West Ham becoming a greater force in the Premiership. It's important that we now build on that.'

While many felt that would mean Dowie being pushed out of future starting line-ups, he insisted, 'There should always be competition for places and if I'm the one not doing the business then I shouldn't be in the team. There's no room for sentiment in football.' Wise words, indeed. Feeling that I'd established a reasonable rapport with Iain, I mentioned the constant jibes he received for his looks (not least from his manager in various post-match press conferences!). 'There's a lot of rubbish talked by certain people and it annoys me because I don't think what is said is factually true,' he said, probably pulling a few faces at the other end of the line. 'If you've got a photo where I'm challenging for the ball at the far post, I'm hardly posing for pictures, am I? As far as I'm concerned, my wife is very happy with my looks and that's all that matters. If people want to make a living out of commenting on other people then so be it, but some of them should take a look in the mirror first.' A reference to Harry, perhaps?

I later discovered that the sales of *HNM* had taken a dramatic drop that month, but argued that the previous three issues had all featured new signings (Bilic, Dani and Dumitrescu) on the cover. 'Don't worry,' I said, 'I doubt if Dowie will be pressing for another cover again anyway.' How right I turned out to be . . .

Around this time I also got to know Rachel Anderson a little better – having finally agreed the contract to write the authorised Julian Dicks biography – and was happy to comply when she suggested that it might be an interesting idea for the magazine to interview her about her role as the world's only female agent licensed by FIFA. I ventured out to Westcliff again and we discussed how she got involved in the game (through the marketing side) and came to represent Dicksy (through knowing his wife Kay). 'Julian was having a few problems,' she told me, 'but there was a reason. There were lots of outside influences and they all had a domino effect. Perhaps the person advising him at that time didn't necessarily have his best interests at heart. I suggested a couple of ways of dealing with the problems and when they worked he said that perhaps I might do a better job of looking after him than the so-called experts.'

But don't people say, "You're a *woman*, what do *you* know about football?"' I asked.

'All the time!' she laughed. 'Some say it and others just might think it, but Julian just says, "She knows nothing about football but she knows how to negotiate a contract and get the best for me." And that's what my job is.'

In later years Rachel would become embroiled in a battle to rid football of discrimination against women after she was banned from the annual PFA awards dinner. She took the matter to the House of Lords, taking advantage of the little known Prayer for Parliament procedure. But she was already aware of how clubs needed to change their attitudes as a whole: 'Football is a form of showbusiness. It's pure, simple, raw entertainment and it's unfortunate that a few clubs haven't quite grasped that yet,' she insisted (without necessarily implicating West Ham). She also felt that agents should be viewed with less suspicion, while supporting the Bosman ruling and its likely effects on the game. I totally opposed what Rachel was saying in respect of the latter, however, pointing out that players would exploit the shifting balance of power and that clubs would be held to ransom, but she was adamant that 'football has to move with the times' and that 'clubs are not stupid – they'll only pay what a player is worth and what they can afford'.

Our discussion also allowed me to find out what had really gone on behind the transfer of Don Hutchison, another of Rachel's clients, to Sheffield United earlier in the season. During previous conversations she'd indicated her displeasure with Harry Redknapp's handling of the player (who was always good for a laugh on the phone) and told me she'd set a deadline as to when she'd force the issue. That time had clearly arrived in the new year.

'Hutch wasn't happy,' she confided. 'He scored 11 goals in 26 games in his first season and was very much part of the reason West Ham stayed up. But it was obvious that he wasn't going to get a regular first-team place this season. He stood the situation until Christmas but he's just too good to be in anybody's reserves. Sheffield United contacted Harry and, even though one or two other clubs were interested, he wanted to play for a manager he really respected. Howard Kendall [he of the 'have a drink, lads' stories during Cottee's days at Everton] knows what it's like having a bit of adverse publicity and Don, unfortunately, will always have that holiday incident thrown at him, whatever he does.'

Yeah, he's older Budweiser now, isn't he?

'He'll be back in the Premiership one day,' she insisted. 'Hopefully it'll be with Sheffield but, if not, he'll move on. I mean, that's the name of the game, isn't it . . .'

Chapter Ten

Brrrr . . . brrr . . . Brrrr . . . brrr . . .

'Oh, no, that's all I need,' I muttered, as the sound of the phone ringing broke the silence just as I was getting comfortable on my favourite seat. Not having the faintest idea of who it could be, I pogoed across my flat – with trousers wrapping my ankles together – and picked up the receiver.

''ALLO!' I barked, somewhat irritated at having been disturbed during a sensitive moment of contemplation.

'Er, is that Kirk Blows?' enquired the polite-sounding Scot at the other end of the line.

'It is,' I replied, in a rather more sensible tone, vaguely recognising the voice.

'It's Graeme Souness here, you wanted to talk about Julian Dicks.'

'Er, yes, Graeme . . . er, could you, er, just hang on a moment, I've just got to attend to something,' I stuttered, before bouncing back across the room. WHOOOSSHHH!!!

I returned to the phone in a more decent state of dress and expressed surprise that Graeme had got in touch – firstly, because my initial efforts to send a fax through to Galatasaray, the club he was managing in Turkey, had resulted in the machine producing a sound that usually emanates from a mosque and, secondly, it had just been confirmed that Souness had got the sack. 'Our last league game is tomorrow and I'm in the process of clearing out my desk, so I thought I'd run up the club's phone bill!' he said. 'We can talk as long as you want . . .'

Just what I wanted to hear. The former Liverpool boss was just one of around 35 names on the list of potential interviewees I'd drawn up for the writing of *Terminator*, the authorised story of Julian Dicks, and I considered it a major coup when he finally made contact. Souness had taken Julian to Merseyside in September 1993 and if I was going to reflect the views of the manager who later bombed him out of Anfield – Roy Evans – I also needed the first part of the equation.

Graeme loved Dicksy to bits. 'I think we're alike in many ways,' he confided. 'Maybe I was slightly better at controlling myself, but he's my type of player and wants to win. He'd definitely be one of the best 11 players I've ever worked with. I felt I had a relationship with Julian but, unfortunately, I didn't get the chance to work with him long enough.'

That was because Liverpool decided to chop Souey (groan . . .) from his position within five months of Dicksy's arrival, at which point Roy Evans – one of the longtime backroom boys – assumed first-team responsibilities. I really didn't fancy my chances of persuading Roy to discuss Julian's brief spell at Anfield under his control. For a start, the pair had been involved in a war of words, both face-to-face and in the press, and Liverpool were just a few days away from meeting Manchester United in the 1996 FA Cup final as I sent a fax to the club's Melwood training HQ . . .

'Roy Evans phoned for you about 10 minutes ago,' said one of my colleagues as I arrived at my desk (typically late). I couldn't believe it. The club was gearing up for its most important match in years and their manager was ringing me up to talk to me about a player he didn't even like! I rang the number he'd left and his secretary immediately put me through to his office. 'Listen, I'm a bit busy today but if you ring me back the same time tomorrow morning I'll be happy to talk. OK?' No problem, Roy, that was fine.

By the time Evans had taken over from Souness, Dicksy was in the process of recovering from a knee injury which clearly worried the Anfield staff and did the player no favours in terms of keeping in shape. Julian may have scored the last goal in front of a standing Kop (a penalty against Ipswich) but Evans must already have had doubts because rumours had been circulating during the close season that a swap deal involving David Burrows could be on the cards. After Julian was bombed out of a pre-season trip to Germany, he blabbed to the press that Evans hadn't 'the bottle' to tell him what he really felt.

'I didn't think Julian was as fit as I would have liked him to be,' Roy told me, pleased that I'd bothered to get his side of the story. 'Rightly or wrongly, I had to make some decisions.' Was it true Roy didn't speak to Julian for 10 weeks after he went public? 'I'd be surprised at that,' he responded. 'I think we always said hello. I don't mind having an argument but I'm not the sort of guy who holds any animosity towards people.' But was Dicks told to train with the youth team, as he claims? 'Only when the first team were away. You've got to train with *somebody*. The majority of the time I found him to be a decent lad. The only problems we had were the injury and his fitness.'

It was clear that Julian didn't take to Roy's style of management, while others have suggested that players signed by Souness were looked upon unfavourably. Whatever the reality, I appreciated Evans offering his thoughts and wished him all the best for the match against United later that week. Sadly, they lost to an 87th-minute Cantona goal.

It had been my intention to talk to all the managers Julian had played under, including those at his first club, Birmingham City. I had no luck with John Bond, but Dicksy had a number for Ron Saunders, the man who took him to Brum at the tender age of 14 and looked after him during those early years. 'Who's the most physical team in the league at the moment?' Saunders asked during our lengthy conversation.

'Er, Manchester United?' I offered.

'Exactly,' he said, using the point to fend off criticism that his Birmingham team had been a bit on the dirty side. With the likes of Mark Dennis, Noel Blake, Pat van den Hauwe, Mick Harford and Martin Kuhl (all known as hard nuts) at St Andrews at that time, it's hardly surprising the team had something of a nasty reputation and that people felt Dicks had been educated in the 'school of hard knocks' (quite literally).

'As a youngster Julian showed great enthusiasm and put tremendous effort into his game,' Ron told me. 'Of course, there's a thin line sometimes between giving 100 per cent and going a bit over the top, but I never really thought he had any problems with his temperament – only that, as a competitor, if anyone beat him he'd get after them very quickly.' Ron commanded tremendous respect as he spoke and it was obvious he had little time for the way the sport was heading nowadays. It used to be a man's game but not any more – and I, for one, shared his sorrow.

More revealing information about Julian's early development came from Martin Kuhl, who shared digs with Dicksy and played in the same Blues team. 'He was a scrawny little kid with big eyes – a real ugly little duckling – but I treated him like a younger brother,' Kuhl told me. 'Ron Saunders was an iron man but he loved Dicksy because he was his sort of player. He was brought up with the fact that you won the ball at all costs. He was also taught the tricks of the trade and I don't think it's done him any harm. We used to look after each other on and off the pitch.'

Martin was on Bristol City's books when I rang him, bringing back memories of my disastrous trip down to the West Country a month earlier to meet Julian's dad, Ron, and brother, Grantley. I'd spoken to both parties on the phone and arranged to meet them at Ron's house in the district of Bridlington on the evening of 9 May. What a way to spend my birthday!

I shot down the M4 and was making such good time I decided to stop off for a quick bite to eat just outside Bristol. Returning to my vehicle (a totally impractical two-seater), I still hadn't drunk the bottle of coke I'd bought and tossed it on to the passenger seat. A few minutes later I decided to take a swig (don't tell me, you can see what's coming next . . .) and as I unscrewed the cap the whole thing exploded. WHHOOOSSHHH!!! It was like being caught in a Coca-Cola typhoon. Sticky stuff was everywhere – all over the windscreen, windows, dashboard, steering wheel and seats. And, more disturbingly, it was all over me. I looked down to see my white shirt and jeans covered in dark spots: not only did I look like something out of *101 Dalmatians*, it also served to act as a magnet for every molecular piece of dust within a radius of 50 miles. I had no choice, though, but to carry on driving and, by the time I arrived at the Dicks household, the strap of my seat belt had left a dirty diagonal line across my chest. It looked as if I was wearing a bad outfit from *Star Trek*. My embarrassment was complete, however, when I arrived at Ron's and was invited in, only to walk into a room packed with virtually the entire Dicks family. 'Er, I had a bit of an accident . . .'

Julian was certainly chiselled from the same rock as his father. A former player and key figure on the local football scene, Dicksy's dad is exactly how you'd expect him to be, on the pitch and off. 'I was always aggressive and I hated losing. I'd rather cheat than lose,' he admitted, reminding me of Julian's claim that his dad had been a 'horrible bastard' as a player.

In terms of personality, Julian had clearly inherited many of his dad's characteristics. Ron sat there quietly, using his words economically, while Grantley displayed the same family features. Maybe we should refer to his brother as Terminator II, given his own reputation at non-league level: sent off four times for (early) Bath and booked around 90 times. 'I get plenty of stick because of who I am,' he declared, 'particularly if we're playing in London. I get called a wanker and told I'm as crap as my brother, as fat as my brother, everything . . . But it doesn't bother me.'

Just as Julian generally takes time to come out of his shell with those yet to win his confidence, Grantley is the same. 'I get louder when I'm with people I like and trust,' he revealed, thankfully increasing in volume. And Ron has clearly provided the template for such traits, appearing sullen and sometimes being accused of moodiness – as is Julian – but it's a façade that disappears once the key to the lock is found.

'Grantley and Julian are like two peas in a pod, but I think Grantley mixes more than Julian does,' said their mother Carol a few days later. 'Having said that, Grantley can seem moody at times – and that reminds me of his father!'

The boys' parents split up in the mid-'80s and Carol now resides near Kingston (Surrey, not Jamaica). 'When I started working at the Post Office they thought I was going to be a big black mama because my son was called Julian and they knew he'd been transferred from Birmingham!' she laughed. Not that there should be any mistaking Carol Dicks. A loyal supporter of her son's footballing activities, she has spent many a Saturday evening in the Boleyn pub next to the Upton Park ground. 'Even the landlady knows who I am now,' she said. 'A chap came up to me one night and said, "Can I buy you a drink? Only I want to say that I bought a drink for the person who brought God into the world."'

A real extrovert with plenty to say for herself, Carol appeared to be the very antithesis of her former husband when we met for an afternoon's conversation for *Terminator*. She may have borne little obvious resemblance to Julian facially or characteristically, but her home gave the game straight away. Dicksy paraphernalia littered the place, with books, videos, magazines, photographs and even West Ham ticket stubs on display. 'I'm so proud of him,' she beamed. 'I wrote a letter to our Ju [as she calls him] once to tell him and the ink was getting smudged because I couldn't stop crying.'

After several hours we found ourselves flicking through her photograph albums and scrapbooks – as I'd done at Ron and Grantley's – and this material was tremendously helpful as I began to unfurl Julian's life in his own words and those of others around him. Kay, his wife, was invaluable in this respect and her contribution alone made *Terminator* a unique offering. 'Basically, he was a selfish pig,' she avowed of her husband when ruminating over the difficult 1992–93 period of their relationship. 'He'd do what he wanted, when he wanted. He'd come home pissed up and made me feel as if he couldn't care less about any of us. I'd had enough.'

Julian had already volunteered candid information on the dark days of that particular season, when he was sent off three times and came under increasing scrutiny from the media, but I was still amazed by Kay's honesty. I wanted to hear the real story but I was surprised by how open both parties had been when it came to more private matters such as how Julian's career was affecting their marriage. 'He was so popular at the club with so many so-called friends telling him how great he was that I suppose it was bound to rub off on him. And I'd be the first to have a go at him if he'd been booked or sent off again, so that wouldn't help,' she admitted.

Funnily enough, the one thing Kay didn't want to disclose was the whereabouts of her wedding pictures. 'I think they're at my sister's up in Birmingham,' she said vaguely on more than one occasion when I asked if I could possibly use one in the book. 'I look awful in them,' she claimed, embarrassed by her choice of dress for the occasion. I'd given up the ghost until one particular day when I mentioned the photos once again in the presence of Kattie and Jessica, the couple's two young daughters. 'We know where they are, Mummy!' they screamed in delight, as they scampered off and returned a few moments later with the incriminating evidence under their arms. (Thanks, kids, I winked.) Kay did not look amused . . .

My first visits to the Dicks household in Latchingdon, just outside Chelmsford in deepest Essex, took place towards the end of April 1996 and the family (plus numerous dogs) always made me feel welcome. Julian's hospitality was perhaps a little too generous during our second interview session when he suggested we go and have a few beers outside by the swimming pool. 'C'mon, it's a lovely day – what are you, a man or a mouse?' he asked, as I squeaked my refusal. It was a great idea, but I was driving and he was playing the next day . . . As it was, the entire West Ham team performed as if they were inebriated as they crashed to a humiliating 3–0 defeat by Queens Park Rangers who were relegated in the process! Harry Redknapp went ballistic in the dressing-room afterwards, attacking the defence in particular, although Dicksy refrained from hitting straight back. 'I used to just say "f*** off, you're wrong!" but now I say "fair enough" and go and see the manager on the Monday morning to make my point, as I did after the QPR game,' he told me, aggrieved that 'H' had singled out the back four.

Julian would happily light up a cigar during our book sessions while Kay would serve up cups of tea on a regular basis. Dicksy isn't the easiest bloke in the world to get conversation out of at times but at least he speaks his mind. Kay is easy-going in her manner but it's possible that she found it easier to talk – especially about the difficulties experienced during certain periods – without her husband sitting next to her, like the time Julian took an end-of-season break in Tenerife with a number of other West Ham players. 'He used to go out with people and they'd have all these women hanging around them,' she complained. 'It's very difficult when your husband's going out four nights a week while you're at home with the kids and people are phoning up to tell you things. I was absolutely paranoid – I didn't trust him as far as I could throw him. And he couldn't understand why.' The press, meanwhile, had not made life any easier. 'They drove us up the wall,' she said. 'They had cars parked outside the house and wouldn't leave us alone.'

If Kay thought that Julian's transfer to Liverpool and his improved behaviour both on the field of play and within their marriage had brought an end to the media mayhem, she was sadly mistaken. Things may have improved generally but the fragile windows of confidence that had developed in the following three years were soon to be smashed to pieces. It was about 10 a.m. on Sunday, 26 May when my phone rang. 'Have you seen the *News of the World*?' asked a friend, rather furtively.

'Er, no,' I responded, still not fully awake.

'Julian's on the front page,' she said. 'You'd better go and buy a copy.'

'SEX ROMP SHAME OF MARRIED SOCCER STAR,' screamed the paper's cover as I picked it up in horror. It could have been any one of hundreds of high-profile footballers but, no, there were Dicksy's fat little features staring out at me, beneath a picture of a bleeding Dudley Moore after being 'battered by wife Nicole'. Thinking that's what Julian would probably end up like if a word of the story was true, I raced home and pondered what impact this would have on the writing of my book. More than anything, though, I felt concern for Kay. The paper claimed that her husband had 'enjoyed nights of passion with a besotted 17-year-old' while in Tenerife and, whether there was an ounce of substance to them or not, the revelations would have a devastating affect on his family.

The allegations were splashed over the first three pages, providing a detailed account of how Julian had supposedly lured two young girls back to their hotel room after 'cuddling and kissing' one of them in Lineker's Bar. The account was provided by the older friend, who spoke of how Dicks had intimated by the way he looked at her that he wanted 'to do the double' with them (leaving readers wondering exactly what kind of face one has to pull to make such a suggestion). The story was so flimsy, though, it was hard to imagine how any newspaper – even the trivia-obsessed *NOTW* – could devote so much space to a tale in which the most extreme charge was that Julian had spent 'several hours kissing and fondling' one of the teenagers. And what evidence did they have to prove that the pair were together? Cue Exhibit A, a photograph showing them within six feet of each other, which had been cropped to obscure whether either was part of a larger group). Yet the caption read: 'Dicks and Leeann head for her bedroom.' You didn't have to be a genius to recognise that if a photographer was tracking their every move, he'd have got a shot of the two of them disappearing through a hotel door together or at least having some kind of physical contact.

Given that the paper also claimed that Dicks had 'tried it on with our undercover reporter' (named as Helen Carter) and advertised for people who've met stars on their holidays to come forward with their stories, it was impossible to take much of it too seriously. That's easy for me to say, of course.

'Kay went ballistic when she saw the headlines,' disclosed Julian on my next visit after the dust had started to settle. I'd deliberately left the couple alone for a while as I could imagine their phone being red hot. As it turned out, everybody else felt the same way. 'It was really weird, but *nobody* phoned,' revealed Kay when I asked her about that particular Sunday. What had been ringing, however, were the alarm bells the day before the paper hit the streets, since a woman from the *NOTW* called to advise Julian that the story was running and was looking for a comment. 'I told her I had nothing to say and that if they printed anything I'd sue them because it was all lies,' he confirmed.

Julian thus informed his agent of the call and Rachel immediately warned the paper of the distress the story would cause the Dicks family and that legal action would be taken if they proceeded with the publication of such allegations. At the same time, Julian volunteered to Kay that something was going to break in the following day's press. 'I've done nothing, so whatever they write will be a load of rubbish,' he told her.

I asked Kay about that conversation and she told me, 'Julian had to be honest with me. He had no idea he was being followed around in Tenerife, so if he had been guilty they could well have had evidence.' She was understandably furious that they'd become targets once again of the tabloids but, fortunately, she realised the report had little substance when she saw it. 'It was a story about nothing,' she said, although that hadn't stopped the waves of controversy crashing at their doorstep.

'It really annoyed me because when stuff like that gets written it affects my whole family,' complained Julian.

Indeed, the tide had even taken the story out to Spain, where his two daughters were on holiday with Kay's sister. 'People were bothering them out there so I had to bring them home,' revealed Kay.

During the following weeks, Rachel advised me of her intention to fight back on the couple's behalf, having taken advice from lawyers and even attempted contact with the girls who appeared in the story. They were understandably reluctant to say anything (talking to their own lawyers at the time), while further suspicion was being cast on the integrity of freelance reporter Helen Carter. With other sensationalistic holiday stories appearing in subsequent issues of the *NOTW*, it became clear that her mission in Tenerife was simply to continue supplying stories of hedonism in order to justify, and prolong, her stay in the sun.

Dicksy's room-mate during the holiday had been Ian Bishop, whom I'd intended to interview for the book anyway, knowing he often shared with Julian on trips with the Hammers. Of course, he was eager to stress his friend's innocence: 'As soon as I saw the story I knew it was total bull,' he declared. 'None of it was true and I just hoped that Kay hadn't believed any of it.'

She may not have, but there was still concern that other people might. 'The thing that upsets me more than anything is that people believe what they read in the papers,' Kay told me. 'Some even said that, if they'd been me, they'd have taken Julian for every penny he's got!'

A regular visitor to shows around the country with her dogs, Kay was forced to put on a brave face. 'People didn't know what to say to me,' she confided. 'True friends were as good as gold but I could tell that a lot of people were uneasy with me. That was hard to deal with.'

But that's the last thing the tabloid press are concerned about, of course. Despite pledging only to make great headlines of stories when it's genuinely in the public's interest (as opposed to 'of great public interest'), following the death of Princess Diana in 1997 and the ensuing furore about the media hounding anybody with celebrity status, Britain's best-selling papers have continued to dish the dirt with gleeful abandon. Predictably, the tabloids would claim that it's infidelity that ruins relationships, not newspapers, but it's the exposure of people's personal matters to the greater public that so often creates the biggest problem. 'That kind of story would split some families apart,' said Kay when discussing the impact of the piece with me. 'For people who can't take the aggravation it could ruin their marriages, ruin their lives. It's not something the media should be allowed to do. It's the nastiest thing they've every done to me.'

I was most appreciative of Kay speaking so candidly. Julian's loyalty was a private issue but with the subject being thrust into the public domain, I'd felt entitled – indeed compelled – to address the story in some fashion for the book. I asked Dicks if he knew the girl in question and he admitted, 'When I saw her picture I could remember speaking to her.' He also recalled the reporter who alleged he made a pass at her. 'She was a pain in the arse,' he moaned. 'She wouldn't leave me alone so I told her to f*** off and she obviously got the hump.'

Given the threat of legal action, I'd initially assumed the topic would have to be brushed under the carpet as far as the book was concerned. Yet Julian and Kay were prepared to discuss it while Rachel was content to allow them to do so. I'd always maintained that my intention was to address all the major issues in Dicksy's life but this was the ultimate test for all parties concerned. Thankfully, everybody remained true to their word. Rachel was always optimistic that the matter would be resolved in their favour and an out-of-court settlement was subsequently agreed.

Exactly 14 months after breaking the story, the *News of the World* published the following statement on page nine of their 27 July edition: 'On 26 May, 1996, we published a story about Julian Dicks, the West Ham captain, in which we suggested that he made sexual advances to, and had sex with, a girl during a holiday in Tenerife. We now accept these allegations were untrue. We apologise to Mr Dicks and his family for the distress and the embarrassment which our story caused them.'

Oh, that's all right then.

Chapter Eleven

Ian Bishop had been one of the more obvious candidates from the West Ham playing staff to interview for Julian's book. The pair had 'hit it off straight away' according to Bish, having shared a night-out at Hollywood's in Romford after his arrival from Manchester City in December 1989. 'If anybody knows him away from the game it's probably me,' he told me, singing Julian's praises both as a player and a person. 'He looks after the people he cares for – his family and his friends – and away from football you wouldn't recognise him. I'd even go so far as to say he's quite soft.'

One place Julian wasn't soft was on the training pitch, especially when Lou Macari, who'd brought Bish to Upton Park, was in opposition. 'It was a bit of shock for me when I first arrived to see somebody booting their manager up in the air,' said Ian. 'To be fair to Lou, he kept coming back for more but it was a bit strange. Julian had been made captain but he seemed to have a love–hate relationship with the boss. It looked stormy at times.'

I found Macari even easier to make contact with than Roy Evans. He was managing Stoke City at the time and within a few hours of faxing his office he was on the phone, laughing and joking about his relationship with Dicks. 'Tell Julian I'm waiting for another chance to kick him!' he quipped, obviously in good mood. Lou had replaced John Lyall in the summer of 1989 and endured a difficult six months or so in charge. With stability evolving into stagnancy at Upton Park, the board had decided to bring in an 'outsider' and Macari, having proved his managerial credentials with Swindon, was their choice to try and take the Hammers back to the top flight. Many weren't surprised when things didn't work out, assuming his round face wouldn't fit into a square hole, but a lot of that had to do with Macari not liking much of what he saw when he arrived – including Dicksy. 'I called him fat,' laughed Lou when I asked about his first meeting with Julian. Macari certainly had his preconceptions of the player ('he had a reputation of being bad news,' he admitted) but his thoughts on the prevalent attitude at the club became more obvious when discussing his frustration with Dicks. 'I would have tried *anything* to make him realise that he was an under-achiever. He still hasn't achieved what he should have in the game given his talent,' he offered. 'But he's a bit unfortunate that he played at West Ham at the wrong time. Had he played in the days of Billy Bonds and Trevor Brooking – the real professionals – he probably wouldn't have been so misguided. But if you're in an environment where everyone's a little bit sloppy and saying, "Let's eat, drink and be merry", you've got a job on your hands to change their attitude.'

Indeed, one of the things Macari had tried to change was the player's eating and drinking habits. He disapproved of Julian downing cans of coke in the build-up to a game and tried to introduce a healthier range of foods at the training ground, but constantly found resistance to his ideas. Some of his views made perfect sense, of course, but Lou's own idiosyncrasies often undermined what he was trying to achieve. I've heard a number of stories of Lou jumping off the team bus on the way to games to place a bet or consult journalists about what side to name that day. 'Same team as last week,' he allegedly once said before disappearing before a match. And club photographer Steve Bacon still tells the one about Macari asking for his verdict on Colin Foster before pushing through the £750,000 deal to buy the defender from Nottingham Forest.

Despite the obvious friction that existed between them, Lou was eager to stress his regard for Julian. 'My main view is that people don't know the real Julian Dicks. Deep down he's a nice lad – not a slob or a thug – and he's a very, very good footballer. There would be many instances I could talk about to give an indication that he was misguided but I don't think I'd want to do that.'

The point made about Julian not playing in the era of Trevor Brooking and Billy Bonds was interesting, though, given that the latter found himself replacing Lou after his controversial departure in February 1990 and subsequently trying to impose his own philosophies. Julian had been totally honest about his relationship with the Hammers legend ('I was a right bastard with Billy Bonds the whole time he managed West Ham,' he once told me) and I was determined to talk to Billy to get his side of the story. At that time he was working at Queens Park Rangers and I went through the motions of sending a fax to Loftus Road. After getting no response I was given Billy's personal telephone number by an acquaintance and even though I didn't really like the idea of ringing him at his Chislehurst home – knowing how much he valued his privacy – I couldn't risk missing out on a key interview for the book.

After establishing nothing but an intimate relationship with his answerphone for the first month or so, I assumed that Bonds wasn't keen to discuss conflicts with players he used to manage. But I kept on ringing and suddenly one day he picked up the phone. Indeed, he was more than happy to talk, revealing a certain understanding – if not sympathy – towards Julian's aggressive character on the pitch. 'I can see similarities between us in that we're both very committed, physical types of players,' he said. 'I spoke to him a few times when he got into trouble because I could see why it was happening and knew how he was feeling. But it's only in the last year or two that it's started to sink in.'

Bonzo was brutally up-front about their dust-ups – 'there were times we could have come to blows. I would have loved to have chinned him a couple of times' – but the real revelations came when I asked about his trying to keep Dicksy from speaking out against the much-derided Bond Scheme. 'Julian wasn't the only one. I never backed the Bond Scheme either,' he disclosed. 'I couldn't come out and say it because it was something the club were proceeding with, but I was asked by the board to do certain things for the Bond Scheme which I refused point blank to do. Nobody knows that because to this day I've never said anything about it. But I thought it was a diabolical liberty and I was dead against it.'

I felt somewhat honoured, not to say surprised, that Billy should take this opportunity to reveal his true feelings on the Bond Scheme and use (or choose) my book to do so. I also feel the introduction of the scheme was a contributory factor in Billy's increasing disillusionment with the game. 'You couldn't blame the fans for feeling the way they did,' he added, 'but the hostility made it very difficult for everybody. The one thing about West Ham United has always been its togetherness. The fans had supported the team through thick and thin and even when we were struggling they knew when to get behind the team. I was at Upton Park for 27 years and I've never known a season like it. It was a nightmare.'

I'm not sure how much Bonzo's words – or the official club magazine's editor providing him with a platform to expose such views – were appreciated by the board of directors, but I didn't see any reason to camouflage such opinion. The impact of the Bond Scheme – a concept demanding that fans pay between £500 and £975 before acquiring the right to purchase a season ticket (which some would define, at best, as extortion and, at worst, blackmail) – on the 1991–92 season could not be brushed under the carpet and Julian had been the one player to publicly voice his dissent. In Dicksy's words, he 'got a bollocking' for it but, when I asked managing director Peter Storrie about it, he insisted that nobody was singled out. 'All that was said to the players was that they shouldn't really air an opinion on something they don't know the full facts about. They were just told to concentrate on football,' he said.

Terminator provided me with the ideal opportunity to address general events during Julian's time at the club, because it was important to set his story against a backdrop that would provide context. With that in mind, it was fascinating talking to Billy about those past years, just as it was in speaking with John Lyall. Manager of West Ham for some 15 years, until the club failed to renew his contract in 1989, John commanded tremendous respect for his abilities as a coach and leader of men. Julian's first full season at West Ham was to prove Lyall's last and I was especially keen to ask him about the club's decline in the late '80s. After setting a world record for a goalkeeper (when buying Phil Parkes for £565,000 in 1979), splashing a club record £800,000 on striker Paul Goddard in 1980, winning the FA Cup that same year, reaching the final of the League Cup plus winning promotion the following season and finishing a club-best third in 1986, how on earth had we found ourselves selling Frank McAvennie and Tony Cottee (the latter for a then British record fee of £2.2 million) and replacing them with two men from the old Third Division (Walsall's David Kelly and Fulham's Leroy Rosenior)?

'That's just the way West Ham had to do it,' he insisted. 'With the likes of Mark Ward and Frank McAvennie, you bought them cheap and they became more valuable. In fairness, David Kelly had a lot of clubs chasing him and we felt we did well to get him. But Kelly and Rosenior were replacing two international footballers. It's not easy to replace Geoff Hurst, is it?' John agreed that the sale of the two prized strikers was a major factor in the Hammers' relegation in 1989. 'We lost very important players, while Billy Bonds was nearing the end and those things have a great effect on the club.'

While fans looked upon the loss of key players and subsequent lack of investment as a direct indication of a lack of ambition within the club, Lyall was philosophical about the position. 'If a player is going to be successful, it can sometimes help him coming into that kind of situation because he'll have to think. Lads like Tony Cottee had to work out how to score goals because they weren't going to have them laid on a plate. Players had to think about the game because the points weren't guaranteed every week.'

That may well have been the case but it had been so frustrating for the supporters. The 1985–86 team had come incredibly close to winning the league, but instead of building on things, the club did precisely nothing and the momentum was lost. The downward spiral had commenced and relegation followed just three years later. I hadn't been disappointed to see

Lyall go in 1989 because, from a fan's point of view, he'd presided over the demise and was consequently guilty of negligence. Yet any feelings of negativity I may have had while speaking to John were ultimately erased by my growing understanding of his compassionate nature. Here was a man, schooled by the likes of Ron Greenwood, who recognised that football wasn't just a game, it was about *people*. This was conveyed in his reflections on bringing Dicks to the club, for example. 'I drove up to Birmingham and I can remember Julian and Kay looking so young as they sat there. In those situations you're hoping that you're doing the right thing for them,' he said. 'He was a nice lad, very respectful. I can remember him coming into the training ground in the afternoons with his children whom he doted over. It was nice to see the fatherly affection.'

Lyall may well have been accused of showing a similar feeling towards his younger players and when he came to leave Upton Park, he wrote to them in a show of appreciation of their efforts. 'Those lads keep you in work and it's just nice to say, "Thanks for what you did and I'm grateful." You get close to players.' John's great loyalty to people may well have ultimately undermined his struggle to keep Hammers in the top flight but he continued to work with the same philosophies. 'Obviously there's pressure when you're at the bottom of the table but you smile as much as you can. You've got to try and lift the players. Relegation is such a disappointment because it affects so many people's lives,' he said candidly. 'Managers, coaches and players can all find themselves leaving as a result and when you multiply their families it can create a tremendous amount of problems for people.' As we spoke, John was part of a committee responsible for the re-writing of English coaching certificates but I'd got in touch with him on his farm in Suffolk. I was immensely grateful for his time and, our conversation finished, I felt that he'd have had far too much dignity to have publicly complained about any restrictions he might have experienced during his later years at the club.

One of the men who would have learnt so much from Lyall's style of management was Alvin Martin, who'd arrived from his native Bootle as a kid in 1974 and had just played his final match at Upton Park when we got together to have a chat for *Terminator* in the summer of 1996. He'd yet to put any of it into practice (agreeing to spend a year at Leyton Orient as player/coach), but as one of the elder statesmen who'd witnessed most of the trials and tribulations of Julian's West Ham career, I wondered what kind of relationship he shared with his fellow defender.

'When I sat down with Julian, I found him different company to when there was a group around us,' he revealed. 'But there's a mutual respect between us as players. If I had to pick a team to win a game to save our lives, he'd be in it.' While some may have assumed that the two men with equally forceful personalities might have bonded well off the pitch, Julian possibly seeking Alvin's advice during times of trouble, I got the impression that for all their 'mutual respect' you probably wouldn't see the pair of them sharing a beer together regularly.

'I would never have expected Julian to talk to me about his problems. Now and again he'd probably have known what I'd have said anyway,' admitted Alvin. 'I've offered loads of advice on the pitch and we've had our little fall-outs when not a lot of common sense has been spoken. But there's a common respect and we both knew that, maybe in training, we didn't wallop each other because then it might get out of hand. I don't think he'll ever go into the diplomatic corps. He wears his heart on his sleeve and if somebody asks him a question and he feels at liberty to answer, he'll tell you the truth.'

The inclination for Julian to speak his mind was all too evident when he turned his back on England in the summer of 1996 – not that they'd given much of an indication that his services were in demand anyway. Dicksy had been playing well, kept his nose clean (going some 20-odd games without a booking) and, with Blackburn's Graeme Le Saux sidelined with a bad ankle injury, the press were pushing for his selection in the build-up to the Euro '96 championships. Indeed, after West Ham's 2–1 win at Chelsea in February, a throng of media men had Harry Redknapp cornered in Stamford Bridge's press room as they prompted Julian's claims to an England place. 'A few people would blink if they saw his name on an England team-sheet, but the ability is there in his boots,' declared 'H'. 'If Terry Venables asked me, I would tell him that Julian is in outstanding form.'

Since the ageing Stuart Pearce (ironically to join WHU as Dicks was leaving it in 1999) was the only obvious candidate to play on the left side of England's defence, I certainly felt Dicks would be worth a place in the squad on merit but I couldn't really see it happening. For that reason I was reluctant to use *Hammers News Magazine* as a vehicle to campaign for Julian's selection, but I did feel entitled to open it up as a forum for debate. Everybody – fans included – offered their opinion in the April edition, while I visited Dicks at home to gauge his mood on the subject. 'I believe I'm good enough to play for England. People might think I'm being big-headed, but I know I've got the ability,' he insisted. 'Of course it would be nice if I do get a call-up, but if I don't then I won't lose any sleep over it.'

Julian may have seemed rather nonchalant about the matter as he sat there in his lounge sipping cups of tea, but his hopes must have been raised when the tabloids ran stories declaring his inclusion for the squad for the forthcoming friendly with Bulgaria as a formality. Needless to say, it didn't happen. Further hope came when Venables visited Upton Park himself for the visit of Bolton Wanderers, but Dicksy turned in a disappointing performance which even assistant boss Frank Lampard admitted; still, team-mate Slaven Bilic had a surprise word in Julian's shell-like ear and told him that he was likely to figure in the squad for the friendly against Croatia on 24 April. Or so Ted Buxton had supposedly said, despite claims that he'd also told Bilic that Dicks should 'grow his hair'. Of course, Julian was once again ignored.

To make matters worse, the likes of Phil Neville and Alan Wright – two players considered by Julian to be inferior – were called up and that, as far as Dicksy was concerned, was the last straw. I spoke to him on the phone a few days after the squad was announced and he told me that he was no longer interested in playing for England. Before I had the chance to break the news in the magazine, however, *The Sun*'s 4 May edition ran the headline 'STUFF YOU, TEL!' Dicksy had spilled the beans to a tabloid reporter when quizzed after a training session and declared, 'I'd sooner build a dog kennel that play for England.'

The implication of Julian's reaction, however, was that he was more concerned about playing for his country than he'd previously suggested. I asked him if it might be considered by some as a classic case of sour grapes on his part and he admitted, 'Possibly. They might accuse me of being bitter but I'd just rather do something else. I don't care if England win or not, it doesn't bother me. The last England game I watched was six years ago.' I then put it to Julian that his lack of interest in the fortunes of the national side could be used by Venables to justify his exclusion. 'Because I don't watch England play?' he retorted. 'That's babyish. I never watched Liverpool play but Graeme Souness still bought me.' I didn't think the analogy really applied and reiterated the point about needing passion to play for your country. 'All Venables has got to do is watch me play for West Ham and he'll see I play with as much passion as anybody,' he insisted.

That was true, of course, and in some respects it summed up Julian's general attitude to the game. Hammers fans love to see Dicksy giving everything in a Hammers shirt but the reality is that he could be wearing one of his brother's non-league strips and he'd still be dying for the cause. Come to think of it, you could stick a ballerina's tutu on him and you'd still not get far off 100 per cent. When he's playing the game he loves he only plays it one way – to win – and in that respect he's playing for himself.

The issue of ego also came into it. Anybody with a true competitive spirit will have belief in their abilities and if, like Dicks, they see rivals they consider inferior being favoured at their expense, it's going to rankle. It's not that he wanted to wear an England shirt, it's just that he considered himself the best. 'Venables must have something against me,' he complained. Who knows if Terry did have something against Julian?

I spoke with Peter Storrie (who'd sat alongside the England boss at the Bolton game) and his theory was that the player's reputation was still a major handicap. 'I spend a lot of time with Terry and I pushed Julian for a long while,' he said. 'He was close to getting a call, but I think one of the reasons he didn't was that Terry already had two players in Paul Gascoigne and Paul Ince who are notoriously a bit volatile. Having three sparks in the team was maybe too much to run with.' It was a perfectly plausible theory, but the presence of other 'sparks' in the squad would only have annoyed Julian even further. The debate about Dicksy's skinhead hairstyle was another irritant.

All these issues would have been discussed with Venables if only I'd have been successful in persuading him to be interviewed for *Terminator*. Faxes were despatched to his Scribes West nightclub and Portsmouth Football Club, where he was a director, but my efforts were in vain.

Another 'no thanks' credit in the book went to Sky's Andy Gray, who was obviously reluctant to discuss the views he conveys so willingly on air. And a third such acknowledgement seemed likely after my attempts to make contact with David Mellor proved fruitless. Again, the fax machine had done its bit, firing off messages to the MP's Westminster office and Radio Five Live, but to no avail. I was moaning to somebody about his lack of response (probably over a pint or two) when they suggested one particular time of the week when everybody knew exactly where he was: in the BBC studio for his Saturday *Six-O-Six* radio show. It was such a simple idea it was brilliant! I'd call him up on his show. Not only would I be able to put Mellor on the spot in the most public way, but I'd be able to give the book – and *Hammers News Magazine* – a plug in the process.

The fact that I made the call on 12 October, with the 1996–97 season well underway and the Hammers returning from Everton (after yet another Goodison Park defeat), suggests how flexible my original deadline for the book had been. The initial agreement had been to have all the text ready by September but I'd stuck naïvely to the task of trying to interview everybody on my original list (including scout Ron Veal, who'd discovered Julian at the age of 10, Janet Rodgers, his landlady when joining Birmingham at the age of 14, plus a load of former playing colleagues) without realising that compromises would have to be made if I was going to bring it home on time.

Not that Mellor's contribution made a world of difference. After successfully making it on to air, I barely got to pose my question about Dicksy's much-improved behaviour on the pitch when David predictably started speaking over me to refer the point to journalist John Ley, his studio guest. Mellor eventually mumbled a few seconds of patronising rhetoric and left me clinging on to the dying words of his sentence which did not make for the greatest of quotes.

Terminator – all 125,000 words of it (some 50,000 more than anticipated) – finally hit the shelves with a resounding thud just a week or so before Christmas and I looked forward to the reviews with a certain amount of suspense. There certainly hadn't been an authorised biography of a sporting star quite like it ('I don't think I'd choose to go and have a pint with the bloke,' was the response from one associate) and nobody could fault my research, but it just seemed unusual sitting on the opposite side of the fence for once. Having spent 10 years in rock journalism, proving that the pen can sometimes be mightier than the guitar chord, I felt strangely vulnerable knowing that other journalists were in the process of critically analysing the worth of a project I'd spilt blood, sweat and beers over.

Fortunately, the book was looked upon favourably, and won several excellent reviews: 'A mad book, but good. Blows, a life-long West Ham United fan and editor of *Hammers News Magazine* has done a stack of research, talked to all the right people and ended up with a football book which is well above the ordinary,' wrote *Total Sport*; 'Kirk Blows shows how an authorised biography should be written,' claimed *The Independent*; *90 Minutes* described it as 'a compelling and entertaining insight'; *Sky Sports* awarded the book top marks, as did several other magazines. There were also a number of interesting perceptions, such as the one made by *Total Football*'s Jon Palmer: 'The author shows the same attitude to writing as his hero has to playing football. It doesn't have to be pretty, it doesn't have to be clever, it just has to do the job.' That was certainly the intention when I set out writing – it had to be accessible to all of Julian's fans.

Over Land & Sea's Gary Firmager, meanwhile, made special mention of the book's cover photograph in his review for *FourFourTwo* magazine: 'You get the impression that the purpose of this book is to let you know that Julian Dicks isn't really the nutter most others would have you believe. But if it was published for that reason, it fails miserably. The front cover itself features a picture of a snarling Dicks and in the back of the book you'll find a match-by-match analysis of his eight red cards,' he wrote in his five-star review. While thanking Gary for the star rating in a letter, I pointed out that we'd chosen the cover photograph with the express intention of changing people's preconceptions. As well as having immense impact, the shot defined the very essence of Julian as many saw him – all ferocity, fire and fury – and it made a definitive statement as to the objectives of the book. We weren't setting out to paint him as an angel, as some might have initially suspected.

The back cover picture also required a bit of work and Photoshop technology to slim Julian down a little (he's never lost weight so fast). If some were surprised by the cover design, however, the material used to illustrate the pages inside also gave the book an independent feel. As well as paper cuttings, showing all the headline-making incidents, we ran various fanzine covers, illustrations and caricatures. There was a spot-the-difference between Dicksy and Sydney from the *Beano*'s Bash Street Kids (no difference); a photo-story that started with Trevor Brooking asking Billy Bonds if he fancied a drink after the match and finished with Bonzo declaring that he'll have 'a Julian Dicks – just one half, then I'm off!'; and a cartoon of Julian asking a copper if Bond Scheme protesters can stay on the goal line ('We need the points, officer!').

The Bond Scheme protests also generated some unique photographs, my favourite being the one in which a crazed-looking fan was cuddling Julian who'd just retrieved a wayward corner flag. 'He looked like the guy was going to punch me but he just said, "I f***in' love you!" I just said, "Oh, cheers!"' revealed Dicksy, when I quizzed him about it. There's also a Liverpool squad line-up with Julian and Neil Ruddock resting their hands on each other's knees (no wonder they were happy to see each other when Razor arrived at Upton Park in 1998) and lots of material from his family archives, including a '70s holiday snap of Julian's dad standing alongside Geoff Hurst and Glenn Hoddle in the Canary Islands. The only picture that caused any concern to Julian, amazingly, was one of Hammers MD Peter Storrie. 'What's that tosser doing in my book?'

Chapter Twelve

'Paulo, how's it going?'

The Portuguese star smiled nervously as he shook my hand with a certain reticence. 'I'm fine,' he said, almost waving me away in the same movement.

'How's the English coming along?' I asked, stubbornly dragging my heels along the floor of Highbury's Marble Halls.

'Yes, yes . . .' he replied, looking decidedly uncomfortable.

It was approximately 2.15 p.m. on Saturday, 17 August 1996 and Paulo Futre had left me somewhat bemused. I wandered up to the Arsenal press room and even before being handed a team-sheet, I somehow knew that the newly signed striker wouldn't be putting in an appearance that afternoon, in our first game of the season. What was he doing standing in the Highbury foyer? Why was he so reluctant to chat? And why was he still in his bloody suit?! All would be revealed shortly . . .

It was a miserable start to a miserable first month of what would be, for the most part, a miserable season for West Ham United. The sun may have shone down on north London but the storm clouds had already gathered ominously over the Hammers' prospects, with an injury-ravaged team going down 2–0.

The close season had seen a flurry of transfer activity; in fact, it all exploded in one frenzied week, with *five* internationals arriving at Upton Park in the space of three days. The spree began on Tuesday, 2 July, with the aforementioned Futre (signed from AC Milan under the Bosman ruling) and former England Under-21 captain Richard Hall being introduced at one press conference, while the record £2.4 million signing of Romanian striker Florin Raducioiu was confirmed just 48 hours later, along with Welsh defender Mark Bowen – a free transfer from Norwich City – and long-time loanee Michael Hughes, who'd agreed with the club to allow his contract with Strasbourg to expire in order to take advantage of the Bosman ruling, to everyone's (apart from the French club's) mutual advantage. Add in former WHU striker Steve Jones, brought back from Bournemouth (for reasons best known to Harry Redknapp) for £150,000 plus Mark Watson, and fans were predictably enthusiastic about the start of the new campaign.

Equally predictable, however, was the West Ham injury crisis and only Hughes (who'd already been at the club for most of the previous 18 months) and Jones of the new signings were in the first-day starting line-up, while the likes of Cottee, Moncur, Bishop, Potts and Dumitrescu were also sidelined. It all seemed so terribly disappointing, but things could only get better . . . or so we thought.

The Sunday papers after the Arsenal game were full of stories of Futre's walkout from Highbury, suggesting that he'd refused to play because he hadn't been allocated his favourite No. 10 shirt. 'What a load of cobblers!' stormed Redknapp when *HNM* quizzed the Hammers boss about the situation.

Something had clearly happened, however. Firstly, I'd seen Futre acting suspiciously (I know, I sound like a policeman) just inside the doorway and it was evident that he was waiting for a car to take him away from the stadium; secondly, the striker's name had appeared on the original team-sheet – as a substitute – which had to be amended in hasty fashion, so some explanation was needed. Redknapp duly obliged: 'On the Friday I'd spoken to Paulo about not playing the next day because he had a thigh strain and hadn't trained. But when I arrived at the ground Frank Lampard had already filled in the team-sheet and put down Futre's name as sub. Paulo was saying "no sub, no sub", obviously meaning he wasn't supposed to be one of the substitutes. Then I pick up the papers on Sunday and I have to spend the rest of my time answering to a silly story that somebody's made up.'

Redknapp failed to acknowledge two things at this point: one, why assistant Lampard hadn't known of the player's 'unavailability' and two, why Futre subsequently did a runner ('thigh strain' and all) before the match kicked off. 'Paulo can't speak English and I can't speak Portuguese so how are we supposed to have a row?' he concluded, attempting to draw a line under the whole sorry affair. Of course, it was all a desperate cover-up on Harry's part and, despite having grave reservations about his explanation, we pretty much had to go along with it.

Needless to say, long after Futre's association with West Ham ended, Redknapp was telling a rather different story; in fact, it became something of a party piece for him. 'We give Paulo the No. 16 shirt at Highbury and he says, "No, me Futre, me No. 10." So I tell him, "We have a squad system here and your number is 16." So what do I get? "Me Futre, me No. 10!" The next thing we know is that he's disappeared, hailed a cab and gone home!' announced Harry on stage at Jongleurs Comedy Club in Bow in February 1998. The story also appeared in Harry's autobiography which appeared nine months after his stage performance, revealing that Futre had offered to fork out £100,000 to reimburse punters who'd bought Moncur shirts with No. 10 on them in a bid to win his favourite number back. 'In truth we'd probably only sold about six,' joked 'H' in the book, acknowledging John's lack of star status with the fans. 'Moncur swapped shirt numbers with Paulo in the end – for a villa in Portugal, I think!' he admitted at Jongleurs.

It was a shame that Futre had become something of a figure of fun after his short spell at West Ham. I'd attended the press conference at Upton Park and my mission had been to get enough material out of the player to dedicate two or three pages to him in our August issue, something that was far easier said than done. Such conferences are often chaotic affairs, photographers and camera crews forming a barrier in front of the rest of the press in a little room and questions sometimes being channelled through an interpreter, as was the case with Futre. The additional problem for me on such occasions was that everything aired in the actual press conference itself was being digested by the daily reporters, who were obviously in a position to have their stories read the very next day. Because my publication wouldn't be hitting the shelves for a few weeks or so, I had to have exclusive material. And that meant having a private conversation with the player on a one-to-one basis. Well, a one-to-one-to-one basis if you included his interpreter.

After Peter Storrie had completed the formalities it was then a case of following the new players (Richard Hall was also being unveiled on the day) out on to the pitch for the photograph session. My usual trick was to stuff a copy of *HNM* in their hands for my photographer to get the shots I needed. This generally ensured exclusivity because other football publications would hardly want to run a picture promoting another magazine. The odd newspaper might run the same photographs but I was happy for them to do so – it was all free promotion for *HNM*.

'I don't think people realise how big a signing this is for West Ham,' said Jerome Anderson, the agent looking after Futre's interests, as we stood out on the pitch together. True, the 30-year-old's accumulated transfer fees amounted to over £20 million, with Reggiana, for example, paying £5.5 million for his services just two years earlier. The last 12 months with AC Milan, however, had seen the 41-times-capped international play just one game due to a serious knee problem, while his record over the previous four seasons amounted to just 10 goals in 33 games for four different clubs. I was sceptical, to say the least, but West Ham had the sense to ensure his contract contained a clause which allowed for the club to terminate the arrangement should Paulo experience any more problems with the knee. The gamble was worth taking, although his weekly wage was considerable.

My interview with Futre wasn't the easiest ever conducted. As soon as the player, his interpreter and I formed a group it seemed as if a dozen microphones had been shoved between our faces, while the net result in terms of quotes was disproportionate to the amount of time spent conveying the questions. Paulo would be waffling away in his native tongue for ages, only for our multilingual friend between us to deliver the terse response: 'yes'.

To try and get a different angle I expressed curiosity about his interests off the pitch and he revealed his liking of music and film, although he insisted that he loved to spend time with his wife and two sons. He also had interesting things to say about compatriot Dani, who'd not survived long at Upton Park the previous season. 'He has a lot of things to learn. If he wants to think about football 24 hours a day and show commitment he can become one of the world's best players,' he confided. It's not easy getting to know somebody under such circumstances but he seemed to speak with sincerity despite being a little surprised by my probings into his life away from the game.

In fairness to Harry, I could fully understand him trying to throw a blanket over the dispute at Highbury. Such bust-ups are embarrassing for all concerned and the onus is hardly on the manager to feed the press a juicy story, although once it's been exposed he's then got an interesting dilemma. Does he stick with his original line or admit to having told a porky?

Things were not going as planned with Florin Raducioiu either. 'He takes his football very seriously,' Rachel Anderson told me after she'd met him and found him to be a studious, deep-thinking character. I was naturally sympathetic when the Romanian striker got the most ungentlemanly welcome to English football via the wayward elbow of Torquay's John Gittins in a pre-season 'friendly'.

'I'm not worried about the physical side of things,' the 26-year-old persisted, not realising how much he would need to reproduce the same line in his defence over the following months. I'd been delighted to see Raducioiu brought to the club. For £2.4 million, I thought he represented value for money. He'd scored 21 times in 35 appearances for Romania, he was his country's top scorer in the 1994 World Cup and he had worn the shirts of AC Milan and Espanyol, among others. OK, he hadn't had the best of Euro '96 tournaments – he had scored just once as the Romanians crashed out at the first hurdle and there were doubts about his condition, but he was surely worth the investment and would set Upton Park alight when fully fit.

It all seemed too good to be true in the final half an hour of the game against Southampton on 24 August. Futre, who had inspired the Hammers to a late equaliser against Coventry a few days earlier, had already got the home crowd buzzing by coming on as a second-half substitute and, with Raducioiu and Dumitrescu coming off the bench against the Saints, the Europeans worked their magic again as West Ham came from behind to claim their first win of the season. It was mesmerising stuff, the Portugeezer and the two Romanians running riot to leave the Southampton defence (and our own poor Iain Dowie, it seemed) completely bamboozled. Their speed of thought and movement was on a completely different level and it left *Match of the Day* commentator John Motson drooling, 'There's going to be a lot of fantastic football to look forward to at Upton Park this season.' Little did any of us know how quickly the imported beer would turn flat.

It goes without saying that *HNM* had a distinctly continental flavour during this time: our coverage of the European Championships extended to Marc Rieper providing us with an exclusive diary from the Denmark camp and we also followed Slaven Bilic's progress with Croatia, who fell to Germany in the quarter-finals. England were also eliminated by the Germans, of course, and I used my 'Ed Mouths Off' column to register my displeasure with a certain Paul Ince. With England's five penalty-takers failing to eclipse the efforts of the opposition in the semi-final, it had been left to Gareth Southgate to volunteer for the first sudden-death kick. 'But where was the "Guvnor" when his country needed someone of steely mind?' I asked. 'To put it bluntly, he was quaking in his boots about 30 yards away. For all the bluster, when it came for actions to speak louder than words, the only activity from certain players was that which took place in the rear of their shorts.'

I thought it was a fair comment to make, even if some of the West Ham directors may have twitched nervously at the thought of me throwing more lighted matches on a bonfire they'd long hoped had been extinguished.

Chapter Thirteen

The Eastern promise of the final 30 minutes against Southampton in August was soon to appear nothing more than a dream, with fans waking up to the grim reality that, once again, the total of West Ham's team did not equal the sum of its parts. In the very next match, a Juninho/Emerson/Ravanelli-inspired Middlesbrough battered the Hammers by a 4–1 scoreline, although Michael Hughes – with a sizzling 30-yarder – did manage to score what arguably turned out to be the team's best goal of the season.

Ironically, Julian Dicks picked up his first booking since he'd last played at Boro, 26 games earlier, and he wasn't a happy chappy when I spoke to him at the North East hotel the team were staying at prior to their match at Sunderland the following weekend. 'I thought the officials were an absolute disgrace,' he stormed. 'I didn't touch Ravanelli but he screamed as he fell to the ground. I thought he was dead! I was so annoyed with the linesman I just told him to f*** off.'

I could relate to Julian's frustration. The European Championships had already issued a stern warning that the game in England was changing shape as a result of the pressure being placed on referees to punish foul play, which in itself was playing into the hands of the foreign players who like to think that the slightest physical contact should be rewarded with a free kick. Increasing the penalties for bringing people down was always going to encourage footballers to play-act, knowing a yellow card will render their opponents less effective. And with the Bosman ruling, plus the greater monies circulating within the game (thanks to Sky Television and increased sponsorship and merchandising activities) resulting in a sudden influx of imports – who are used to playing football almost as a non-contact sport – it was inevitable that we'd start to see bad habits infiltrating the Premiership. I was so perturbed by this predictable development that I dedicated my column to the debate that month. 'A mere second after shirtsleeves have come into contact, players have been seen flying into outer orbit – no doubt accumulating air miles in the process – with expressions of anguish spread across their faces,' I complained.

Some of the foreigners may have had trouble staying on their feet, but those at West Ham were having difficulty even getting on to the pitch. Futre's run of (five) games ended with a pulled hamstring in the 2–0 home defeat by Wimbledon in mid-September and, even though he returned to make another four appearances as substitute deeper into the autumn, it always seemed inevitable that he'd be released. I contacted Peter Storrie towards the end of November to enquire about the rumours that Paulo might choose to call it a day, but he insisted: 'No decisions have been made.' When we asked Harry Redknapp about Futre after the 0–0 draw at Sheffield Wednesday on the thirtieth of the month, however, he conceded: 'We know he'll never recapture his old form but, even so, he's been struggling. You've got to be able to do it week-in, week-out if you're going to survive in the Premiership.' Clearly, his patience had run out. Less than a fortnight later, it was mutually agreed that Paulo should retire from service and *HNM* duly caught up with him at his Algarve outpost to allow him a chance to say farewell. It had been a gamble on the club's part that failed to pay off, but I thought it rather harsh when Futre's name was used to build a case against Redknapp for making errors in the foreign transfer market.

This all came to a head around the Christmas period, the Hammers having had a dire time in the league (slumping into the bottom three after just four wins from the first 18 games), Ilie Dumitrescu lacking fitness, form and favour and Florin Raducioiu apparently suffering from the same.

There were some highlights: a 2–0 win at Forest, Tony Cottee scoring the second within seconds of Marc Rieper being sent off; a dazzling 4–1 Coca-Cola Cup victory over the same side in which Dowie scored twice (yes, you read that correctly) and loan-signing Hugo Porfirio produced (to my mind) the best individual performance seen by an outfield Hammer for years; plus a thrilling 2–2 draw with Man. Utd in early December, in which Raducioiu pulled away and imparted sufficient curl on the ball to beat Peter Schmeichel from a tight angle. The highlights, however, were greatly offset by the disappointments and they didn't come any bigger than the débâcle of the Coca-Cola Cup defeat at Second-Division Stockport.

Raducioiu, in one of his few starts, had scored his first goal for the Hammers to put them ahead in the initial fourth-round game at Upton Park, but wasteful finishing (by that man Dowie again) was punished when County took advantage of Dicks's mistake to grab an equaliser and take the tie back to Edgeley Park on 18 December.

What a rotten day that was. I'd stopped off to collect copies of *Terminator* from the publishers in Leicester in the afternoon and completely underestimated the second half of my journey, especially as I'd chosen a disastrous route across the Peak District and had to drive through torrential rain. By the time I got anywhere near the fringes of Manchester I had the radio on and was being informed that Dicksy's opening header had been erased by a rather less impressive one by another Hammer up at the other end. (Nuff said!) As I swung the car into the nearest gap I could find near the ground, I didn't need the radio to hear the cheers of the home faithful as Brett Angell scored the winner.

By the time I found my place in the away seats (under cover fortunately), the locals were rolling in the aisles of their own stands as Dowie – he of the farcical own goal – left the pitch with a broken ankle. 'A tie eked from the finest traditions of English knock-out football,' claimed *The Independent*; 'A tie eked from the bowels of hell,' was my verdict as we trudged out into the sodden streets of Stockport with nothing but our embarrassment to shield us from the rain. If ever there was a night to make you wish that football had never sunk its claws into your soul, this was the one.

As has been well documented since, Raducioiu had no role to play in that game (lucky him), the player having decided to occupy his time elsewhere on the night in question (in Harvey Nichols, so legend would have us believe). By the turn of the year, however, most fans had come to resign themselves (as had Florin himself) to the fact that the Romanian was never going to be fully utilised at Upton Park.

The Hammers took on Sunderland on 28 December and, once again, Raducioiu had to sit out most of the match as Porfirio (hardly an out-and-out striker) and another loanee, Mike Newell (embarrassingly past his sell-by date), laboured up front. 'We want Radi on the pitch!' sang the crowd in unison, with yours truly giving full vocal support in the East Stand, as the team clung to their one-goal lead (courtesy of Slaven Bilic). Reluctantly, Redknapp brought the player on with only five minutes remaining, but Florin needed just four to slip his marker, gallop 50 yards and bang the ball into the back of the net. That wasn't good enough for Harry, though, who dismissed the goal as 'not all that good' and later claimed in his autobiography that Radi only lost his opponent because he'd jumped out of the way of his challenge!

I was convinced that there was more to the Raducioiu situation than met the eye and, with the season at the halfway mark, I thought there was no better time to arrange a meeting with Harry to discuss how things had been going. That was the general pretext, but as I headed to the Chadwell Heath training ground I was determined to put him on the spot about the Romanian's lack of first-team opportunities.

I hung around in the foyer for a while before 'H' came past and invited me to join him in his office. Not wanting to press him into a corner immediately, I opened up the conversation by reminding him of his quote at the beginning of the season when he'd admitted that we might find this campaign a lot more difficult than the previous one. He'd brought in several new faces but, of the key ones, two had been lost through injury (Futre quitting and Hall damaging a foot in a pre-season friendly) while Raducioiu had 'found it difficult to settle'. I seized on the opportunity to bring Florin into the debate and drew attention to the fact that the fans were singing, 'We want Radi on the pitch . . .'

'Well, I want Florin on the pitch,' he retorted, 'I bought him, remember! The easiest thing for me is to pick him and the hardest thing is not to pick him.' So why hadn't Florin played more games? I asked. 'He had a terrible start,' insisted Redknapp. 'Everywhere we played pre-season he looked like he didn't like the physical side of English football. He was always getting knocks and complaining. I started him at Middlesbrough and he was disappointing. I started him at Sunderland and again he didn't have a good day. So at that time I felt he lacked the strength to come to terms with what was needed to play in this country. But when he's come on as a substitute he's done ever so well. I've no doubts that he's got terrific ability – I wouldn't have bought him otherwise – but he's had real problems adapting to our game.'

And here was my bone of contention: if you don't play someone, they're not going to adapt, are they? I made the point by stating that 'the fans would argue that he needs a run of 10 games or so if he's going to adapt' (because it's always more productive to offer the view of the supporters rather than push the theories as my own). 'It's all right people saying that,' he shrugged, 'but if he ain't doing it I'm not going to keep playing him for the sake of it. The team is more important.'

Did the fact that Radi was taking time to adapt imply that he'd turned out to be a different type of player to the one Harry thought he was buying? 'I knew what kind of player he was,' insisted 'H', 'but I didn't think he'd be so intimidated by English football.' I asked if our not getting the best out of Florin reflected badly on the club and he was forced to admit, 'If it reflects badly on anybody, it's me. But I can't make him stand up to challenges when people want to get physical.'

The strange thing about the Raducioiu scenario (as opposed to Boogers, for example) was that the fans – usually the first to get on the players' backs – were sympathetic towards him. 'Yeah, but were they up at Middlesbrough or Sunderland?' Redknapp countered. 'Where are all these great performances I'm supposed to be picking for?' Incredibly,

Harry came out with a gem of a quote when I least expected it, after I'd asked simply if Florin had spoken to him about his frustration of sitting on the bench. 'Yes, I'm sure he's unhappy, but there have been other reasons why I haven't played him and eventually they'll come out. When I'm ready I'll let people know.'

'Ah, now we're getting somewhere,' I thought. In fact, I felt like I'd swung a winning punch. OK, it may only have been a jab, but it achieved more than all my previous efforts. Of course, Harry wasn't going to tell me what those 'other reasons' were just yet, so there was little more I could do on the day apart from ask about the player's likely future. 'I'd like to keep Florin,' he said somewhat disingenuously, 'but in reality that wouldn't be possible if I wanted to bring somebody else in.'

So what were these 'other reasons'? Was Harry referring to Florin's no-show for the trip to Stockport, which only became public after the player was sold (back to Espanyol)? Or was there something else, which seems plausible given that the Cup game was five months after the striker's arrival and he'd long been out of favour? There were other questions to put in front of Redknapp, too. What made Radi's exile from the team even more difficult to comprehend was the fact that Harry had perservered with Iain Dowie, who'd failed to score in the 18 league games he'd played that season. Had the boss not been tempted to drop him (before that unfortunate ankle injury)? 'I was tempted but I didn't really feel that I had anybody to replace him,' he said, stressing that he needed a big man who could 'hold the ball up and bring other people into play. What I also needed was somebody around him who could score goals.'

While most were still of the opinion that Raducioiu was that man, there was also reason to question the sale of Tony Cottee back in November. Did Harry regret that? 'Yeah, I do,' he conceded. 'I would like to have kept Tony but I didn't have a lot of choice at the time. I'd spent £4 million in the summer [on Hall and Raducioiu] and had to recoup some of it.' It wouldn't be the last time Harry would find himself in such a position.

Chapter Fourteen

Tony Cottee might never get the opportunity to fulfil his ambition to return one day to West Ham and manage the club, but at least he can say he realised one of his goals when he became a columnist for *Hammers News Magazine*. OK, it hardly compares but the position did at least allow Tony to retain some kind of profile in England at a time when he wasn't sure whether he'd ever get the chance to ply his trade in his home country again.

The pint-sized striker joined the *HNM* team as the 1996–97 season kicked off and he was more than keen to put pen to paper every month to provide readers with a special insight into life at Upton Park. In additional, the column offered him the chance to comment on the game's topical issues and I was delighted with the standard of work he produced. After just one month, however, it looked as if we'd started something we couldn't finish when Tony revealed that Harry had received a good offer from Selangor FC of Malaysia for his services. With all sorts of speculation appearing in the press over the next week or so, Tony admitted that it didn't look as if their interest was going to come to anything and subsequently used his column to explain how the agent concerned had failed to substantiate the offer in the form of a contract. He therefore announced his intention to stay at Upton Park and fight for his place along with Raducioiu, Futre, Dowie and whoever else might arrive. We naturally took the piss a bit by running a postcard of the tropical tranquilities of the Malaysian coastline alongside a shot of the Boleyn public house, saying how he'd given up the chance of experiencing the former to stick with more of the latter!

Fortunately for TC, the deal was resurrected with new intermediaries and, following a quick trip out to Kuala Lumpar with wife Lorraine to take a look at things, he eventually confirmed that after 335 games and 155 goals for West Ham during his two periods with the club, he was saying goodbye. We duly designed a commemorative *HNM* cover and publisher Tony McDonald did the honours by presenting the framed item to Tony on the pitch at the home game with Derby County (which he watched from our executive box) on 23 November.

With just a year left on Cottee's contract I could understand why the club thought £800,000 was a good deal for a 31-year-old with no divine right to a first-team place. Tony was intelligent enough to realise that the squad needed reinforcing in terms of strikers and, considering the long-term interests of the club itself, he'd have been happy seeing quality walk through the door as long as he got a fair crack of the whip alongside them. What he was less content about, in my opinion, was a lack of opportunity (he had been substituted in three successive games) and playing second fiddle to the older Iain Dowie.

I soon realised that TC's move could also benefit *HNM*, in a funny kind of way. If anything, Hammers fans would be more interested in keeping in touch with Tony's fortunes in the strange climes of Malaysia than they would of his ins and outs with West Ham. We therefore agreed for him to continue writing for the magazine.

Financially, at least, it was a great move for Cottee but the first of his several disappointments out there came when he discovered that the Malaysian season wasn't kicking off until the following April! That basically meant he'd lost the best part of a year without serious soccer and, when you're in your thirties that's the last thing you need. He also didn't need the food poisoning that put him in hospital for two days; the unbearable heat and humidity; political unrest within the club; or the mystery virus that killed over 30 children under the age of six (which meant flying Lorraine and five-year-old daughter Chloe back to England). Add to this the fact that his team-mates were jealous of his success, preferred to fire in 30-yard shots from angles of 25 degrees rather than pass and generally made him feel about as popular as Salman Rushdie in those parts – and it's no wonder he was always talking about an imminent (and permanent) return to these shores. His column ran until September 1997 when he secured a return to the Premiership courtesy of Leicester City.

A lot was happening at Upton Park as Tony headed east. For a brief period it looked as if Slaven Bilic might also be leaving, with speculation linking him with a £2.5 million switch to Spurs. The Croat had quickly established himself as a pivotal figure in the Hammers' defence and enjoyed a successful Euro '96 tournament with Croatia, so it was inevitable that other clubs would start sniffing around and offering tempting bait. I was irritated by the stories, as a three-and-a-half-year contract had been signed earlier that year and I couldn't understand why, just because other parties started showing interest, the club should have to start opening negotiations for an improved deal (as seems to happen all the time these days). Rumours suggested that there was a clause allowing

Bilic to go if a club offered £2.5 million, so we could only assume somebody (not an agent, surely!) had leaked that information; but before we knew it the player had signed a new contract which, according to my reporter in *HNM*, 'will keep him at Upton Park until June 2000.' 'Yeah, right,' I thought, as Slav pleaded his side of the story, although I found it amusing to see him insisting: 'I would only leave West Ham to join a big, big club and Spurs are just not big enough.' It was a great quote and, just to rub Tottenham's noses in it for missing out (whom I suspect were deliberately brought in to force new contract talks), I blew it up for all to see. I also ran off a picture of him making a point to Marc Rieper with the caption, 'Look, Marc, at least *you* must believe me!' to indicate in subtle fashion that some of us still doubted the sincerity of his words.

Just over a month later, Bilic found himself unwittingly contributing to Tottenham's winner at White Hart Lane, as he uncharacteristically allowed the ball to escape him for Chris Armstrong to score. And luck wasn't on his side as a brilliant late shot smacked against the inside of Ian Walker's post to deny the Hammers any sort of reward for dominating the game. The result left an unpleasant taste in my mouth for days but I was able to console myself a few weeks later by having a laugh at Spurs' expense: assuming that our home game against Stockport was guaranteed a hatful of goals (I really should know better by now), I'd allocated an extra page to Coca-Cola Cup action but when the match produced a disappointing 1–1 draw I decided to make use of the space by running shots from Tottenham's 6–1 defeat by First-Division Bolton Wanderers the same evening. 'Let's face it, the result brought the biggest cheer of the evening at Upton Park!' I wrote, alongside the heading 'HO! HO! HO! (A Bit Of Pre-Christmas Cheer)'.

With not too much else to grin about in the build-up to the Christmas period (the win against Sunderland on 28 December being the first in 10 games), we felt entitled to take a light-hearted look at events. Little did we realise, however, how much worse things would get in the new year . . .

Chapter Fifteen

The thick snow resembled a luxurious white duvet as it blanketed the pitch of Wrexham's Racecourse Ground. It could almost have been plucked from a picturesque Christmas card scene before being dumped at the venue for West Ham's FA Cup third-round test in north Wales on 4 January. 'There you go, lads, play on that,' said referee Mike Reed, as he gave the controversial go-ahead for the game. It was a stupid decision by the official and pundit Trevor Brooking quite rightly complained on *Match of the Day* that it was 'ludicrous' for such an important match to be played in such circumstances.

Along with some 2,000 other Hammers fans, I'd coughed up £13 to witness something I could have seen for nothing on *Ski Sunday* but, once again, the paying punter was the last to be considered. Entertainment value was non-existent as players slipped and slid all over the place in their laughable attempts to gain some semblance of control over the orange ball. The referee, meanwhile, had placed himself in a hopeless situation, booking seven players for falling arse over tit as it became impossible to distinguish a legal challenge from an illegal one. With the conditions making it difficult for the Premiership side to impose their superior skills, we could see why Wrexham had been eager to get the game played and when Bryan Hughes put the Second Division boys ahead within six minutes, the BBC were rubbing their hands at the thought of a juicy cup upset. Fortunately, Portuguese striker Hugo Porfirio (whose claim that he had never seen snow before was perhaps tough to believe) did the right stuff in the white stuff, curling in a fantastic 20-yard equaliser to earn the Hammers a deserved replay. If Harry Redknapp's fury at having to play on a 'scandalous surface' had been able to thaw the ice from his frozen crystal ball, however, he might have told his loanee not to have bothered.

By the time the second game against the Welshmen was actually played, on the Saturday intended for the fourth round following a midweek postponement due to fog, the mood of the Upton Park faithful had dipped alarmingly. Successive home defeats by bottom-of-the-table Nottingham Forest and Leeds United, either side of an unlikely draw at table-topping Liverpool (with a strikeforce of Steve Jones and Mike Newell indicating how bad things were) wouldn't have helped, but much of it had to do with stories that were emerging from the pitch.

The name of Michael Tabor had by now entered the consciousness of West Ham supporters. A multi-millionaire, Tabor was a former bookmaker who, claiming to have been a lifelong fan of the Hammers, made a proposal at the club's AGM to inject £30 million into the club and earn himself a place on the board. With things falling apart on the pitch and cash desperately needed to fund team redevelopment, it was hardly surprising that some fans saw the 54-year-old as some kind of knight in shining armour, naïvely assuming that big money would suddenly become available for player purchases. Of course, there were several strings attached to the offer: firstly, Tabor wanted the shareholders to vote out chairman Terence Brown, and have him replaced by Essex lawyer Henry Montlake, while MD Peter Storrie later revealed that the figures being mentioned would take the form of interest-bearing loans, which would obviously have to be repaid.

It come as no surprise that the club were reluctant to accept such a deal but, while the proposal sat on the table, Tabor was putting another plan of action into gear. Recognising that despondent fans could easily be manipulated to put pressure on the West Ham board, he set about winning the support of the fanzines to help orchestrate a campaign – and *Over Land & Sea* (among others) were happy to play ball. Editor Gary Firmager may well have been sincere in wanting to bring about change but I think he'd also have been aware of the self-promotion gained through helping to bring that about. We'd already seen the role a fanzine could play four years earlier when *Fortune's Always Hiding* (by now defunct) was instrumental in galvanising public support against the Bond Scheme. Through its initiation of red-card protests, it played a key part in cementing fans' resistance to the concept and could proudly pat itself on the back when the scheme was radically amended. *OLAS* clearly saw a parallel in the two situations and thought that history could repeat itself, appointing itself as a medium to communicate propaganda on behalf of Tabor. To be fair to Gary, he always insisted that he was simply encouraging debate – the red cards issued at Upton Park carrying the phrase 'it's good to talk' – since Tabor complained that West Ham were showing no inclination to discuss the deal with him. That was the club's prerogative, of course, as it was to keep the matter as confidential as possible. And that's what initially made me suspicious of Tabor's motives. If he really had the best interests of the club at heart, as he so forcefully claimed throughout his media campaign, he wouldn't have been using such cynical methods.

It all came to a head when Wrexham scored a 90th-minute winner in the replay with Wrexham at Upton Park, the result sparking a pitch invasion in which fans chanted 'sack the board'. I'd taken a seat in the press box and looked down from the West Stand upper tier with genuine horror as I realised the situation was in danger of snowballing out of control.

I conveyed my feelings through my monthly column, writing: 'Hands up who had a distinct feeling of *déjà vu* when the protests against the board started again? All those horrible memories of the Bond-Scheme outcry came flooding back, leaving a rather unpleasant taste in the mouth. The scenes of dissent after the Wrexham game may not have carried the same conviction of those in the dark days of that relegation year, but they certainly could do if the agitators have their way. There's no doubt that certain people have seen the current situation as representing a great opportunity to stir up unrest, propelled by an inflated view of their self-importance and motivated by the idea of carving themselves a piece of history. Drunk on ignorance and naïveté, they blindly assume they know all the facts, jumping to conclusions and whipping others up into a frenzy. The danger is that the outside world will assume these self-appointed spokesmen are representing all Hammers fans. Most intelligent supporters and observers realise that, unless we're equipped with the full details of the Tabor proposal, it's impossible to make any judgement. Granted, if the club had explained its initial reservations the brakes would have been put on the anti-board bandwagon that so many have jumped on. But why should the directors instantly release confidential information relating to a proposal that was still on the table at the time? Just because other parties want to wage a campaign in public, it doesn't mean that West Ham have to compromise themselves and go against the established ethic of keeping business matters private.

'Of course, the suspicion is that a proposal (which may, in theory, be in the club's long-term interests) might be rejected as a result of directors being more concerned with self-preservation. It's a natural fear but I can't help thinking that some people are going to feel silly when they realise they've been used. And in that category I include tabloid newspapers who've also manufactured a campaign. My main concern is the affect all this might have on the team. We don't want to undermine our own chances of survival, so I'll just say this to the agitators: when you rock the boat you only increase its chances of sinking.'

Naturally, everybody would have expected me to defend the board in the club's official magazine, but I believed every word I wrote and felt entitled to put my views across. One thing that amazed me around that time was how the club continued to entertain fanzine personnel. I remember one such publication describing the chairman as 'the f***ing liar Brown' in big words across a double-page spread, and I asked myself why the people responsible were rewarded with privileged access. The answer, of course, was that the club had woken up to the power of the fanzines in the wake of the Bond Scheme and continued to see them as a threat. And while not quite attempting to defeat the enemy by singing his song, the likes of Peter Storrie thought it far better to keep these people on their side by avoiding confrontation. The theory would be confirmed on other occasions during the next few years.

While I defended the club's right to deal with its business affairs in a confidential manner, I was disappointed that Storrie had failed to elaborate at a later stage on certain things he'd divulged in the heat of the battle (admittedly under pressure from the likes of *OLAS*). 'We have to investigate all our options and Michael Tabor is not the only benefactor to have expressed an interest in the club,' he told *HNM*. 'For example, there is an American businessman who is interested in becoming involved in Premiership football and has a substantial amount of money to offer. There are people who don't want to negotiate through the newspapers and want to keep their business confidential. We have to do what is right for the club, the fans and the shareholders.'

The identity of the mysterious American was never revealed, of course, while the question of what is right for 'the club, the fans and the shareholders' is never a straightforward one. As editor of *HNM* I received a number of telephone calls from supporters keen to express their doubts concerning the chairman and his fellow directors' priorities. That's understandable when those with a major shareholding are indicating a reluctance to give that up, although I always made the point that nobody was in a position to reap any major rewards on an ongoing basis as profit is only made on shares when they're actually sold. That doesn't mean that people aren't going to hold on to their shares stubbornly in the knowledge they're only going to increase in value, but – as in all forms of business – a sale is made when the price is right.

The problem for West Ham over the years is that its directors have never been in a position to pour huge sums of money into the club once they've made their initial investment. There is no Sir John Hall, Sir Jack Hayward or Jack Walker, who've bankrolled Newcastle, Wolves and Blackburn (not that it's brought those clubs much success in recent times), nor a high-profile businessman such as Tottenham's Alan Sugar or Chelsea's Ken Bates. No, the power at Upton Park is in the hands of a banker (Terry Brown), vice-chairman Martin Cearns and director Charles

Warner, people who have to rely solely on sound business principles to steer the ship towards profitability. That's not been easy when the Boleyn Ground has needed redevelopment and the team required strengthening.

Following the Taylor Report, which demanded that top-division stadia become all-seater by August 1994, West Ham replaced the old South Bank with the 7,600-capacity Bobby Moore Stand (opened in February 1994) and North Bank with the Centenary Stand (operational from January 1995, accommodating 5,900 people) at a cost of some £7.5 million, with the lower tiers of the West and East Stands having seating installed (and let's face it, there wasn't much from the Bond Scheme to invest, was there?). This made for a reasonably decent 26,000-capacity ground but as the effects of the Bosman ruling have gradually taken hold during the mid-to-late '90s, even more financial pressure has been placed on clubs wanting to compete at the highest level. Sure, huge increases in television, sponsorship and merchandise revenues have splashed more cash around the top end of the game but transfer fees and salaries have spiralled out of control as the balance of power has shifted from clubs to players (and their agents). With turnovers increasing year by year, it's now imperative that clubs retain their Premiership status or, at the very least, bounce straight back from relegation. Otherwise it's a financial disaster, where income diminishes to such a level that players' contracts can no longer be comfortably honoured. The top earners are subsequently sold and clubs are left trying to get back into the big-time with less talented players, some of whom are still earning Premiership wages. Whereas relegation in the old days needn't have seriously threatened a club's future, it's now akin to being swallowed by quicksand.

The Hammers were certainly beginning to get that sinking feeling in January 1997, with one leg caught firmly in the bog. Harry Redknapp was also beginning to feel suffocated, admitting in the Upton Park press room after the Wrexham defeat that he'd stand down if that's what was considered best. 'If people don't want me here then I understand, the club is more important that me,' he said with a hangdog expression. Visibly shaken by the dramatic events of the last few minutes (Kevin Russell's thunderbolt sticking a knife through his heart and the angry mob on the pitch simply twisting it in even further), it's possible that Harry's crimson features were further deepened by a sense of embarrassment over the Tabor situation, the latest episode of which suggested that it was he who introduced the potential investor to the club (which he later confirmed in his autobiography).

Nevertheless, Redknapp's words were interpreted by the rest of the media men around us as an offer to resign and the following day's papers made horrible reading for Hammers fans. As if the Wrexham defeat didn't leave enough of a nauseous feeling in our stomachs, now 'H' was threatening to quit. Things really were falling apart.

Some would have been happy to see Redknapp go, of course. It was all very well for Harry to complain about having his hands tied for players, but wasn't it he who'd bought Florin Raducioiu (now returned to Espanyol) and Ilie Dumitrescu, gambled on Paulo Futre, sold Tony Cottee and placed so much faith in Iain Dowie? In many people's eyes he'd made numerous mistakes and was now simply suffering the consequences. Redknapp's argument, certainly was that he'd been forced to operate at the bottom end of the European market and when you're doing that you've got no option but to take risks. I've lost count of the number of times Harry has told me how simple it is to buy Dennis Bergkamp – somebody you *know* is going to produce – as opposed to trying to unearth talent that you *hope* is going to come good. And it's a valid defence. Of the five pre-season signings, Michael Hughes, Mark Bowen and Futre were all free transfers, while a tribunal had placed a value of £1.9 million on Richard Hall (whose injury could not have been foreseen, although sources around his former club Southampton suggested problems were always likely) and £2.4 million for such an experienced international as Raducioiu was not exactly the earth. Hugo Porfirio was another loanee, as was Mike Newell, so Redknapp certainly had a case.

In my mind, Harry was never going to resign and had declared no such intention: he simply responded to a reporter's question by saying he'd be prepared to leave if people thought it in the club's best interests. That's not the same thing, although Redknapp later revealed in his autobiography that he *had* offered to quit during conversations with the chairman behind closed doors. To cover myself, however, I'd used the headline 'What next for Harry?' on the cover of the February issue of *HNM*, which was ambiguous enough to still apply should the manager have done something drastic before fans got the chance to read my interview with him.

While things couldn't have got much worse, they didn't immediately improve, with 2–1 defeats by Arsenal (Ian Wright scoring the winner) and Blackburn Rovers (Rio Ferdinand's first goal) leaving Hammers with just one win (against Sunderland) in the last 17 outings. Thank God for the two-week break in February.

Chapter Sixteen

My boss looked a little worried as he gave me the nod to come into his office. What have I done now? I wondered, as I entered his den with a sense of foreboding. 'Shut the door,' he said, walking back to his desk. This was serious. 'We're signing John Hartson from Arsenal,' he said. 'Four million quid.'

It was a shocker for a number of reasons. For a start, the Hammers had already just shelled out £2.3 million for Newcastle's out-of-favour Paul Kitson and, being widely understood that the club were prepared to spend a maximum of £5 million to build a new striking partnership, we'd assumed the second arrival would be somebody of similar price (possibly Stoke's Mike Sheron). I was also surprised that Arsenal had been prepared to let Hartson leave, but with Ian Wright and Dennis Bergkamp the obvious first choices up front at Highbury, manager Arsene Wenger thought the offer was too good to turn down and that the 21-year-old Welshman deserved regular first-team football.

We immediately went to work on replacing the cover of the next issue. The original version (with Kitson on his own) was ditched and we generated an image with the hitmen's faces side by side. 'TWIN STRIKE!' boomed our one coverline, before I came up with the idea of 'rubber-stamping' the fees on the players' heads, just to emphasise the amount of money the club had spent. By the time Hartson's signing had been confirmed, however, it was announced that his fee would 'eventually exceed £5 million'. Right, £5 million it was then, as we smacked the figure on his forehead. Needless to say, it wasn't long before Harry was downplaying the fee: it had been around £3.2 million, he had claimed, and the the rest dependent on West Ham enjoying all types of success. 'To pay £5 million he'd have to score the winner in the European Cup final!' was the sort of thing he said, making my cover look rather silly a few weeks down the line. I thought this kind of inconsistency was typical, though. First the club wanted to make a big fanfare of how much money was being invested, with Peter Storrie proudly revealing the figures, then the manager reduced the fee as the critics started to question the wisdom of the deal. It had happened once before, with Marco Boogers, when Harry admitted over our dinner in Germany that 'you can't buy a player for less than a million', conceding that the figure of £1 million in the press statement was not entirely accurate (£800,000 is thought to be the actual fee).

The Hartson deal did attract a lot of criticism, however, with the likes of David Mellor (yeah, him again) accusing the Hammers of making a 'panic buy' and investing far too much money on somebody with questionable temperament. 'How much John cost isn't the issue,' I wrote. 'He's been brought in to do a job and whether he's a good acquisition or not depends on him doing that job, end of story. A player is worth whatever it takes to prise him away from the club he's with. Those people who suggest that the recent buys are an act of desperation couldn't be more wrong. In recruiting Hartson and Kitson, the Hammers have a 21-year-old and 26-year-old as their twin strikeforce which, in theory, should remain in place for years to come. I believe the money spent shows ambition on the club's part and point more to long-term aspirations than just hopes for short-term survival. Hartson will prove to be a good investment, an asset whose value is unlikely to drop unless he suffers a complete loss of form.'

I was also asked to defend the purchases on Liberty Radio prior to the two new strikers making their débuts at Derby on 15 February. I predicted a 1–1 draw and if referee Gerald Ashby had been remotely awake during the game he might have awarded the two obvious penalties the Hammers deserved. And yet bizarrely, he pointed to the spot for the least likely of the day's claims and handed the Rams the points on a plate. The detractors were quick to smirk after the 1–0 defeat, particularly with Hartson getting booked for an alleged elbow on Igor Stimac and immediately incurring a two-match suspension. The incident formed the basis of my first conversation with John for *HNM*. 'There was nothing malicious in the challenge but he went down as if hit with a sledgehammer,' insisted the softly spoken Welshman as he reflected on the moment which saw the Croat clutch his face, fall to the ground, get up, stagger a few yards as if bullets had riddled his body and then theatrically hit the turf again. *Encore! Encore!*

'I didn't elbow him, there were no marks on his face and he was perfectly OK when he took the free kick,' he said. 'Stimac knew he'd done his job very well and is probably really proud of the fact that he got me booked and suspended.' The youngster sounded philosophical about it all but future clashes with the Derby defender would suggest the matter was not forgotten. 'I don't like to think I'm stupid and I don't do stupid things, but sometimes I know I have to start using my head a little bit more. It's something that will come with experience,' he added, although the passage of time would prove otherwise.

I'd get to know Hartson a little better after his first full season, but the immediate priority was for the two new men to set about the job of hauling the Hammers to safety. Both scored on their home débuts in the thrilling 4–3 win over Tottenham on 24 February and, although the team suffered another awayday hiccup at Leeds the following Saturday, Kitson hit a double to bag three vital points in the next home game against Chelsea. Kitson and Dicks had overturned the Blues' lead gained through Gianluca Vialli's first-half goal and the victory was almost there when Mark Hughes popped up with a heart-breaking equaliser in the dying moments. 'F*** it!' spat a fan in front of me up in the East Stand, grabbing the raised flap of his seat and slamming it down in anger before trooping off towards the exit. Others followed but, as sick as I was, I decided I wasn't going to disappear, even though it looked as if two crucial points had. Incredibly, though, with the seconds of injury time ticking away, Michael Hughes' corner found its way to Kitson's head and the ball crept inside the far post and over the line. 'In a week of great escapes [a reference to Liverpool's dramatic 4–3 against Newcastle], West Ham's vanishing act from the bottom three must go down as the most stunning of all,' wrote *The Sun* in the aftermath of a moment that arguably made the difference between staying up and getting relegated.

Buoyed by the late lifeline, draws were gained at Aston Villa (where the emerging Frank Lampard was ruled out for the rest of the campaign after cracking a bone in his right leg) and Wimbledon (in which Stan Lazaridis popped up with a 90th-minute equaliser). The third successive away game was a classic 'six-pointer', though, Coventry also deep in the brown stuff. I was contacted by BBC Radio Coventry to preview the match and cautiously predicted a 1–1 draw. Thankfully, a Hartson double and another goal from rising star Rio Ferdinand secured a decisive 3–1 win and survival appeared to be within our grasp.

By this time the fuss over the proposed Tabor takeover had well and truly died down. The West Ham board had somehow come up with the cash to provide Harry with 'the tools to do the job' and the new striking partnership had made an immediate impact. With the pacy Kitson making intelligent runs to exploit the damage caused by the presence of the muscular Hartson, the boss deserved the credit for recognising how well the two players would complement each other. Not that everybody was as generous, however: one of my writing colleagues complained that Harry had got lucky. 'He only got them because they were reserve players,' he moaned. 'He didn't *know* it was going to go so well, did he?'

I thought it was a stupid thing to say and it just proved how some people are never going to be happy if they've made their mind up about somebody. The bottom line was that Harry had gambled again – with bigger stakes and less room for error – and this time it looked like paying off.

Now that Tabor had lost credibility with the fans, some of the fanzine personnel changed their tune somewhat, admitting they'd always known exactly what he was all about. I had to laugh when one of them complained that Peter Storrie had failed to acknowledge them. 'That's the thanks I get for encouraging those signings!' he said, with reference to Hartson and Kitson, as if he'd personally been instrumental in their arrival. In a funny kind of way, though, maybe he had a point. 'Looking back, I think the fans clamouring for Tabor's money – and my offer to resign – perhaps forced the chairman's hand,' admitted Redknapp in his autobiography. The likes of *OLAS* may simply have been trying to encourage dialogue between the board and Tabor, but the fervour of the fans may well have had some influence on Terry Brown taking the initiative, while Harry won't have been shy of telling the chairman what he thought was needed to resurrect the team's fortunes.

Yes, the directors were well aware of the need to redevelop two sides of Upton Park, but the funding of that work would disappear if the club was relegated. The priority had to be on guaranteeing survival and, with that very much in mind, a further big-money signing was made on transfer deadline day, 27 March. I'd taken advantage of the break in action after the Coventry game to drive down to the West Country for a week or so and was surprised to pick up the paper one day to see the Hammers discussing terms with Manchester City's Steve Lomas, with a view to a £1.6 million transfer. When the 23-year-old midfielder returned to Northern Ireland's international base just outside Belfast without having signed, however, it was reported that Lomas had rejected the prospective move. On deadline day itself, however, a fax arrived at Upton Park to confirm that the player had agreed to join the Hammers. 'I simply asked Peter and Harry if I could take a day to speak to my family and mull it over because it was such a big move for me,' revealed the flame-haired fella when we linked up to discuss the circumstances behind the deal. In his thick brogue, Steve admitted how difficult a decision it had been to leave the club he'd spent the last eight years with following his move from Coleraine at the age of 15. But Lomas had his head screwed on, as our conversation revealed – particularly when I quizzed him about the *Daily Mirror*'s story which suggested that City had to 'pay Lomas to go!' 'It's just the way football works,' he informed me. 'I never asked for a move, so City in turn had to pay as the contract states. But the club hadn't offered me a new contract yet and they knew how unhappy I was about that. I considered that they'd reneged on a promise.'

I welcomed his honest, straight-talking approach; it's that characteristic which has propelled him to the top. Lomas has since captained both club and country and his leadership qualities are there for all to see. He may be slight in build but he has character and commitment, qualities that can take people a very long way. We duly placed Steve on the cover of the next *HNM* and, while it may not have been the most aesthetically pleasing picture, screwing his face up as if having a premonition of City's results over the next 15 months, at least he could console himself with the fact that he had a better-looking girlfriend than the majority of those reading my interview with him. In fact, with the young lady in question being a glamour model, the chances were that the magazines revealing her talents were far more likely to be, let's say, safely filed away by our readers than the ones displaying his.

Surprisingly, none of the new arrivals seemed particularly concerned about the very real threat of relegation, although their confidence – an essential part of a professional's make-up – may have been amplified somewhat for the sake of making a positive impression. 'If I thought for a minute that we'd go down I wouldn't have signed,' insisted Hartson.

'I wouldn't have joined if I didn't think I'd be playing Premiership football next season,' echoed Kitson, whose laid-back persona has often been seen as moodiness.

'We've got more than enough talent to get out of trouble,' avowed Lomas, who'd played under five different managers since experiencing the drop himself the previous year. The fact was that Hartson was playing reserve-team football at Arsenal; Kitson wasn't even doing that, with Newcastle dispensing with their second string; while Lomas was already playing in the First Division in a side that would slip into Division Two the following season. Add in the attraction of playing in London and earning a nice slice of the transfer fee in each case and it's not hard to see why players were still happy to come to Upton Park.

There were others heading through the exit gates, however. Striker Steve Jones – considered surplus to requirements following the arrivals of Hartson and Kitson – was offloaded to Charlton (the club making a £250,000 profit in the process), while the likeable Kenny Brown, who will forever be remembered for scoring the goal that denied Manchester United the championship in 1992, joined Birmingham for £75,000. Mark Bowen had negotiated a free transfer out to Japan's Shimizu S-Pulse

Wrighty puts the boot in
(courtesy of Dr. Martens)

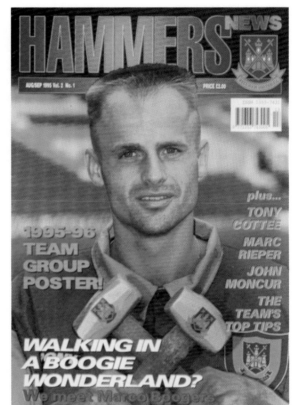

RIGHT: Well, it seemed like a good idea at the time! (© Independent Magazines)

BELOW: Dicksy and agent Rachel Anderson catch up on some reading (courtesy of the author)

SHAME ON YOU BOOKIES–Pa

I'M SO SORRY

Rio drink-drive ban
earns England axe

By PAT SHEEHAN

RIO FERDINAND has promised to pick up the pieces of his shattered career and admitted: "I've been so naive."

The West Ham star's dream of an England debut against Moldova became a nightmare when he was convicted of drink-driving yesterday.

The teenage defender was immediately told by England boss Glenn Hoddle he was **OUT** of next Wednesday's World Cup qualifier at Wembley.

Ferdinand, 18, was banned from driving for one year. He said: "I'm just so sorry. I've been very naive and I am being forced to pay a heavy price.

"It's a harsh lesson for me to learn, being so close to gaining my first full England cap.

"I made a mistake for which I am dreadfully
Turn to Page 43

EXCLUSIVE

FRANK SKINNER LIVE

Mitre

Rio's regret

ABOVE: Hutch and
Moncs: a right pair
of cowboys?
(© Steve Blowers)

RIGHT: Can I have my
shirt back now, TC?
(© Independent
Magazines)

HAMMER AND SICKER ... Wright is restrained by team-mate Sinclair after being sent off. Pic: PAUL WEBB

WRIGHT NUTTER

Sent-off star takes it out on ref's room

FURIOUS West Ham striker Ian Wright damaged the referee's dressing room after being sent off in yesterday's 5-1 home defeat by Leeds.

Now Wright faces action from the FA, who are bound to take a dim view of a player taking the law into his own hands. Wright was furious at the

EXCLUSIVE by JACK STEGGLES

dismissal and went on the rampage after being shown the red card for an off-the-ball challenge on Ian Harte.

Blazing-mad Wright tried to get at referee Rob Harris on the pitch - but was dragged away by his team-mate Trevor Sinclair.

But he took it out on the referee's dressing room and he is certain to pay a heavy price for that moment of madness.

A West Ham spokesman said: "We can confirm an incident took place. But until we've seen the referee's report and conducted our own investigation we can make no further comment."

Two other West Ham players — keeper Shaka Hislop and

midfielder Steve Lomas — were also sent off as the Hammers ended up with just eight players on the pitch. And the club could face a heavy fine as an angry fan tried to get to an assistant referee. Six fans were arrested.

But Leeds boss David O'Leary had no complaints with the referee. "I thought he had an excellent game," he said.

Match report – Pages 64-65

Wright gets it wrong

(© *Sunday People*)

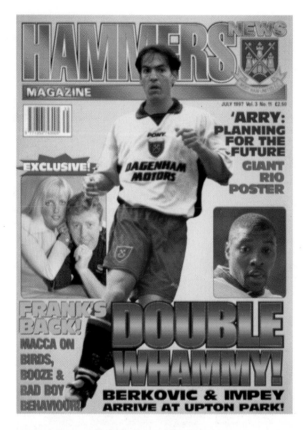

LEFT: Computer trickery puts Berkovic in Hammers kit (© Independent Magazines)

BELOW: Another Pub Talk session gets underway (hic!) (courtesy of the author)

ABOVE: The editor of *HNM* gets buried in his work (courtesy of the author)

RIGHT: Our farewell offering (© Independent Magazines)

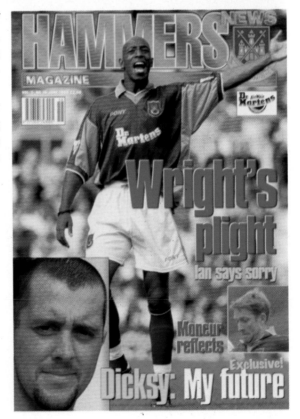

ABOVE: Steve Harris of Iron Maiden plays the Claret & Blues
(© George Chin/courtesy of EMI)

BELOW: Come on you Irons!
(© George Chin/courtesy of EMI)

and Aussie goalkeeper Steve Mautone (having made just three appearances) was shipped out to Reading for £250,000. These departures took place with little fuss but the big talking point (once again) was the future of defender Slaven Bilic.

While I'd been happy to see a West Ham man making an impact in the Euro '96 games, I was naturally concerned that his success would encourage the sharks to start swimming around. Tottenham and, allegedly, Manchester United had already been fought off earlier in the season, but it wasn't long before it came to light that Bilic had been discussing terms with Everton with a view to a pre-deadline move. EVERTON?! The last thing we needed was to lose our key figure in defence, especially with our Premiership status hanging in the balance, but with the Goodison guys offering £4.5 million – the very fee which allowed the player to talk to other clubs, as written into his contract – it seemed inevitable that Slav would be lured away, not least by the double-your-money wages sitting on the table. Redknapp was predictably cheesed off by the whole affair. He had enough problems on his plate already and recognised how the development had been orchestrated by the player's agent. How else could Everton have known of the clause in Bilic's contract?

In a surprise move, Slaven returned to Upton Park with an 'I'm staying . . . for now!' message, which everybody generally accepted as meaning that the deal would go through immediately after the season had finished. 'I was impressed with Everton but I also told them I can't come now. If I had gone and West Ham go down I would never forget it,' insisted the 28-year-old in the news pages of *HNM*. Such loyalty to the Hammers' cause was admirable but you couldn't help thinking there was more to the situation than met the eye. It's not impossible to believe that a player might let his conscience get the better of him but it was difficult to accept that Bilic had developed such a relationship with West Ham in just 18 months, particularly when somebody representing him must have leaked the necessary information to the Merseyside club.

I dedicated the lead news page of our April edition to the story, allowing the Croat to express his 'commitment' to the club, while acknowledging Harry's indignation at being able to do absolutely nothing about the situation. We followed up by canvassing the views of the fans, most of whom were resigned to seeing the player eventually leave. A few questioned the player's determination to give everything in his final months, while others made references to the Paul Ince situation back in 1989. 'He's just money-minded, let's get rid of him,' said Dale George.

When you consider that such opinions were being voiced in the club's official magazine, while Bilic was still a West Ham player, this was fairly controversial stuff. But I felt we were entitled to assess the mood of the supporters as long as nobody got abusive or nasty. If anything, most of them were bemused by the attraction of Everton, if Slaven's insistence that 'it's not just about money' was to be believed. 'I can't understand why he thinks Everton are such a big club,' said David Wicks.

Scott Nicholls declared, 'You can't knock him for having ambition, but going to Everton's not having ambition, is it?' Indeed, to say the Toffees had been going through a sticky patch was an understatement. Since winning the championship in 1987 they'd taken a considerable nosedive and, with the exception of the surprise FA Cup success in 1995, avoiding relegation was their most notable achievement.

Bilic duly battled it out at Upton Park until just two days after the season's closing game with Manchester United, when he was unveiled at a Goodison Park press conference. The funny thing was that Joe Royle, who'd set the deal up in conjunction with chairman Peter Johnson back in March, had since got the boot and it was caretaker boss Dave Watson (still playing in defence himself) who found himself presenting the new acquisition to the media. What upset Hammers fans at this point in time was Bilic's declaration that he'd moved to a club 'to win things'. He added: 'With no disrespect to West Ham, I don't think they are in a position to regularly win trophies.'

That may well have been the case but given that Everton actually finished below the Hammers that season, it was somewhat ironic that the player should start talking about the sky raining success, particularly as he didn't even know who his next manager was going to be. Furthermore, it soon became known that Bilic was to receive part of his signing-on fee that was to be given to him if he was still at the club at the end of the season. Suddenly things started to make sense. Not only did the fans have to listen to a load of baloney about Everton's potential prospects (when they all knew the £20,000 a week had more to do with his decision to move north) but they also had to swallow the player's assertion that he'd delayed his decision through loyalty to the club and its followers. Loyalty is a dangerous word to use in front of people whose only understanding of it is when used in the context of discussing the likes of Billy Bonds, Trevor Brooking, Alan Devonshire and Alvin Martin. And now they were suddenly realising that a payment thought to be around £300,000 – ironically termed a 'loyalty bonus' – had been his main incentive to stick around in London. No wonder they were singing 'There's only one greedy bastard' when Bilic turned out for his new side against the Hammers at Goodison Park just three games into the following season.

To be fair to Bilic, what many people failed to acknowledge was that he probably wasn't quite cashing in to the extent they thought, given that he was earning half of what Everton would have been paying him for the final two months of the campaign. And as he later pointed out, there was also the danger of injury. Had he broken his leg or suffered a serious problem playing those final games for the Hammers the deal would have been off, so there was an element of risk involved on his part. Again, that's overlooked by most people eager to condemn him. Football fans are often guilty of hypocrisy. How many punters would spurn the opportunity of doubling their own salaries if the chance presented itself? In any case, it's usually OK for a duff player to sling his hook but when it's somebody they value, they're up in arms about it.

Hammers fans were certainly justified in feeling aggrieved at the way Bilic left Upton Park. They felt not only deserted but deceived by him. Ultimately, though – and somewhat ironically – it was Slaven himself who had reason to feel deceived. While the monetary aspects of his transfer would have been of major consideration, he'd have been induced by all sort of promises from the Everton hierarchy that great things were just around the corner. He'd have been told his big-money arrival was the first of many, as the club looked to make an assault on the game's major prizes. Sadly for Evertonians – and amusingly for Eastenders – the bright new era failed to materialise, and Howard Kendall was brought back for a third period in charge while the new manager was wheeling and dealing in the transfer market at bargain-basement level as another season-long struggle against relegation ensued.

I couldn't help but take the mickey when running a photograph of Hammers players celebrating a goal against the Merseysiders when they next visited Upton Park. Inserting a speech bubble above Bilic declaring: 'Oh well, there goes the title!', I thought it encapsulated our style of humour while making a valid point, but I'm not sure everybody appreciated our tongue-in-cheek approach. Those that did laugh, however, might also have considered the contrast in West Ham and Everton's fortunes somewhat fitting. Since engineering the move, Bilic has suffered from loss of fitness, form and favour, to the extent that he was transfer-listed and very nearly returned to Upton Park with his tail between his legs for virtually nothing in the summer of 1999 until he failed a medical.

What many people also forget is that West Ham made a near £3-million profit when the player made his club-record departure, and it was that money – the board knowing the transaction was going to take place – that ultimately paid for Steve Lomas's recruitment from Manchester City. And the midfielder's arrival has since proved to be a key factor in the Hammers turning things around.

Chapter Seventeen

Rather depressingly, by the time Steve Lomas got to make his début for the Hammers, nearly a fortnight after his move south and a full 18 days since the 3–1 win at Coventry, the team's momentum had been lost. The match against Middlesbrough at Upton Park on 9 April (which finally saw long-term injury victim Richard Hall emerge from the shadows) was a scrappy affair, as confirmed by Steve when I asked him about the 0–0 draw. 'It was very frantic. Boro made it very difficult by packing the midfield and trying to stifle us,' he said, following one of the few successful things Bryan Robson's men did in the final weeks of the season. The Teesside outfit were deep in trouble themselves, their position made all the worse for having had three points deducted for failing to fulfil a fixture at Blackburn Rovers earlier in the campaign. Thankfully, by the time they arrived at Upton Park, it was confirmed that their appeal to have the points returned had failed, although for months nobody at the bottom of the table had known where they truly stood. 'Boro's position in the table must not be allowed to influence matters,' I wrote, worried that the FA would back down if they knew the club were going to be relegated as a direct result. This, in turn, naturally, had a bearing on our position and although everybody (outside the Riverside Stadium) was delighted to see justice prevail, it looked for a while as if none of it was going to make a huge difference anyway, given that the Hammers were doing their best to shoot themselves in the foot.

As if the pitiful 2–0 away defeat by 10-man Southampton (with Israeli playmaker Eyal Berkovic scoring one of the goals) wasn't a big enough example of West Ham waving the white flag ('that's the worst we've played in a long time,' admitted Harry afterwards), they went one further the following week in a match from which the fans took weeks to recover. The home date with Everton was considered to be crucial and, with Paul Kitson scoring twice in the first 32 minutes, it looked as if everything was going to plan. But this was Upton Park and nothing's ever that straightforward. Shortly into the second half the Hammers were awarded a penalty and since Dicksy had been injured in training prior to the

Middlesbrough game, it looked as if John Hartson was going to take the all-important spot-kick. Incredibly, rather than placing the ball on the spot, the big Welshman walked towards Kitson and offered him the chance to complete his hat-trick. The whole ground could see Kitson shaking his head and refusing the opportunity, but that wasn't good enough for Hartson, who insisted his partner take the kick. Whether it was a generous gesture by John to let his mate enjoy a magic moment or whether he simply bottled it, we'll never know, but either way it was a nervous-looking Kitson who shot rather tamely at goal, allowing Neville Southall to make a vital save.

Knowing that a third goal would have made it game, set and match, a wave of disappointment blanketed most of the crowd and having crashed off at least three sides of the ground, it quickly dissipated into sheer nervousness. Most teams would have had the resolve to protect the two-goal advantage but a large percentage of the supporters in the dozen rows immediately beneath me in the East Stand have not spent years losing their hair for nothing. Anxiety increased as the Hammers sat further and further back and invited Everton to apply pressure and, once Graham Branch pulled one goal back, it became suffocating. As if anyone needs reminding, with just seconds remaining on the clock, Duncan Ferguson duly netted to make it 2–2 and leave home supporters feeling as if the ground beneath them had just given way.

It was like being stabbed in the stomach and having the knife twisting your guts into a knot. The blood rose to leave a sickening taste in the mouth and it was little wonder that people were spitting flames of fury as they left their seats. 'You f***ing wankers, West Ham!' shouted one bloke nearby amid the din of seats being kicked and slammed and the flurry of programmes being ripped up and tossed in the air. The second half had been an act of sheer suicide and the Hammers had got what they deserved, slipping into the bottom three as a result of the points dropped. A game that started with us riveted had left us feeling filleted.

Fortunately, the next game at Leicester was just four days away, so there wasn't too much time to dwell on things. And given that the Hammers had won their previous eight meetings with the Foxes, at least recent history was on our side. Fate once again smiled down on us favourably, John Moncur deciding a game which could easily have gone either way. His goal in the 75th minute was just a bit too early for my liking, however – the final quarter of an hour seeming like a week. In truth, I'd have taken four points from the two games just played, but it was typical of West Ham to go and get them in an arse-about-face manner.

With two successive home games before a final day-trip to championship-chasing Man. Utd, it was imperative that another four points were picked up to cross the safety threshold. Surprisingly, they came in a relatively simple manner: Sheffield Wednesday collapsed in style as Kitson finally got his first Hammers hat-trick (without needing a penalty!) in a 5–2 win, and a strangely muted Newcastle ground out a 0–0 stalemate that decided issues at both ends of the table. West Ham had got to the 42-point mark and would now go to Old Trafford for a meaningless match against the champions, as long as Middlesbrough failed to win at Blackburn in their re-arranged fixture on the Thursday beforehand.

I somehow found myself in a Mexican restaurant on the evening of that televised match and despite a certain female doing her best to divert my attention by trying to lubricate my tonsils, I still managed to keep one eye on the TV screen behind her back as the final moments of the draw were played out to confirm the Hammers' place in the Premiership. TEQUILA!!!

Chapter Eighteen

'Bloody foreigners!' For just a few seconds it would have been easy to assume that Harry Redknapp was suffering a flashback from the middle of the previous season. But this time it wasn't Futre, Raducioiu or Dumitrescu who were driving him round the bend, just an innocent pedestrian who'd provided the wrong directions as 'H' desperately sought guidance while behind the wheel of his motor.

''Scuse me, love . . . Runnymede Hotel? Yeah, Runnymede . . .'

We returned to our conversation via Harry's car-phone for a few moments before it suddenly took a sharp turn. 'Ere, I think that bird's gone and sent me on a wild goose chase!' he exclaimed, getting all flustered as his destination continued to elude him.

The purpose of the West Ham manager's drive from his home in Bournemouth to the hotel in question on the outskirts of London was never revealed but it was natural to assume that he was meeting a player or agent to discuss a potential transfer deal. Not that Hammers fans were expecting any further arrivals, with the capture of Israeli international Eyal Berkovic and winger Andy Impey having been confirmed just a few days earlier on 2 June for a total outlay of £3 million. In many ways they were surprise buys, given the money spent on Hartson, Kitson and Lomas in the final third of the previous campaign but, like a window-shopper at the January sales, nothing stops Redknapp from taking advantage of a bargain when he sees one.

'I've just been out to see some games in Italy and I'll tell you what, their league is nowhere near the standard of ours,' he said, while still in pursuit of the Runnymede. 'I went to see a match between Roma and Udinese and it was pathetic. The thing was, the fella I mainly went to watch (attacking midfielder Francesco Moriero) wasn't picked to play because he was going to be out of contract. That meant he could move for nothing if he went abroad and he came up to me with his agent after the game to have a talk. I said, "I had a great recommendation, but I haven't seen you play yet so I can't do anything." I couldn't believe it – two days later I heard he got transferred to AC Milan for £3.5 million!'

I had to laugh, but 'Arry's anecdote provided a unique insight into how hit-and-miss the continental transfer market can be if you're not operating at the very top end, although some would say that if Harry really knew his stuff, he'd have been well aware of the player in question's credentials and wouldn't necessarily have needed to watch him again in action. Nonetheless, I found it amusing to hear him happily tell the tale – as if looking for a laugh at an after-dinner speech – and it proved that dealing with 'bloody foreigners' hadn't dimmed his sense of humour.

One player who rarely brought a smile to Redknapp's face in the final phase of the season had been Portuguese dangerman Hugo Porfirio. Like Raducioiu, he was another player I had a lot of faith in who wasn't benefiting from a run of games in the team, being used sparingly as a substitute for much of his loan period. I'd asked Harry about him after the 0–0 draw at Villa Park in March and he insisted that he couldn't accommodate the player within the formation he wanted the team to play. It was a valid explanation but I was still of the view that Hugo offered us something in attacking terms that was unique (in a similar way that Dani had the year before), something which we saw to great effect at Selhurst Park just a few days later when he came off the bench to help orchestrate a rescue operation against Wimbledon.

Porfirio had apparently been available for just £800,000 after arriving on loan (or, more specifically, on a short-term contract basis) from Sporting Lisbon in the autumn but an impasse soon developed. Knowing he'd be out of contract with Lisbon in the summer, Hugo was not in any hurry to commit himself because he'd later have a choice of clubs to move to (and profit from); indeed, West Ham could also benefit from that situation (as they had done with Michael Hughes a year earlier). But rather than run the risk of losing him, the club made a definite offer to the 23-year-old, and required a response before the end of February – the agreed deadline with Lisbon.

'He'll be a West Ham player for years to come,' declared Redknapp just before Christmas, convinced his man would sign, but as Porfirio dithered and delayed a decision it was no coincidence that Harry felt less inclined to select him for his starting line-up. He certainly wasn't going to pick Hugo just to keep him sweet. At the same time, the less involved the player felt, the less inclined he was to commit himself to a team he couldn't regularly get into. It was no wonder the situation dragged on into the close season, although, by that time, it was obvious his future lay elsewhere (he signed for Racing Santander). I kept my chief reporter Steve Blowers on the case, however, and was much amused by his attempts to make contact with Hugo back home. 'My Porfirio, he in the hills!' cried his mum on one occasion after he'd disappeared on holiday.

Quite why MD Peter Storrie was heading out to the Algarve – save for topping up his suntan – for talks with Hugo in mid-June I couldn't quite understand, given that another playmaker in Berkovic had already been signed at that stage. The Israeli had played for Southampton the previous season and, although he'd been technically on loan, everybody assumed his success would see him join the Saints on a permanent basis. Some even thought he'd already signed, but outgoing boss Graeme Souness was quick to have a word in Harry's shell-like that the player's registration remained with Maccabi Haifa and he was available for £1.75 million (which seemed like a steal even then). Hilariously, he'd turned down Tottenham to sign for the Hammers, feeling our attractive passing game was more suited to his style. I knew it was a great acquisition and was determined to put Berkovic on the next cover of *HNM*, except that there hadn't been a press conference and he wouldn't be seen in a West Ham shirt for another two months. We therefore came up with the idea of transplanting Eyal's head on to the body of another Hammer – Steve Potts being similarly diminutive – and Bob's your uncle, there was our July cover. Readers were scratching their heads and thinking: 'But how did they . . ?'

Come to think of it, we were tempted to try a similar ploy with Andy Impey (although I'm not sure whose body we'd have used) after we learned that his arrival had been delayed as a result of his being diagnosed with a foot condition known as 'hammer-toe'. It could only happen to a West Ham player, of course, and there were plenty among the Upton Park faithful who were convinced he was still suffering from the ailment well into his Hammers career, so disappointing were his performances. 'He's always caused us problems when playing against us,' insisted Harry during our close-season conversation, yet as far as some were concerned, QPR had sent a different player across town.

The close-season transfer business further confirmed my theory that West Ham had made two very conscious decisions in recent times: one, to prioritise the development of the team ahead of the ground, knowing there was little point in having a super stadium if it was going to host Nationwide First Division football, and two, to invest in younger players so that their transfer fees could be recouped in later years. The latter concept made perfect business sense, because team replenishment then funded itself. With Kitson the oldest of the new arrivals at 26, Impey and Berkovic both 25, Lomas just 23 and Hartson the baby of the lot at 21 when signed, the Hammers were suddenly taking the long-term view and building for the future. It hadn't always been that way and it was something I was keen to discuss with Harry at that time. He subsequently confirmed the change in philosophy: 'When we were spending money in the past, it was always, "Well, we need a striker, let's pay £300,000 for one." We'd end up with somebody like Lee Chapman, for example, who was obviously only going to be a short-term investment. But money was made available in the second part of last season and I thought the chairman and the board did ever so well there. You only get what you pay for and we bought quality.'

The irony was that, despite the club spending nearly £10.5 million to bring five new players to West Ham (and committing itself even further with their wages), Peter Storrie chose this particular time to unveil his plans for a redeveloped Boleyn Ground. I can't say I was particularly happy to see him providing an 'exclusive' to the *Recorder* group of newspapers, pictured as he was alongside a visual of the proposed new ground complete with a rebuilt 17,500-capacity West Stand. The MD should have been using the club's own publications to publicise its activity, not doing favours for the local press. Certainly the club's official photographer, Steve Bacon, may have been employed by the *Recorder*, but you'd still expect stories of this nature and magnitude to be fed through the official channels first. Sadly, there was nobody at the club at the time to encourage or co-ordinate such thinking and the magazine lost out.

For the record, Storrie announced that the rebuilding of the West Stand – which would see the capacity of the ground increase by 10,000 to 36,000 – would commence in May 1998 and be completed by the beginning of the 1999–2000 season. In addition, the £15 million development would include the replacement of the primary school in Castle Street (behind the Bobby Moore Stand) and the construction of a club-run leisure centre. But then it all went quiet.

OK, maybe the development of the ground had to be put on the backburner as a result of the substantial financial commitment to the playing staff, but surely Storrie should have held back from revealing the club's plans at that time. Five new players had been bought and although further dilemmas may have arisen when the success of rising stars such as Rio Ferdinand and Frank Lampard meant that contracts had to be re-negotiated, these should have been anticipated and taken into account before jumping the red light and announcing bold plans about a new stand. Needless to say, the redevelopment did not take place as intended and Storrie found himself discussing the matter at the official fans' forum in Collier Row in November 1998. On the night itself, Peter claimed that work on developing the school area would start in February or March in 1999 and that three further stages of construction included the new West Stand, the two corners of that side and a new East Stand. 'In three to four years it will end up as just about a 40,000-capacity stadium,' he declared.

Again, it would appear that his enthusiasm had got the better of him, because he subsequently asked to see what had been written once he learned that *HNM* would be running an abbreviated transcript of the evening's debate in the next issue. We faxed an advance copy of the text to Peter's office and he duly returned it with amendments to the wording of the paragraph that related to the redevelopment. 'February or March' was changed to 'as early as possible in 1999' while the new West Stand and its corner areas were now simply 'being looked at by the chairman', with no mention of the East Stand.

Given that around two hundred fans had heard what Peter had said at the time and that the fanzines had also recorded the evening's events for possible publication, I took the opportunity to question the logic of rewriting his responses. While I accepted Storrie's explanation that the club's official magazine shouldn't be printing certain claims as fact when planning permission was still being sought, I still wondered why he hadn't shown similar caution at the forum itself.

Another problem for Storrie (whose title was to change to Chief Executive/Director of Football) in the summer of 1997 was the not inconsiderable matter of team sponsorship. The five-year agreement with Dagenham Motors had run its course and details of new sponsors were expected to be announced at any moment, coinciding with the launch of new home and away strips. 'We are 99 per cent certain that the deal will be in place in time for the sponsors' name to be on the shirts for the Tottenham game on Wednesday, 13 August,' declared Football Secretary Neil Harrison when I rang him for our pre-season issue. Yet the first home game of the season came and went without further news. My understanding was that negotiations had been taking place with a new South African airline and the rumour was that the company's licence had yet to be granted, hence the delay. Storrie more or less confirmed as much when questioned about the matter at the aforementioned forum, declaring: 'We were in the running for the second-largest sponsorship deal in the Premiership.' He also claimed that Dagenham Motors had only shown interest in extending the relationship by a further two years, when the club had been looking for a longer agreement. With the benefit of hindsight the club may have been better off retaining their current sponsors if the option was there, given that the Hammers ultimately found themselves playing the entire

1997–98 season in shirts bearing no sponsor's name. That may have been good news for fans who preferred the new strip without such advertising (such as *moi*), but it was embarrassing for the club to be the only one in the entire Football League without a deal. It had been suggested that the airline in question had started pumping in money to reserve its place should the licensing problems be solved, while other rumours circulated that Jiffy condoms might be the new sponsors (much to everybody's amusement).

The failure to secure an acceptable agreement, either with the intended party or an alternative company, was considered by some to represent failure on Peter Storrie's part and may well have been a contributory factor in the club's decision to relinquish his services in the summer of 1999.

The July '97 issue of *HNM*, with our computer-generated image of Berkovic on the cover, also included an interview with former Hammers hero Frank McAvennie. The flamboyant forward had captured the imagination of the fans in spectacular style, hitting 26 First-Division goals in his first season after arriving from St Mirren in the summer of 1985, but the golden glamour-boy succumbed to a lavish lifestyle and was unable to repeat such feats in either of his two spells with the club. His cheeky charm and contribution to West Ham's best-ever season, however, won him a permanent place in the supporters' hearts and he was an ideal candidate to interview – if only he could be found.

I'd initially tried to track him down the previous summer when talking to former playing colleagues of Julian Dicks for the *Terminator* biography. Julian had described the roguish Scot as 'a great bloke' during one of our chats, declaring: 'Frank liked to enjoy himself and we used to have a good time together. I don't think anything really affected him – all he seemed interested in was going out and drinking!'

Dicksy admitted he'd lost contact with McAvennie and the last I'd heard was that he was back in Scotland. I therefore rang a journalist on the sports desk of a Glasgow-based newspaper – whom I thought would have an idea of his whereabouts – and he told me that Frank had 'gone to ground' and not been seen for a while. My timing couldn't have been any worse. Knowing his participation wasn't particularly essential to the book I concentrated on making contact with various other parties and it was just as well that I didn't waste any further time chasing him. On 21 November, 1996, the *Daily Star* ran a story detailing how McAvennie had been fined £750 for possession of cocaine, following his arrest at Glasgow airport in April that year. The story also alleged that it had been his third court appearance of the week, having been declared bankrupt after failing to pay off a car loan and losing a legal battle to recover £100,000 confiscated by customs who 'claimed it was being sent to the Continent to buy drugs.' No wonder Frank had 'gone to ground'!

And yet, here we were, just under a year later, being offered the chance of an exclusive interview with the man himself – if we could agree a fee. My publisher, Tony McDonald, was keen to conclude the deal and even though it had generally been our policy never to pay for interviews, we both felt it would be worth our while in this case – as long as Frank was prepared to discuss some of the more controversial chapters of his life. We somehow found the cash and Frank certainly didn't disappoint, addressing all the highs 'n' lows of his turbulent life, which allowed us to run a coverline of 'FRANCK'S BACK! *Macca on birds, booze and bad-boy behaviour!*' In retrospect I think the West Ham directors may have been a bit embarrassed by having their magazine used as a platform for one of the club's former players to deny being a junkie while admitting to having taken coke while on their payroll.

'I tried drugs only on a few occasions and when I did I was out of my head on drink anyway,' he claimed, before explaining how he'd been asked to look after a small quantity of cocaine by a friend and had forgotten about it until was discovered in his pocket when making a flight a few days later. According to the *Daily Star*, Frank's response to being caught white-handed was simply: 'It's only a wee bit of Charlie!' We got great mileage out of the piece, dedicating 11 pages across two issues to it and we felt rather proud of ourselves that *HNM* had once again ventured into dangerous territory.

Featuring a player the fans love is one thing, talking to a player the fans love to hate is something else. Just a few months after our McAvennie exclusive, Tony Mac suggested we follow up with an interview with Paul Ince. Yeah, him. I applauded his initiative but really couldn't see Ince giving up his time to be featured in a magazine read by those who'd been torturing, tormenting and terrorising him on every return he'd made to Upton Park since his acrimonious departure to Manchester United in 1989. It just wasn't going to happen, but if Mac thought he had a chance of persuading him to co-operate (having known him in the late '80s) then we had nothing to lose by trying. He therefore wrote a friendly letter to Paul c/o Liverpool Football Club, whom the player had recently joined after a two-year spell in Italy with Inter Milan, explaining that the time might perhaps be right to set the record straight once and for all. Since Liverpool was arriving at Upton Park for a league match on 27 September, the plan had been to feature Ince in the issue that came out in the middle of that month, and if he turned round, held his hands up and publicly apologised for his error of judgement eight years earlier, then maybe the match wouldn't be marred by the incessant abuse he'd otherwise probably have to face. Not only would it be a good public-relations exercise on Paul's part, we could also feel satisfied that *HNM* had done its best to smooth things over (while selling a few more magazines in the process!).

When we failed to get an immediate response we assumed he wasn't interested, but suddenly Mac received a call from Paul's wife Lynne, apologising for the delay but confirming that he'd be available to talk. And, sure enough, within a day or so the conversation took place (over the phone), and Ince was happy to allow us to donate a small fee to the Princess Diana Memorial Fund instead of paying him. Had we been the *News of the World*, of course, his response would have been very different, as he confirmed.

Like elephants, West Ham fans have very long memories and one of the biggest problems over the years was that Ince had not apologised for posing in a Manchester United shirt several weeks before actually transferring north. The picture had created an untenable situation and, despite the Hammers' lack of enthusiasm at the prospect of selling him, they really had no choice in the end.

As Ince established himself as one of the game's most determined characters during the '90s, many interpreted his confidence as arrogance while even United manager Alex Ferguson had called him a 'big-time Charlie' following his departure from Old Trafford. The biggest problem for West Ham fans, though, was that Paul had done little to improve the situation, simply burying his head in the sand as if he'd done nothing wrong.

By the time the piece hit the streets Ince had already received a predictably hostile reception during Liverpool's 2–1 defeat at Upton Park, but at least we were able to gauge the mood of the fans at the Hammers' next game, at Southampton. 'If he was big enough to admit he was wrong, then fair enough. But until he does that, he's going to get it every time,' said Les Cullen of Wallington, confirming my feeling.

For that reason I was pleased to see Paul show some remorse in the article. 'It's the only thing I regret in my life, posing in that shirt,' he conceded, explaining that he'd allowed the picture to be taken in the belief that the deal would go through while he was on holiday and if nothing happened it would be destroyed. 'I just hope the fans can accept that people make mistakes.' OK, it wasn't exactly an apology, but for the first time he'd admitted he'd been naïve and done wrong and I considered this a major coup for the magazine. We commenced the feature with a double-page spread dedicated almost entirely to the heading 'THE MAN

YOU LOVE TO HATE', with just half of Ince's face looking in from the right. I still think it's the best two pages we ever produced because, apart from looking great, it hit the nail on the head perfectly.

While everybody concentrated on the shirt issue, however, many overlooked what was perhaps the most controversial part of the piece, in which he attacked the West Ham directors for sacking John Lyall. 'It was a disgrace. I thought that if they could treat somebody as loyal as John like that, then what was the point of me being loyal to the club?' he stormed.

I wasn't too sure how the club would react to having such views expressed in its own magazine, but Mac's view was that it was a previous hierarchy who'd made the decision in 1989 so there shouldn't be a problem. That was true, but Martin Cearns and Charles Warner were already on the board at that time and in theory they could have taken exception (even though Len and William Cearns were in the senior positions). After all, it's still the club as an entity that was being criticised. There were no complaints but I still wonder what comments were made about it over tea and biscuits somewhere deep within the Boleyn Ground.

Chapter Nineteen

The word 'injury' may be considered a six-letter expletive as far as footballers are concerned but it became a vital part of *HNM*'s vocabulary during the build-up to the 1997–98 campaign. First the Hammers sent a team to Charlton on 4 August to play a pre-season benefit match for defender Simon Webster, whose career ended following a two-year fight for fitness after breaking a leg in a training clash with Julian Dicks just 14 days after leaving the Valley. And you had to feel a certain sympathy for Charlton fans as they watched their two new signings, former Hammer Mattie Holmes and striker Clive Mendonca, being taken out by trialist Steinar Neilson. 'He's just the sort of player we're looking for,' said Peter Storrie, much to our amusement, as the Charlton medics worked overtime after the 1–1 draw.

Within a week we'd got word that midfielder Danny Williamson was being traded for Everton international David Unsworth, Harry desperate for a left-sided defender following confirmation that Julian Dicks was still struggling with the knee injury incurred during training in April. We'd last seen Julian collecting his Hammer-of-the-Year award at Upton Park's final game of the season, and I'd kept tabs on his progress during the summer after he'd had a piece of inner cartilage removed and the left knee washed out.

'I really don't know when I'll be playing again,' he admitted, when I rang him at home in early July for an update. On revealing that he'd had yet another operation – having a piece of flapping cartilage shaved (how much cartilage had he actually left?) – he insisted that rumours of his imminent retirement were once again premature. 'Stories about this being career-threatening are rubbish!' he blasted. 'It annoys me because people believe what they read in the papers and my family get worried. But I've no worries about the future. I'll be back.'

Predictably, such claims fell on deaf ears in certain quarters. 'Dicksy's had it, he'll never play again,' became something of a catchphrase from one of my contributors, who was adamant he had it 'on good authority' that Julian's knee would never recover sufficiently to enable a return. It had all been said before, of course, when Dicks suffered major ligament damage in October 1990 but made a successful return after 14 months. 'That injury would have finished 75 per cent of the players I know,' said Billy Bonds when we spoke for the *Terminator* book. Julian had set out to prove everybody wrong then, but the fact that his current problem was with the very same knee hardly inspired confidence, especially as the prognosis seemed to be getting worse. 'This cartilage problem won't be affected by my old injury,' he insisted, when I first quizzed Julian back in May. 'If it was anything to do with the ligaments then the swelling wouldn't go down, but it has, so that's pleasing.' By July the swelling was causing concern, however, and Dicksy confessed to me: 'Because of the past problems I've had with the knee, it will take longer to heal than usual.'

As the season got underway, new rumours started to circulate that Julian was going to have to quit the game, so I rang his agent Rachel Anderson for a response. 'It's absolute rubbish to say that Julian's career is over. He had expected to be further down the road to recovery by now but the knee still has some swelling. Going abroad to see a specialist may be the answer but we have a number of options.'

Dicksy did indeed have to dig out the passport, jetting off to Alabama to consult Dr James Andrews, the surgeon who'd worked on Paul Gascoigne's problem knee in past years. After a number of examinations and tests, it was decided that an operation could be performed in which an artificial cord would be attached to the anterior cruciate in the knee. This would hopefully stabilise the cruciate and stop the swelling.

'It's feeling f***ing sore!' complained Julian when we spoke shortly after he emerged from Mile End's London Independent Hospital in October. 'The specialist said I could either have the operation or just crack on with my general rehab and see if it strengthened that way. If I decided to leave it and found it was not better in eight months time, then I'd consider myself silly for wasting that time. Either way it was going to be next season before I could return.'

Dicksy had made the logical decision but the pain had certainly made him doubt the wisdom of going through with the operation. 'When I came round afterwards I thought, "F*** it, is it all worth it?" I was drugged up to the eyeballs and in absolute agony.'

It was perhaps a bit too early to really press Julian on his state of mind, but I was still eager to discover how great a chance he really felt he had of making a successful return. Having gone through the recovery process once, he certainly knew what was in store over the next year and this time around he had the added advantage of having matured sufficiently. 'I was only 22 before and didn't know how to cope with things,' he candidly admitted. 'I was going out drinking every night to relieve the boredom but now I've got other things to occupy my mind, such as my dogs and family, for example.'

As we spoke he seemed relaxed and philosophical about things, but did he honestly believe he'd play first-team football for West Ham again? I pushed him for an answer. 'I don't know what odds other people would put on it. They could tell me I've got a 1 in 10 chance but that wouldn't make any difference to my determination to come back,' he persisted. 'Regardless of what people might say, I'm 99 per cent certain I'll be playing again. That's the way I am.'

Exactly. As his wife Kay once told me, 'Julian doesn't like having decisions made for him. He'll retire when he wants to, not when other people tell him he might have to.' He might be a stubborn git at times – as Kay will certainly testify – but that attitude is essential when faced with such a long haul back to fitness. It's one characteristic that always sets Dicksy apart from most other players. While others talk about determination, he's proved he's got the stuff running through his veins. If Julian had gone back to his Latchingdon home with anything less than a full belief he'd make it back, he'd have had no chance. If anybody could do it, I knew he could.

By this time David Unsworth had begun to win friends in the position Julian would have been occupying, having completed his move down from Merseyside. The 23-year-old found himself on familiar territory within days, making his West Ham début against his former side at Goodison Park on 23 August. With Danny Williamson heading in the opposite direction as part of the deal (with an extra £1 million following Unsworth south), the young Londoner pulled on an Everton shirt for the first time before the very same game, probably making a little bit of history in the process.

Bilic also faced the Hammers for the first time following his close-season move, so there was plenty of spice to the game but, despite going ahead when Dave Watson diverted Hartson's shot into the net, the Hammers eventually fell to a 2–1 defeat to continue their dismal run of results at Goodison Park (10 losses in the last 11 visits). What made it so annoying on this occasion was that it had been one of our better performances up there, while a win would have made it nine points out of nine for the campaign so far (following wins at Barnsley and at home to Spurs). Bilic got stick from the visiting crowd, Unsworth was applauded by everybody, while Williamson . . . was sort of invisible, really. Danny boy had a disappointing début and soon disappeared completely from view as he succumbed to ankle problems. The fact that he missed 25 games for West Ham the previous season because of injury to his ankle cannot be considered merely coincidence and there are some who hold the view that his career was doomed before transferring north.

It was yet another brilliant bit of business by Harry. The likeable 23-year-old may have been a home-grown talent – he lived just round the corner in Plaistow – but he'd clearly become surplus to requirement in the middle of the park following the arrivals of Lomas and Berkovic. And to get an England international (albeit with just one cap) of the same age with twice as much first-team experience under his belt, in a position which badly needed filling, *plus* a million quid, was too good to be true.

Before too much activity on the pitch there was yet another change in defence, when centre-half Marc Rieper departed for Celtic and Ian Pearce was signed from Blackburn as a replacement. This was yet another astute move from Harry. I'd never been entirely convinced by the less-than-great Dane, despite improving hugely after his nervous start in our colours, but when he started to intimate his future might lie elsewhere, with less than a year left on his contract, it was a relief to get £1.5 million for him. Some fans might have complained about Pearce being overpriced at around £2.3 million but I argued that we'd replaced a 29-year-old with somebody six years younger at a net cost of just £800,000. If Redknapp could do that for all the players approaching 30 he'd be more than happy.

In next to no time the Hammers had completely rebuilt their backline. Bilic and Rieper had gone, Dicksy was out for another season and Richard Hall had suffered yet another setback with his foot injury. Rio Ferdinand had established himself as the new fulcrum at the heart of defence and Unsworth and Pearce were his new partners on either side. And then there was Steve Potts.

Despite racking up nearly 400 games prior to his testimonial against QPR a week before the new season kicked off, he'd become the eternal extra man of late, having made just 20 league appearances the previous campaign – usually as an emergency stand-in. Despite impressive performances, mopping up trouble with perfect precision in the tackle, Steve always seemed to be rewarded by being squeezed out of the side as soon as others became available. Many might consider his unstinting loyalty as a lack of ambition – surely he should be looking for first-team football on a permanent basis? – but he's not the kind of guy you can imagine rocking the boat. I remember first interviewing him for a 'Profile on . . .' piece back in 1995 and his struggling to get three adjectives to describe himself as a player. 'I dunno really,' became something of a stock answer, as we ran through the questions and, as affordable as he was, I found it hard to understand how somebody with such a placid personality could find himself skippering the team (as he eventually did for nearly three years until being sent off at Newcastle in March 1996, when Dicksy took over).

Harry had complained about the lack of vocal authority at the back on more than one occasion but was happy to return the captain's armband to Potts when Julian was sidelined towards the end of the 1997–98 season. Just three games into his run we witnessed the penalty débâcle in the crucial relegation clash with Everton, as Hartson and Kitson both showed complete disinterest in taking the kick. But it wasn't just the two strikers Harry was unhappy with. 'I was very, very annoyed and had the raving needle about it,' said Redknapp, when I later asked him about the incident. 'The whole thing was very unprofessional and I also blamed Steve Potts, in a way, because he was the captain. He should have taken responsibility and made sure things were done right on the field. His job was not just about tossing the coin.'

The funny thing is that Steve probably had no idea who should have been taking the penalty anyway. When the Hammers had yet to be awarded a spot-kick after 23 games of the 1998–99 season, I asked Harry who would have the honour, should one eventually come our way. 'Dicksy,' he said, 'if he's on the pitch. If not, then maybe Wrighty or Frank Lampard.' Mmm, that's a bit vague, I thought. At the same time I spoke to Julian (who'd made a first-team comeback by this time) and he denied having been awarded the responsibility. 'It's down to the players. I'd probably let Wrighty take it although, if I did, I'd probably still get the blame if he missed!' he said, indicating his sense of disillusionment at the time.

With no evidence to suggest things were any more organised a couple of seasons earlier, is it any wonder that the scenes witnessed during the Everton match were 'like you'd see at a testimonial', to quote Harry's words to me once? And if he knows Potts is hardly Mick Jagger when it comes to making himself heard (resembling, rather, Charlie Watts or Bill Wyman), why make him captain at all? Steve agreed to be interviewed for *HNM* to coincide with his testimonial but wasn't overly keen on discussing Harry's merits as a manager. He took the diplomatic line, which is what you'd expect from a player a little unhappy at being pushed out of the picture. The last thing you'd expect to see from Pottsy would be him courting controversy and, in any case, Rio Ferdinand had enough of that on his plate at this particular time . . .

Chapter Twenty

The news came into the office via a brief phone call. Rio Ferdinand had been nicked for drink-driving. I must admit I was shocked. Not just by the thought of the young defender knocking back the beers and jumping behind the wheel of a car (hey, we've all done it, according to John Hartson), but by the appalling timing of it all: the 18-year-old had won a call-up to the full England squad just two days earlier.

Probably the finest talent to emerge from the Upton Park youth ranks since Bobby Moore, Rio was fast climbing the ladder of success and his progress was monitored by the news pages of the magazine. He was called up for England's Under-18s in April 1996, signed a new three-year contract the following month as he made his West Ham first-team début as a sub in the final match of the season, flew out to take part in the European Under-18 championships in France that summer; had a three-month loan spell at Second-Division Bournemouth midway through the '96–97 campaign; made his first start (against Wrexham) in January; made his first Premiership start (against Derby) in February and scored his first senior goal (against Blackburn); signed a new five-year deal (said to be worth £1 million) in March; made his England Under-21 début in April when he was carried off with an ankle problem); and saw a reported £6 million bid from Manchester United dismissed by Peter Storrie in August.

Incredibly, with just 20 league games behind him as September arrived, he was the elder statesman of the first-choice defence – in terms of Hammers appearances – with Pearce and Unsworth only just being recruited. And now Glenn Hoddle had called him into his full England squad for the World Cup qualifier against Moldova. It had been a meteoric rise but, just as we all experience when we run too fast, we find ourselves tripping over and Rio did just that when the boys in blue nabbed the boy in claret and blue.

I tried to picture the scene and remembered a story from my music journalism days when the old keyboard player of cobwebbed rockers Uriah Heep was asked to step out of his car by an officer of the law after consuming a few brown waters too many. 'Only if you put your arm on my ssshhoulder and ssshhay, "You're nicked, me old beauty!" he slurred. Somehow I think Rio conducted himself with a little more dignity, don't you?

It was quickly confirmed that Rio had received the minimum one-year ban and a fine of £500, but the biggest penalty came with the news that the Football Association had withdrawn him from the England squad. It was a huge blow, not just for Ferdinand but everybody associated with West Ham. Had Rio played against Moldova, he'd have been the second youngest player to appear for England (behind Duncan Edwards) and the first Hammer to play in the full XI since Tony Cottee in 1988.

But there was something else. Something big. Rio's indiscretion took place within a day or so of Princess Diana losing her life in a car pursued by Paris paparazzi and driven by somebody who'd been drinking. With the nation gripped by grief, the football authorities had to be seen to be coming down hard on somebody guilty of getting behind the wheel of a car with excess alcohol in their system. 'Don't kid yourself that football's governing body is making a decision in the interests of setting an example to other kids,' I wrote in my monthly column. 'No, the real reason – understandable as it may be – is that with all the publicity surrounding the circumstances of Diana's death, the FA realised they would be crucified by the press if they allowed Hoddle to select somebody recently convicted of drink-driving. It would be tantamount to condoning the alleged behaviour of Dodi Fayed's driver. The FA had no choice, but let's be clear on exactly why the decision was made.'

My real beef was the lack of consistency. 'What explains the FA's reluctance to take such a firm stance when dealing with the actions of other, more established England internationals in the past? You've got Gazza supposedly smashing up aeroplanes and hotels (not to mention the wife!), Tony Adams has spent four months in jail after forgetting that people walk on the pavement and cars drive on the road (and not the other way round), while Dennis Wise forgot that it's a football he's paid to kick and not a taxi cab. Yet all these people continued to play for England. Then we're being told Rio is to be taken 'under the wing' of Adams and given advice, as if he's some kind of alcoholic who's lost all sense of self-control. What rubbish!'

It was typical of the press to link drink-related stories in such a way and much of it was done purely for the sake of generating sensational headlines. Rio was still allowed to train with the England squad — indicating that once the dust had settled he'd be back in contention for a place — and it was little surprise that the media were in hot pursuit. Quite rightly, he refused to talk although he agreed to be interviewed for *HNM*. We stressed that we'd handle the situation sympathetically and provide him with the perfect platform to express his remorse. Within days word had got out that the next issue would include an exclusive conversation with Ferdinand and I soon had Harry Harris of the *Daily Mirror* on the phone. The chief soccer writer and twice British sports journalist of the year had been contributing a column to the magazine for just over a year as part of a deal that covered more than one title published by *Independent*.

Harry was most interested by the fact that we had Rio lined up for our next issue and wanted to make a proposal. If I were to fax him the article when it came through, he'd reproduce some of it in advance of *HNM*'s next appearance and run our cover to promote the issue. The *Mirror* would gain an advantage over its rivals while *HNM* would enjoy national promotion and reap the benefits with increased sales – a perfectly feasible offer of the kind that takes place all the time in publishing.

But this situation was different. Footballers have a natural cynicism for most of the press and one of our aims, as an official club magazine, was to establish relationships of confidence and trust with the players. If you've struck a rapport with them and they're comfortable speaking honestly to you, their conversations will be more candid, their personalities will come across and readers can get to know the people they pay to watch on the park every week. *HNM* prided itself on the fact that all interviews conducted on our behalf were exclusively for the magazine. There are many journalists I could have commissioned work to over the years but their pieces would have been no good to me if elements were going to be seen in various other publications as well.

That's a principle we tried to abide by, even in the most modest of circumstances, but Rio's drink-driving bust was obviously a controversial subject and if he'd refused to talk extensively to the tabloids then there was good reason for it. To have traded the copy in such a way would potentially have damaged a very important relationship for the magazine. And then there was the matter of timing. If a piece appeared in the *Mirror* in advance of our issue going on sale, then we'd effectively have given our exclusive away.

I had no choice but to reject the offer. I was warned what would happen otherwise – that the copy would just be lifted anyway by the papers (as is often the case, as if copyright laws didn't exist) and we'd get no credit or publicity at all. I didn't appreciate having such leverage used against me – particularly by a contributor to the magazine – and wrote to say that if so much as one sentence from the final interview with Rio found itself into the pages of the *Mirror*, then Harry could consider his arrangement with our company terminated. My response was not to his liking and, needless to say, his column never appeared again.

'I JUST CAN'T FIND THE WORDS TO SAY HOW SORRY I AM' was the heading we chose to run alongside a morose-looking Ferdinand on the opening spread of the feature when it appeared in our October 1997 issue. He was genuinely apologetic and seemed incredibly embarrassed by the furore, but admitted it was a legitimate mistake on his part, having underestimated the amount of alcohol in his system after celebrating his international call-up the previous evening.

As the printing presses started to run (and the Upton Park players' bar suddenly turned dry) another Hammer found himself making headlines as the stale breath of the story continued to linger. 'DRINKING AND DRIVING? WE'VE ALL DONE THAT' were the words that stood at the head of a page in the *Daily Mail* on 11 September, in which John Hartson declared: 'I'm not telling tales out of school if I say that Rio's bad luck was to be caught. If we are honest, we must admit we have all done it. There but for the grace of God . . .'

The strong suspicion was that the quotes were lifted from the Welsh striker's weekly column in the *Recorder* and even though the story expanded to acknowledge that he would 'never again take one drink and drive', it was still a classic case of John's honesty (or some would say stupidity) getting the better of him and landing him in hot water. The *Mail* predictably focused on 'football's unhealthy alliance with alcohol' and interpreted his words as meaning that 'drink-driving is commonplace among top-level players in England.' That may or may not be the case, but John was more likely to be referring to blokes in general rather than just members of his fellow profession. In any case, he should have realised how such claims would be used by the media and, in being drawn into a conversation about a fellow colleague's naïveté, he revealed his own. I'd see more of that first hand during our next meeting.

It's not so much that Hartson and headlines would go gracefully hand in hand over the next 18 months or so but rather that they would entwine themselves together in erratic fits of passion and rage. And it was something Hammers fans were going to have to get used to.

Chapter Twenty-One

If John Hartson could have been bottled and corked during the opening four months of the 1997–98 season, he'd have been a vintage claret. In the way that David Cross had terrorised defences 20 years earlier, John had the enemy running for cover and the only brown stuff on display was that running down opposing defenders' legs.

Having formed a 14-goal partnership with Paul Kitson to haul the Hammers to safety in the closing months of the previous campaign, the Welshman stormed off on a solo mission and rammed in an incredible 17 goals in 20 games by 3 December . He opened the team's account in the 2–1 opening-day win at euphoric Oakwell as Barnsley celebrated their first ever top-flight match; he took just three minutes to get on the scoresheet against Spurs in the next game and even put the side ahead in the top-of-the-table clash (yeah, you read that right) at Old Trafford to suggest an unlikely victory (we lost, of course). Huddersfield's Coca-Cola Cup hopes were sent fizzing with a hat-trick and four goals in a week, against Villa in the same competition (in a 3–0 win) and in the Premiership against Bolton (3–0 again), he proved he could do no wrong.

Hartson was on cloud nine as he headed the Premiership scoring charts, leaving the likes of Bergkamp, Sutton, Cole, Vialli and Wright trailing in his wake, but trouble was just around the corner. First he called referee Mike Reed a shithouse (the least he deserved) after the official's erratic handling of the 2–1 defeat at Leicester, incurring an FA charge for bringing the game into disrepute (for which he was fined £1,000 but fortunately escaped a ban); then it emerged that he'd received a police warning after a reported drink-related incident at an Essex hotel.

'That was blown out of all proportion,' insisted Harry Redknapp when I mentioned the episode to him. 'Apparently he had a relative who got into an argument about something and somebody panicked and called the police. John was just trying to calm the whole thing down.'

Harry did concede that when it came to football issues, however, Hartson had to start using his head before opening his mouth. 'John's got to be careful in what he says. I don't think he can afford to open his mouth straight after a match. John wears his heart on his sleeve and that's how he plays the game, so you're not going to see him saying, "I thought the referee was very good today", after something like the Leicester match. If he thinks the ref was shit he'll say so. I don't necessarily think that's a fault in him – if that's a fault it's rather sad. But John's not a problem. If you look around carefully we haven't had problems like some other clubs have had – and I'm talking about those at the very, very top.'

To be fair to Hartson, it was easy to understand his frustration after the game at Filbert Street in which the Hammers had pretty much dominated but came away with nothing. The free-kick count went heavily in the home side's favour while five Hammers were booked to Leicester's none. 'I was sitting among the Leicester fans for the match and if it hadn't been so infuriating, I could have laughed at the way Reed took the sting out of the venom of the home supporters who were determined to give him a hard time following his terrible penalty decision against the Foxes at Chelsea last season,' I wrote, in order to offer John some defence. 'Harry had already gone on record prior to the match, airing his concerns that Reed might subconsciously offer the benefit of the doubt to Leicester on the night – and so it proved. You had that big lump [Emile] Heskey hitting the turf at every opportunity, seemingly being sent flying every time anybody near him so much as botty-burped. And the ref fell for it. "I was pleased with my performance," said Reed afterwards. Yeah, I bet you were, mate. I think Johnny and I will have to stick together on this one.'

HNM also spoke to the fans for their view on the whole shenanigans. 'Even some of the Leicester fans sitting near us thought the ref was having a peculiar game. But that's irrelevant, Hartson should have kept his mouth zipped because the result of what he said is so inevitable,' said Mike and Elaine Forrester of South Woodford, who feared he might get banned, while Steve Allen of Waltham Cross declared: 'Hartson was right to say what he did. Although the ref didn't affect the result, some of the decisions he gave were diabolical.'

West Ham had fallen to a late Ian Marshall shot after Eyal Berkovic had struck in the second half to wipe out Heskey's opener. The Hammers playmaker had run over to the visiting fans to celebrate his goal and somebody in the crowd just happened to have an Israeli banner for him to wave. 'Berko gets out his very big hanky' was the caption we ran with the photograph in *HNM*, although quite what the player thought of us referring to his national flag as a snot rag we'll never know. After all, he wasn't known for his sense of humour.

Hartson could count on the support of the fans while he was banging in the goals. Everybody loves you, baby. But when you're not doing the business it's a different situation. Following his goal in the 4–1 win over Crystal Palace in December, the Welshman was to score just once more in the next 11 Premiership games (netting the fifth in the 6–0 thumping of Barnsley). The cups, meanwhile, brought agony and ecstasy. The Hammers had been propelled to the fifth round of the Coca-Cola Cup thanks to John's six goals in the competition so far, but after hitting three against Huddersfield, two against Villa and one against Walsall, the sequence suggested he was going to fire blanks against his former Arsenal team-mates. And so it proved, despite having the golden opportunity of a penalty to give West Ham a 17th-minute lead. Hartson's weak spot-kick was comfortably captured by keeper David Seaman and within seven minutes Ian Wright had given the Gunners the lead to send them on their way to the semi-finals (via an eventual 2–1 win).

In the FA Cup, John had spared our blushes with a late third-round winner against non-league Emley. West Ham had a tradition for struggling against lower division sides but surely the Unibond Premier League outfit couldn't cause a problem, could they? Well, 'WHU' doesn't stand for 'Well Hilarious Upset' for nothing. Frank Lampard scored within three minutes of the kick-off to leave us wondering if the 10–0 Milk Cup win over Bury in 1983 could be surpassed, but when chemical worker Paul David nodded in an equaliser from a 56th-minute corner, any kind of victory would have sufficed. Fortunately, the head of Hartson had the final say with just 10 minutes remaining and we could all breathe a huge sigh of relief.

A fortnight later, at Tottenham, John made his presence felt in a different way, butting into a touchline confrontation between his manager and Spurs defender Colin Calderwood. It had all sparked after Samassi Abou – an early-season signing from Cannes – retaliated after clashing with Ramón Vega, who collapsed to the ground as if struck by lightning. It was a performance of histrionics by the defender as he clutched his leg and (Swiss-) rolled around in apparent agony. Headmaster, oops, referee David Elleray responded by waving red in the face of Abou who in turn waved black in the face of the official with his finger. The Ivory Coast-born striker wasn't going to leave the park without telling the ref exactly what he thought of the decision – albeit in French – so, enter Harry Redknapp who ran along the touchline to sort things out. Enter Calderwood, who for no good reason decided to have a go at Harry. Just as it looked as if 'H' was going to stick one on him, enter Hartson who grabbed Calderwood and told him to f-f-f-f-f-find something else to do.

I witnessed the fray from the front row of the press box, alongside José Domínguez sitting in the Tottenham dug-out. For one moment I thought Spurs boss Christian Gross was pointing at me to start warming up and I was almost tempted to jump out and give Mr Elleray a few words of advice myself as the throng around him expanded. Abou was eventually led away – arm around shoulder – by French compatriot Bernard Lama, on loan from Paris St Germain as goalkeeping cover.

In the post-match press conference Harry defended Abou and complained about Vega's theatrics. 'I thought he'd broken his leg but it was only a broken tie-up!' he mocked, before downplaying his clash with Calderwood. 'It was nothing. I know Colin and he's a good lad. It was just a misunderstanding.' As Redknapp got up to leave the room he turned and quipped, 'Anyway, John's my minder – he'll look after me!'

As usual, we roared with laughter; the press crowd always do when Harry's on form. And let's face it, when the stern-faced Christian Gross is around, somebody needs to make a joke. It was purely a glib remark and obviously not meant to be taken seriously, but some papers decided to quote him verbatim and include it among the rest of his comments after the 1–0 defeat.

This was all well and good but it hardly did Hartson any favours, helping to build the image of a hefty heavyweight you'd expect to see more on the doorstep of a Swansea nightclub rather than a football pitch. But staying on a pitch for 90 minutes started to prove a problem for John in the latter half of the campaign. West Ham headed to struggling Bolton on 21 February needing a win to boost hopes of finishing high enough in the league to qualify for a UEFA Cup place; and their chances were hardly helped by Hartson being given his marching orders in the second half for an unnecessary flick of the arm at midfielder Per Frandsen. It wasn't much but it was petulant and a clear sign of John's frustration as his goal drought extended. Recently signed Trevor Sinclair then put 10-man Hammers ahead, and it looked as if the three points were in the bag until Bolton's Nathan Blake had the last laugh with just a couple of minutes remaining.

Four days later, West Ham were back in Lancashire, this time at Blackburn Rovers for an FA Cup fifth-round replay. Despite having a press pass for the game, a sixth sense suggested I might enjoy the night more with the visiting fans even though logic told me it was going to be a cold and miserable affair. All eyes were on Berkovic, who'd complained of being the victim of anti-Semitic remarks from a Rovers player in the 2–2 draw at Upton Park and was also blamed by Ewood Park fans for over-reacting to Kevin Gallacher's wayward arm to prompt a red card. But it was Hartson who looked as if he was going to steal the honours when poking in from close range in the first period of extra-time. As Hammers fans began to anticipate a place in the quarter-finals, though, Stuart Ripley forced the tie into a penalty shoot-out with a late equaliser. To say the atmosphere was tense would be an understatement, but Hartson converted his spot-kick with little fuss – along with Unsworth, Lampard, Pearce and the four Rovers players – and when Craig Forrest saved the final effort from Colin Hendry, it was left to Steve Lomas to fire home and send West Ham back to London with Wembley's twin towers looming on the horizon.

It was without doubt the most exhilarating moment of the season. I remember driving back down the M6 feeling totally elated: it had been a long time since any cup competition had inspired such euphoria. What a shame we had to face Arsenal in the last eight for the second time that season. The Bolton sending-off had disqualified Hartson from taking part in the match at Highbury – which finished 1–1 but should have seen a Hammers victory if only Berkovic had taken a great opportunity to double a lead provided by Pearce – but he was back for the Upton Park replay. And this match was to prove the most gut-wrenching of the year. With Dennis Bergkamp having been sent off for throwing an arm into Lomas's face, the opportunity to beat the Gunners repeated itself but yet again the Hammers failed to capitalise. Hartson eventually wiped out Nicolas Anelka's first-half injury-time goal, proving wrong those who said he'd never score against his old colleagues, but he joined the ranks of Berkovic and Abou who failed to score from the spot once the game went into a penalty shoot-out. What made it worse was the fact that Arsenal – kicking first – twice failed to convert and we misfired on both occasions when following up.

Harry Redknapp later admitted to me that it had been the lowest moment for him, too. 'I thought we could have gone on to win the competition,' he said ruefully. Privately, and very soon publicly, he was becoming increasingly concerned at the deteriorating form of Hartson. Initially I'd sprung to the 22-year-old's defence, writing in January: 'The big Welshman hasn't enjoyed the best of times recently, but after scoring 17 goals in 20 games it was inevitable that he'd eventually go a few games without hitting the back of the net. Nobody could maintain that kind of form.' All strikers experience barren periods when nothing seems to work but John seemed to let his head drop badly. It wasn't as if goalkeepers were pulling off death-defying saves or his shots were hitting the woodwork either: he simply didn't look like the same player after a while. Whereas before his size had once been a powerful weapon, now it had become a handicap and he'd degenerated from hardnut to lardbutt in the space of a few months. The one thing everybody used to say about Iain Dowie (who left around this time as part of the deal that brought Trevor Sinclair from QPR) was that at least he'd always given 100 per cent, but Hartson didn't even look as if he was trying, strolling about and bemoaning his luck when he hadn't worked hard enough to deserve any.

Fans can be fickle but they can generally see when a player isn't giving his all and their patience was beginning to wear thin. Harry's, meanwhile, disappeared completely after Hartson was sent off for the second time in two months in the home game against Derby on 11 April. 'If he wants to fight he should get in touch with Frank Warren and ask him to put him on at York Hall on a Tuesday night,' said Redknapp in disgust after watching his heavyweight hitman smack Igor Stimac in the back of the head as they both went tumbling on the half-hour mark. John's feud with the crafty Croat ran back over several games; one reporter had even tried to dig the dirt up at Pride Park earlier in the season when Stimac appeared briefly in the press room. 'I've not much to say about Hartson,' he said, 'he's an OK player but . . .'

'Get off the pitch, Hartson, you fool, get off . . .' screamed the fan sitting next to me in the East Stand as John saw red again. In some quarters of the ground, however, he was applauded and cheered for giving Stimac what they thought he deserved. 'Something has got up Igor's rather large nose because he's done nothing but play to wind up Hartson and get him into trouble,' I wrote. 'The ugly East European was at it again in this match, making a fuss like a big girl's blouse and falling down and crying like a three-year-old toddler when he couldn't get his own way.'

Referee Graham Barber, meanwhile, did little to prevent the match from degenerating into an anarchic mess. 'He was never in control of the game and had a shocking afternoon,' said the *News of the World* after the 0–0 draw (in which Derby – or should I say Debry, as the electronic scoreboard read, suggesting that County were rubbish – also had Eranio sent off).

None of this had any impact on Redknapp who described Hartson as 'stupid' if he had indeed thumped Stimac, who had the last laugh in playing with the fiery Welshman's short fuse. 'He may be laughing but at least he's laughing with a sore head,' said John afterwards, obviously happy to have made his mark. Within a week or so I was chatting with Julian Dicks and mentioned the incident, knowing he's been in plenty of similar scrapes himself in the past. 'John had to go, there's no doubt about that, but he reacted instinctively and I know from my own experience what it's like to be in that position,' he told me. 'I know I can't exactly talk much – it took me 10 years to learn how to control myself – but if John ever wants to speak to me for advice he only has to ask.'

John certainly had plenty of time to sit and listen: his latest indiscretion resulted in a four-match suspension. It's arguable as to exactly what the effects of his absence on the team were. He signed off in style with a brace in the 2–1 home win against Blackburn but, boy, did the wheels fall off big-time after that. BIFF! The Saints showed no mercy as they cruised audaciously to a 4–2 victory at Upton Park. THWACK!! Liverpool smashed five past World Cup hopeful Lama at Anfield with no reply. KAPOW!!! Relegated Palace swept into a 3–1 lead at Selhurst Park before Manny Omoyinmi scored twice as a late substitute to at least salvage a point. Hammers finished that particular match in the ludicrous position of having just ONE defender (Pearce) left on the park, Ferdinand and Potts unavailable through injury and Unsworth sent off in the final minutes, before we equalised, funnily enough. Frank Lampard had scored in the fourth minute and the two points lost through failing to retain the lead meant that West Ham went into their final match against Leicester needing a win and hoping that Aston Villa would succumb at home to newly crowned Premiership champions Arsenal.

The Upton Park finale was a thriller, in which Abou inspired Hammers to a 4–3 win that again exposed our defensive frailties. Ultimately, it wasn't enough to gain the final UEFA Cup place (seventh): Villa defeated an Arsenal side that 'maybe wasn't 100 per cent committed' according to boss Arsene Wenger who was looking forward to the following week's FA Cup final. Oh, thanks very much! As if knocking the Hammers out of both cups at the quarter-final stages wasn't good enough, the Gunners also had to destroy our league hopes by mincing about like a bunch of fairies to give Villa an easy three points.

With the rearguard disintegrating (as much through lack of resources as anything else) and shipping 15 goals in the final four games, Hartson had the ultimate defence against those accusing him of costing the club UEFA Cup qualification. As far as he was concerned, the problem wasn't the attack – nine goals were scored in the four games he missed – the problem was at the other end.

That's not exactly how Harry saw it, however. 'If Hartson had played at Palace we'd have won that game,' he told me. Yet at the same time he acknowledged: 'We leaked goals in the final games and that's nothing to do with John.' Clearly, he didn't want to be seen to be blaming the Welshman but I knew he felt the unnecessary loss of his 24-goal striker, for a total of seven games during the season, was a major factor. 'John had

FORTUNE'S ALWAYS HIDING?

that spell when he went off the boil but I'm still his biggest fan and to score that many goals in a season is a tremendous achievement. When he's on his game, like he was against Blackburn in his final match, he's absolutely frightening.'

Not frightening enough to convince West Ham supporters to vote him as their Hammer-of-the-Year, however, which went to the outstanding Rio Ferdinand in his first full season. Nor did he make the runner-up position either. It was skipper Steve Lomas who received that particular accolade. Hartson wasn't happy, feeling as if his efforts hadn't been appreciated enough by the fans and, according to some sources, threatened to 'drink Wales dry' during the close season. We would meet within a couple of months to discuss such recreational – or lubricational – activities . . .

128

Chapter Twenty-Two

'I like a beer, although I wouldn't say I drink more than the average f***ing 23-year-old. But I like having a drink and to enjoy myself. I haven't got a drink problem by any means – I haven't got a drink now and I'm not bothered – but when I go out and have half a dozen f***ing pints I can put weight on. So it's only if I pig out and binge.'

John Hartson was revealing rather more than just his bare feet as he stretched out across the bed in his hotel room in Uphall on the outskirts of Edinburgh. It was 24 July 1998, the Hammers were on a pre-season tour and 'Custard Hart', as I was tempted to call him after seeing his newly dyed blond thatch, was responding to a question about how difficult it was for him to keep his weight down. It's one that had to be asked, too, since the striker had looked increasingly lead-footed as the previous season progressed.

I was amazed by John's honesty. Players have always been reluctant to talk about their social activities at the best of times, but in the current climate – with much greater emphasis being placed on healthy diets and various new fitness techniques – it was incredible to hear him talking about pigging out, bingeing and knocking back the ale. The fact that he claimed to drink no more than the average bloke his age hardly inspired confidence, after all. In fact, to protect John to some extent, I thought 'a few pints' might sound a bit more acceptable than 'half a dozen f***ing pints' when writing my feature for *HNM*. Imagine the tabloids picking up on the story and writing about the player's 'six-pints-a-night benders'. All the same, Hammers fans must have got the drift that self-discipline was probably not one of Hartson's strong points.

In fact, Harry Redknapp had gone on record earlier in the year about how the Welshman was in danger of going off the rails and losing his way. 'John has got to get down to some serious hard work to get his game back together again. He's a good player when he puts his mind to it but he has let his performance and discipline drop and if he is not careful he could end up in the same situation he found himself in at Arsenal,' he warned.

As I sat on the corner of Hartson's bed and drew him into a

conversation about how his first full season at West Ham had gone, I reminded him of what Redknapp had said publicly. His response was astonishing.

'Round about the January or February time, I personally felt I'd shot my bolt,' he revealed. 'I'd scored 17 goals in the first 20 games and that was f***ing frightening. Then I scored twice in my next 14 games and obviously the expectation was that I was going to keep scoring as I had done. But I went off the boil and wasn't training so hard. I think I got a bit complacent. I honestly felt that I'd got my 20 goals and thought, "That's me now, I've done my bit."'

I was truly shocked by what I was hearing. Sitting in front of me was a top professional, earning more in one week than some Hammers fans do in an entire year, admitting – as if sitting in a confessional box to recount one's sins – that he'd literally given up!

'It's not the right way to think because there was a long way to go; we were pushing for Europe and I was trying to finish the season as the Premiership's top scorer,' he added. 'I honestly don't know why I got complacent. But it happens in all walks of life, doesn't it?'

Well, at least he admitted it was wrong, although in most 'walks of life' you get the sack. I was surprised that success had diminished his desire in such a dramatic way and found it difficult to comprehend why he should be so open about the way he'd felt. In some respects I was pleased, however. Not only did certain things about the previous season start to make sense but I was honoured that John should feel so comfortable in my presence to speak so candidly. Indeed, I thanked him for his sincerity and honesty, although some might consider his willingness to confess as naïveté or, at worst, idiocy.

I must admit, I could have been forgiven for questioning his intelligence myself when I first contacted John in his room. *Clubcall* reporter Chris Raistrick and I had flown to Scotland to cover the Hammers' friendlies against Hibernian and Motherwell while also taking the opportunity to speak to some of the players and find out how the preparations for the season were going. My two targets were Hartson and new signing Ian Wright, both of whom had been faxed of my intention to gain some interview time on the free day between the two games. After driving to the hotel and being invited into the restaurant to share some of the dinner prepared for the players, I saw Hartson disappear off towards his room. Knowing he was there for the entire evening I took my time in finishing my meal and later wandered out to the reception area to ask for John's room number. I then rang him from the lobby.

'John, it's Kirk from *Hammers News Magazine*.'

'Hello, mate.'

'Listen, did you get my fax about us having a quick chat for the magazine?'

'Er . . . no.'

'Well, with all the spotlight being on Wrighty's arrival at the club, I thought it might be nice to remind fans of the bloke who scored 24 goals for us last season, especially as you're a former team-mate of Ian's as well. Are you happy to talk?'

'Yeah, no problem.'

'Where do you fancy doing it, down in the lobby here or in your room?'

'Er . . . shall we just do it on the phone?'

'Well . . . seeing as I've come all the way to Scotland to see you it might make more sense if we actually did it face to face, especially as I'm only about 50 yards down the corridor from you.'

'Oh yeah, that's a good idea.'

Yes, I thought it was, too. Less than a minute later I knocked on his door and was greeted by a firm handshake, a warm smile and a friendly welcome into his room. His familiarity surprised me given that we'd only really spoken over the phone (although he had once given me a ticket for a sold-out game at Southampton when the press box was full) and I felt sufficiently buoyed to make a glib comment about his new hairstyle. 'I was just messing about with it really,' he confessed, as he made himself comfortable on the bed. 'Obviously I got some stick from the lads at first but they've settled down. My girlfriend doesn't like it, though.'

I made myself comfortable down by his toes and asked if he felt any pressure in trying to follow up a season in which he'd just lost out to Manchester United's Andy Cole in the Premiership goalscoring stakes.

'I don't feel under pressure because I've got confidence in my own ability, as long as I'm fit and in the team,' he said in his soft Welsh accent. 'But if I don't do the business then obviously I will come under a bit of pressure. As will Andy Cole or [£7.5 million Blackburn signing] Kevin Davies. That comes with the job.

'But people like Wrighty and Paul Kitson will always score more goals than me,' he insisted. 'I'll always set up more goals for Wrighty than he ever will for me. I don't mean any disrespect but he won't f***ing outjump the likes of [Gary] Pallister or [Liverpool's Neil] Ruddock to knock balls down for me, but what he will do is make runs and that might take some of the responsibility off my shoulders. Last year I missed Kitson for f***ing months, I played with Abou, with Eyal, Trevor, Manny, on my own . . . and still managed to score 24 goals after missing seven games. But I'm confident I'll score lots of goals – I *know* I will – but to do that I've got to keep myself fit and avoid the silly things which got me suspended last season.'

Again, Hartson was coming clean. 'What I've got to get out of my game is the f***ing stupid stuff – the elbowing and the silly punches. That's ridiculous schoolboy stuff, the sort of things I'd do when I was playing for the Under-14s,' he admitted, obviously referring to the red card against Bolton and Derby. 'I did that last season and it cost us. I wouldn't say it was the *only* reason we failed to qualify for Europe. I thought the lack of defending at times cost us. We let in five at Liverpool and even if I'd have played I couldn't have f***ing scored six! But I admit that it affected the lads when I was out.'

John was adamant he'd probably have finished as the division's top scorer had he not missed seven matches, but in doing so he was inadvertently accepting more responsibility for the team's failure to get into Europe. He couldn't on the one hand claim he would definitely have scored more goals ('if I'd have played every game I like to think I'd have got 28–30 goals,' he told me) and then, on the other, insist they'd have made no difference. Just one more goal against Palace would have seen the Hammers into the seventh place required.

'My biggest target now is to keep myself fit and in top condition. It's basically down to how well I look after myself and how much I want to do it. But I will do it, I *know* I'll do it. The football itself is not a f***ing problem – I can play, I can score goals, I can head the ball, I can shoot, I can run . . . I can do everything. But if I'm not fit I can't f***ing do any of it.'

As well as voicing his concerns through the media, Harry Redknapp had taken John into his office on more than one occasion to discuss things. 'Harry saw what was happening last season and spoke to me a number of times, when he felt I was sluggish or had put a bit of weight on. He told me: "You're not the same player you were earlier in the season." You have to listen to Harry – he's been in the game a long time and I respect what he's got to say. After he pulled me in I got my head down, but then there was the sending-off against Derby, which Harry publicly said he didn't like.'

BANG! BANG! BANG! BANG! BANG!!!

We both jumped as the door did its best to hang on to its hinges. We suspected John Moncur was making his presence felt in the corridor outside. 'We'll f***ing ignore it,' said Hartson, happy to allow me to explore his psyche. I probed as to what impact his success and increased public profile had had on his character, wondering if it had been difficult to keep his feet on the ground.

'It can be hard at times,' he conceded. 'The success hasn't affected the way I am and I'd like to think I'm not a big-headed person. I go back to Wales to see the boys and I'm the same as I always was. The only thing that gets you down is when you get people coming up to you who don't know what they're talking about, when they're pissed up. It's great when somebody nice approaches you and says, "Excuse me, sorry to bother you but my son supports West Ham and could we have your autograph?" It's a pleasure, but when you get pestered by rival fans you just feel like f***ing having a go.

'Obviously you can't but, with the type of person I am and the way I've been brought up, it's in my nature to f***ing tell 'em where to go. It happens all the time and you have to walk away, but sometimes it's very, very hard. I've been out when people have said things and my family have gone: "We can't believe they've said that to you." Because I'm just like those people myself – I'm a football fan and support Swansea City. People don't understand – they think you're some kind of f***ing nugget when you're just a happy-go-lucky boy. But that's the price you have to pay.'

With that, there came a somewhat milder knock on the door and John opened it to allow Eyal Berkovic into the room. I shook the Israeli's hand and he emitted a brief smile, but he seemed eager to discuss something with his team-mate. I thanked John again for his time and left, knowing I'd just taken part in probably the most personal, probing interview ever conducted on behalf of the club's magazine. Hartson had admitted to taking the foot off the gas, described some of the things he'd done as stupid, confessed to struggling with his weight when 'I pig out and binge', revealed how difficult it was avoiding confrontation when out in public and acknowledged that his biggest target was to keep himself in shape. As well as making for sensational reading, it also provided a unique snapshot of the player's mentality. Credit for that must ultimately go to John because a less sincere character would just have brushed some of the points aside with a series of diplomatic clichés. Having said that, I'm still a great believer that to get strong answers you need to ask strong questions and Hartson gave me the confidence necessary to do that.

Whereas some journalists would have taken a sensationalist approach, I tried to create a more intimate atmosphere when I wrote the feature, presenting it more as a sort of character analysis. I entitled the piece

'FROM THE HART' and maybe my sympathetic handling of it played a part in discouraging the daily press from ruthlessly hanging Hartson with the rope he'd supplied in his very own words. His boots were still on the ground but they were entrenched firmly at a crossroads. 'The world may be at John Hartson's feet,' I wrote to sign off, in acknowledgement of the feature's opening line, before completing the sentence, 'but his future success is in his own hands . . .'

Chapter Twenty-Three

John Hartson may have been one West Ham player who decided he didn't really want to play during the 1997–98 campaign, but there was another who *did* want to perform but couldn't get into the team.

'I think the dinner ladies are nearer the front of the queue than I am,' complained Ian Bishop as we sat in a West End wine bar to discuss his (dismal) prospects. The 32-year-old had been sighted in public on less occasions than Elvis Presley, Howard Hughes and Salman Rushdie – three times, to be precise – when we got together in late January, and the midfielder was not happy. 'Even before the season Harry said I wouldn't be starting,' he moaned, as the likes of Steve Lomas, the fast-improving Frank Lampard and particularly playmaker Eyal Berkovic all pushed him further out of the frame. 'Personally, I don't think it was the right thing to do. This was before we'd even played a pre-season game! I needed an incentive. If I hadn't performed better than other players then that would be fair enough, but he'd already made his mind up.'

Bish had incurred the wrath of the fans the previous year when a wayward (and negative) pass at Upton Park found Gianfranco Zola and Chelsea immediately scored. With the boo-boys making their feelings heard in the remaining games, Ian avoided the traditional lap of honour at the end of the season while my publisher Tony Mac was so incensed he wrote a three-quarter page article speaking out in the player's defence.

'I don't like boos . . . well, I do like booze sometimes,' he quipped, winking as he clutched his bottle of Becks. Despite some of the crowd giving him a hard time, however, his love of playing for West Ham was obvious. 'I've always had a great relationship with the supporters and never thought I'd consider leaving the club,' he admitted. No, Ian's resentment was against his manager.

'I was annoyed with Harry for taking me off in that Chelsea game. We had an argument and I told him I wanted to get back out there and put things right but I wasn't given the opportunity.' Bish then went on to elaborate how he'd done Redknapp a huge favour by playing with damaged back ligaments but felt let down when he was later pushed out of the side when he was fit. 'Me and Harry were friends once but I don't know where it went wrong,' he added.

Arriving in the East End (along with Trevor Morley) as part of the deal that took Mark Ward up to Manchester City in 1989, Ian's other major concern was to have his contract (due to expire in the summer of '98) extended by 18 months, entitling him to a testimonial match. 'I asked Harry for a free transfer a few months ago, saying, "If you're not going to keep me until my testimonial, let me go for nothing." He said, "I can't let a player of your quality go for nothing." So I said, "Well, why can't you give a player of my quality a new deal?" I just feel I'm going nowhere and I have days when I'm really depressed about everything.'

With that, Bish then revealed a display book containing some cartoons he'd done in his spare time to take his mind away from the game. 'What d'ya think?' he enquired as I pored through the pages.

'They're very interesting,' I said, wondering what advice he thought I could offer in terms of using them in some commercial way. Each drawing (some in colour, the rest in black and white) was of a fictional football character and the lengthy captions indicated some kind of storyline. The best ones were quite impressive and I offered to reproduce one in the magazine for him, saying that perhaps a publisher of children's books might be interested.

As it turned out, we never got round to it as Bish was on his way back north within a couple of months, making a deadline-day move down a division to Manchester City as they struggled to avoid their second relegation in three seasons. I hoped for his sake alone that the club would survive as the idea of Ian stroking the ball around in his usual cultured fashion amid the hurly burly of Second Division football seemed unthinkable. I was in a Spanish bar (missing my first WHU game of the season in the penultimate weekend as the Hammers crashed 5–0 at Liverpool) when Sky's cameras confirmed City's fate, making the drop despite a final-day 5–2 win at Stoke. I could see Bish trudging along the touchline with manager Joe Royle looking like his world had just caved in and I felt genuinely sorry for him. He said he'd go anywhere for first-team football but could he really motivate himself to face the likes of Macclesfield and Colchester on a weekly basis?

I got the opportunity to ask him more quickly than I anticipated. It was FA Cup final day but I bumped into Ian, not at Wembley but in Brixton, of all places, at a party thrown by Iron Maiden. The heavy rockers had just played at the Academy and bassist Steve Harris – the band's founder member whose alliance to the Hammers has long been evident – had restricted the invitation for the after-show bash to personal acquaintances (as opposed to hordes of record company personnel). I was surprised at being asked along myself – particularly as the group were in Holland when Steve rang me (reading a copy of *HNM* to help pass the time on the road?) and I hadn't spoken to him for some time – but I'd been sending him the magazine following a number of interviews at his home about his love of West Ham and it was a typically amiable return gesture on his part. Dicksy is another mate of Steve's and I'd interviewed him that month about Maiden's new album, *Virtual XI* (it's hardly their best but, strangely, Julian described it as just that), which featured a photograph of the band in Hammers kit with a number of players, including Bishop.

'So, what was it like in the dressing-room after that final game against Stoke?' I shouted into Bish's ear after spotting him among the partying throng.

'What do *you* think?' he replied, clutching two bottles of beer in an effort to blot out the memory. I was genuinely intrigued to know how it might have felt to be part of that day's dramatic scenes and emphasised that I felt sorry to see things turn out that way. 'So, are you coming out or what?' he asked while later, as the party started to die down.

'Er, I thought I was out already,' I replied, wondering what he meant.

'No, let's go into town. It's early yet,' he said, determined to have a good time.

Minutes later we were out in the dark streets, trying to find a cab. One bloke decided he didn't fancy taking us ('us' being myself, Bish and one of his mates) and considering Ian had pogoed his way across the road looking like a fan at a Sex Pistols concert, it's perhaps not too surprising. 'Calm down, calm down,' I said, before realising that as a Scouser it's something that Bish should have been saying to *me*, and we eventually got a ride into the West End.

Half an hour later we were approaching Stringfellows nightclub and I reckoned our chances of getting in were approximately one out of a hundred. I looked more at home in a dodgy rock 'n' roll watering hole, Bish was still bouncing up and down as if the pavement were made of sponge and his mate was dressed like a labourer. Suddenly, it was as if the club's red carpet had been rolled out especially for us: the doormen swept us in with one gesture as the queue of waiting punters looked on in astonishment. Something told me 'Ah, Mr Bishop has been here before.'

Inside the club Ian complained once again about Harry's policy. 'It's not right. The likes of me and Moncs have been pushed out just because of our age but we can still play,' he grumbled. I nodded in approval but found it hard to feel too much sympathy given that I'd just stuck £20 into a whip, knowing I earned less in a year than he probably did in a month. I made the point that the team had to evolve and it was good for the supporters to see new faces arriving at the club, especially younger ones. He'd already acknowledged how things had improved on the park – 'the lads have done well and Eyal has been superb' – while he was still at the club, but you could understand him viewing things from a personal perspective and feeling unhappy that he'd been forced to move in order to secure first-team football when he continued to have full confidence in his own abilities. All players think that way. He also felt that he'd shown loyalty to the club but hadn't had that loyalty returned and that was understandable.

It was perhaps ironic that his final game for West Ham should have allowed him the opportunity to erase the memories of the previous year's home fixture against Chelsea, since this time Ian played a key role in the 2–1 victory. 'Bish'll never let you down,' said Redknapp after bringing him in for the suspended Steve Lomas (the midfielder who'd left Manchester City a year earlier) a full five months after his previous league appearances in the 4–0 annihilation at Arsenal and 3–0 sinking at Southampton in the autumn of 1997.

Thankfully, the misfortunes away from home, which seemed never-ending as the Hammers lost nine on the trot in the first half of the season, including a Coca-Cola Cup game at Huddersfield (1–0), were countered by a run of 10 successive wins at Upton Park (yep, you read correctly), including a Berkovic-inspired victory over Liverpool (just four days after the collapse at Arsenal) and emphatic three-goal margins against Bolton and Palace.

The latter game was actually the Hammers' second attempt at getting a result against the south Londoners, after the initial match on 3 November was abandoned in the 65th minute due to floodlight failure. The team had managed to rescue a two-goal deficit through second-half goals from Hartson and Lampard, but with the crowd still jumping out of their seats over the equaliser, the lights suddenly failed, leaving everybody in Upton in the dark. With the problem – diagnosed as contactor coil failure in three units – impossible to rectify on the night, the plug (literally) was pulled on the match.

But this was not the first time a Premiership match televised by Sky had fallen victim to electrical failure (Derby and Wimbledon also suffered problems that season) and some people started to smell not just burning but foul play. News of Far East betting syndicates trying to influence results of games in the Premiership had already started to filter through, and allegations were also made that people had profited through Paul

Kitson's wayward cross-field pass almost immediately from the kick-off at Old Trafford in May '97 as a result of spread-betting on the time of the first thrown-in. These theories were confirmed when a sabotage attempt at Charlton's Valley Ground was thwarted during the 1998–99 season (leading to the jailing of three Chinamen). Huge amounts were being staked on the outcome of games here and it came to light (no pun intended) that scorelines in abandoned matches were valid as long as more than 45 minutes had been played. With the odd Malaysian or two having a few quid on West Ham drawing 2–2 with the Eagles, it's no wonder Frank Lampard never made it to the corner flag in November.

Less than a week later a spat took place between John Moncur and Eyal Berkovic during the game against Chelsea at Stamford Bridge. With the score still at 0–0 in the first half, it appeared that Berkovic reacted to Moncur's verbal lashing by slapping him in the face. I was watching from the press box close to where the incident took place and found it rather more amusing than Harry Redknapp did. 'You can't have players pushing and shoving each other like that. It's not on,' he complained to the media, after the 2–1 defeat. 'These things happen in football but it's not something I want to see and it will be dealt with internally.'

Moncur planted a kiss on the cheek of his team-mate during the match – probably more to avoid punishment from the referee than to repair his relationship with Berkovic – but things blew up again when Eyal returned to Israel for a family occasion. 'I am not sorry. Moncur is one of the most jealous people I have ever met and he has goaded players and fans against me,' he was reported to have said to the media back home. Those who knew the two men were not too surprised by either the confrontation or the fact that Berkovic chose to speak out when abroad. Redknapp himself described Moncur as 'a bit of a mickey-taker' and the serious Israeli simply couldn't relate to much of the Cockney clowning he occasionally felt victimised by. It was a classic clash of characters and cultures and even though Berkovic's introverted nature made some consider him to be miserable and moody, it was also likely that some deliberately took advantage of his different sense of humour – or failed to take it into account at all.

Certainly, the players used to take the piss out of his clothes, both behind his back and in the pages of *HNM*. 'It's not so much that he's scruffy, it's just that he thinks he's wearing nice stuff and it'll be from Mr Byrite or somewhere,' said Frank Lampard, while Moncur went even further: 'Eyal's gear ain't the best. He was telling me today that he's sponsored by a certain clothing firm but I told him to go out and spend the money he gets from them on some decent stuff!'

Not surprisingly, our 'Team-Mates' page – in which we encouraged players to reveal all about what their colleagues are really like – dried up in the end because some were reluctant to say anything controversial about the others in the squad. Persuading players to take part in something that's just a light-hearted bit of fun could often prove harder than anticipated.

His dress sense may have brought a smile to the other players' faces but Berkovic's sober personality did little to discourage anybody from considering him something of a schemer. This view was particularly endorsed when he made a trip home, with quotes regularly appearing via the Israeli media that the player was looking to move on. How much this could be attributed to Eyal himself or his agent Pini Zahavi is open to debate, but it happened on such a regular basis that the argument about his comments being badly translated was proving difficult to swallow.

Berkovic hadn't been around for more than a few months when the first stories appeared of his apparent yearning to play for a bigger club, and in our November '97 issue he insisted: 'I'm very happy here at Upton Park and it's wrong for people to think that I'm not settled.' By the following spring it was suggested that he'd be on his way in the summer if the Hammers didn't qualify for European football. 'I don't want to talk about whether I'm staying or going,' he declared, leaving the door open for a quick escape even though Harry Redknapp told me: 'I don't see any reason why Berkovic should leave West Ham. He's happy, he's under contract and he's never been to see me to say he wants a transfer. But if somebody wants to give us £6 million and he wants to go then obviously we'd have to think about it.'

As far as I was concerned, the very fact that the manager had named his price made the Israeli's departure inevitable, yet the summer of 1998 came and went without any of the player's favoured clubs – Liverpool and Manchester United – showing any definite interest. Berkovic was also guilty of declining interviews with *HNM* to avoid the issue, pretending that the management had banned him from talking. Of course, you'd then go to Redknapp or Frank Lampard and they'd know nothing about it. 'Ask him what you like, we don't care.'

Another player whose future at West Ham seemed doubtful during the 1997–98 season was goalkeeper Ludek Miklosko. I felt sorry for the Czech because he'd worked hard at getting himself in shape for the campaign, but found it impossible to keep a clean sheet (the team's first one in the league coincided, as luck would have it, with Craig Forrest's début between the sticks following his move from Ipswich Town). Harry blamed Ludo for two of the goals which saw Leeds wipe out Frank

Lampard's 75th-minute goal at Elland Road, in which the youngster re-enacted his father's famous 1980 corner-flag jig, but his public damning of the keeper was to be far more intense after the match at Derby County on 6 December.

First Ludo clutched at the ball as if he'd coated his gloves with Fairy Liquid when Costa Rican striker Paulo Wanchope nodded towards goal – suddenly it was in the back of the net for the Rams to claim a 10th-minute lead. Then, with the second half just four minutes old and the Hammers still hopeful of getting back into the game, he booted a goal-kick directly to Dean Sturridge who said, 'Hey, Christmas has come early!' before rifling it back past him to make it game, set and match. Derby boss Jim Smith, the old bald eagle himself, is usually red-faced at the best of times but Harry made him look ghostly white by comparison as he sat down and lost his rag. 'What did I say to him?!' he said in response to one reporter's question. 'I said, "D'you think you could chip the ball just a bit higher next time when you're aiming for their striker?!" He's not paid to make mistakes but he made two rickets.'

I was surprised by Harry's reaction but could understand his frustration. Certainly, Miklosko wasn't happy with his manager's public response – 'I made the mistakes at Derby because I had suffered with knee problems, but nobody believed me,' he complained, when he eventually left Upton Park on Christmas Day, 1998 – and Harry later confessed to me that he'd been a bit rash in his comments. 'That happens when somebody in a press conference asks you what you thought of the goalkeeper when you've lost 2–0 because he made two terrible mistakes,' he said. Again, I had a certain sympathy for Ludo. As 'H' confirmed in his autobiography, Miklosko is a sensitive guy and, like Berkovic in some respects, mixing with the other players and establishing a matey rapport wasn't his speciality. It wouldn't surprise me if he thought the players' humour to be immature and juvenile (and let's face it, it often is) but when you're bringing in personnel from eastern Europe and even further afield you have to accept that mentalities are going to differ. That can sometimes make it more difficult for a manager who's looking to integrate foreigners and create a genuine team spirit.

The Derby game was also memorable for the appearance of striker Paulo Alves, the third player to have been brought in on loan from Sporting Lisbon (following Dani and Hugo Porfirio). The funny thing was that the Derby fans mistook the Portuguese international for former Ram Paul Kitson when he replaced Stan Lazaridis as a late substitute. The poor bloke got booed every time he went near the ball (which admittedly wasn't often) while the sound of 'Kitson is a wanker, he wears a wanker's hat . . .' rang around the Pride Park stadium. 'That Kitson slagged us off,' complained one supporter afterwards to justify the ill-feeling, while another described him as 'an 'orrible bloke'. Again, Paul isn't the most outgoing of types and his demeanour has occasionally been interpreted as moodiness. But whatever he's like, he still doesn't look like any Portugeezers. The whole episode was even more bizarre when you consider that Alves actually had his name spelt out on the back of his shirt!

Perhaps more confusing for Paulo was why Redknapp actually bothered to recruit him in the first place. 'I'm not sure why Harry asked me to come here if he wasn't going to play me. I'm always sitting on the bench and I could do that back in Lisbon,' he moaned, after playing just 54 minutes in four appearances as a substitute. He could have played for 54 years and he probably wouldn't have scored a better goal than Lazaridis did at Newcastle on 7 February to win the game. Skippy fired in from all of 38 yards in the 16th minute to leave the Toon Army wondering what had hit them – it was without doubt the best goal scored by a West Ham player that season.

The local media's big concern in the press conference after the game was why Shaka Hislop hadn't played in goal for Newcastle after recovering from injury, with Shay Given being retained at his expense. Manager Kenny Dalglish mumbled something about a contract dispute – ' it's his prerogative not to sign a new contract and it's my prerogative not to pick him for the team,' he said – and it became obvious that the big keeper would be leaving for nothing under the Bosman ruling in the summer. It's possible that West Ham's presence in the city that particular weekend gave them an advantage in the race to lure Hislop elsewhere.

It was certainly the hot whisper that Shaka would be heading to the East End but Harry was prohibited from confirming anything until the player's contract had expired with Newcastle on 30 June. 'I knew he was out of contract and there's no doubt he would make an excellent free transfer for somebody. If I can't do a deal with Bernard Lama then he'd be the one that would interest us,' he said, diplomatically, when I later quizzed him about the situation.

Lama had been kicking up a stink about his lack of first-team games because the only reason he'd joined the Hammers on loan was to try and force his way back into the French World Cup squad after having incurred a three-month ban for smoking funny fags. 'I really must question why Harry wanted me here in the first place,' said the 34-year-old whose bum was getting sore on the bench, echoing the sentiments of Alves around the same time.

'As much as I want to help Bernard, it's all about today and I've got to do what's right for the football club. Craig Forrest has done a great job for me and I can't just kick him out,' insisted 'H'.

Redknapp was right. He needed to have genuine competition in the squad and if the man in possession of the shirt was doing the business, as 'Stopping 'em Forrest' certainly was at that time, it was only right that he keep his place. The question I was asking was whether Harry had actually promised the Frenchman an automatic first-team place, but Lama admitted: 'He made no promises but he knows I want a World Cup place. If the club don't want me I am sure there are other teams in Europe who do.'

Bernard duly got his wish when Forrest picked up a neck injury after his heroics in the FA Cup win on penalties at Blackburn, and he made the first two of his 14 appearances for the Hammers in the league and cup games against Arsenal. Ironically, it was French Gunners boss Arsene Wenger who'd insisted: 'You can't take Lama as cover. He is one of the top three keepers in the world. All along West Ham have had gold in their hands.'

With goalkeepers flying about all over the place, I thought it appropriate to agree to Allen McKnight being interviewed for a Vintage Claret piece in *HNM*. Less of a gold nugget and more of a rusty bit of scrap iron while representing the Hammers between 1988–90, McKnightmare (as he was dubbed) put in some truly calamitous performances. Many were aghast that he'd been allowed to enter our hallowed pages. I argued that we could occasionally include the odd villain among the heroes for the sake of an interesting feature and the Irishman certainly didn't disappoint. 'Not to put too fine a point on it, I was taking the rap for other people's blunders and that was very unfair,' declared Allen who was, incredibly, still only 33 but now consigned to running a timber business in Hainault. 'To blame me for everything that went wrong was ludicrous. Yet I was the one they picked on,' added the keeper, whose last league appearance came in that 5–1 defeat at Anfield in 1989 that resulted in relegation. He signed off his West Ham career by conceding five against Luton in the Zenith Data Systems Cup and a ridiculous *eleven* against Crystal Palace reserves. To be fair to McKnight, he was playing in a poor Hammers side in the late '80s but that could hardly excuse some personal performances that could only be described as erratic.

Another player whose status among Hammers fans was rapidly reaching clown-like levels was that man Iain Dowie. The hapless striker hadn't scored a goal in 40 league appearances since the 4–2 win against

Manchester City in March 1996 – quite an astonishing record – and he was eventually offloaded to Queens Park Rangers (along with Northern Ireland left wing-back Keith Rowland and a suitcase containing £1.6 million) in exchange for winger Trevor Sinclair. What a deal!

'I didn't score as many goals as I would have liked to have done, but I like to think I earned the respect of the fans through my efforts for the club I love,' said Iain in *HNM* upon his departure, while Harry was later to declare:

'Give me Dowie over Raducioiu any time.' Just as it had been when we'd waved misfit Sandy Clark *bon voyage* back in 1983, though it had been a relief for some to see him go. Sinclair instantly made his mark with a brace on his début against Everton and has become something of a utility man although he continues to insist his favoured position is up front. Every time I've seen him down at Chadwell Heath he's got a smile on his face and he was even laughing when Harry cracked jokes about the size of his arse at the Hammers Forum a year later.

Chapter Twenty-Four

SPLAT!!! I knew it had been a bad idea to wear that suit. Walking down the path that separated the two groups of cages housing Dicksy's dogs – of which there seemed to be dozens given the amount of noise – I'd been speckled from head to foot with mud as the howling hounds had hurled themselves in my direction. But then, I should have known better than to go lurking down the bottom of Julian's back garden, shouldn't I?

Still recovering from major surgery on his left knee, Dicksy had invited me round in February 1998 to remind *HNM* readers that he still existed, despite another year out of the game. He was upbeat and in good spirits as we chatted indoors before venturing outside to have some photographs taken. His daughters Kattie and Jessica had a new toy in the form of a bastketball net and somehow I found myself being roped in to do my Michael Jordan impersonations. I knew I shouldn't have worn that suit.

Julian was as candid as I've ever known. 'I'm not in love with the game of football any more – that died years ago,' he said quietly. 'It's just a job for me now. After all the shit I've taken over the years, from managers, directors and the press, there comes a time when you think, "There are more important things in life."'

I could understand frustration getting the better of him as he sought to climb Everest for the second time in a bid to return to action, but I still considered it a startling admission from somebody who'd always personified the essence of passion for the game. And yet his determination remained undiminished, purely for the sake of proving people wrong. 'What I'd really like to do is just play one game, with no injury problems or anything, and then just say bollocks to everybody and retire. Then I'll have made my point,' he added, revealing a slight bitterness. 'I could have claimed a million pounds on my insurance policy but I don't want people telling me when I've got to retire.' As his wife Kay once told me, Julian just wouldn't be told.

Later that week I attended 'An Audience with Harry Redknapp' at Jongleurs Comedy Club in Bow Wharf. With ale being quaffed faster than during a half-time session at Upton Park, the first four-letter word was aired on stage within five seconds and the recurrent topic of discussion (both on stage and off) was the size of pop star (and Jamie Redknapp's other half) Louise's tits. After playing to the crowd at so many press conferences, Harry was playing the comic in a public environment and getting paid for it to boot. 'Raducioiu? I find it strange how some of you liked him. He got a smack in the gob at Torquay and he f***ing deserved it!' Adopting an East European accent – well, as close as an East Ender can get – he pretended to be Slaven Bilic: 'I love West Ham . . . but I love money even more!' So, Harry, how long have you been an Iron? 'Ever since I met Justin Fashanu!' he said, with all the diplomacy of Saddam Hussein. Can somebody have a photo of him for their mum? 'Why, does she need to stop the cat from pissing up the wall?' And so it went on. All sense of political correctness was tossed out of the window as references were made to Samassi Abou 'eating people' and, for the hundredth time, the size of Louise's tits. With former Chelsea and Leicester star Alan Birchenall acting as compère to keep the momentum going, it was a highly enjoyable evening, even though I lost out to fellow *HNM* scribe Steve Blowers when the champagne was dished out for winning a competition to name Harry's all-time Hammers (simply because he was sitting closer to the stage!).

Redknapp was in slightly less outspoken mood when we got together in the summer to reflect on the 1997–98 season as a whole. 'If you'd told me at the start of the year that we'd finish in the top eight I'd have snapped yer 'and off! The new signings all came off and it's the best football people have seen at Upton Park for many a year,' he told me. I quizzed him on where he intended to play French international Marc Keller, newly signed under the Bosman ruling. 'He can play in three or four positions,' he said. 'I want competition for places and it's very rare when you can play everybody you want and say that's your best team. You've always got injuries and suspensions.'

I asked the question because I wondered whether 'H' had a specific idea in mind as to how Keller was going to be accommodated or if the player was simply a free transfer worth a gamble. I accepted the manager's point, though, because there's never any such thing as a fully fit squad at Upton Park – despite the presence of John Green, one of the best physios in the country.

I also had to ask what was happening with David Unsworth. The defender had enjoyed a good first season at the club but stories about his wife being unhappy in the south had continued to circulate as the year unfolded. 'I dunno, it seems as if it's the women who wear the trousers nowadays,' complained 'H' off the record. 'Dave loves the club and is happy here but his wife has said she can't settle in London and his family are obviously very important to him. We'll just have to see but I'm not optimistic. I can't understand it myself. You've to accept these things when you're married to a professional footballer. The money is good and you have to go where you're wanted.'

Within a few months Aston Villa manager John Gregory was echoing the very same sentiments, only in more explicit terms. Myself and *Clubcall* man Chris Raistrick had been the first to learn of Unsworth's £3 million sale to Villa when Harry revealed to Chris during the club's pre-season trip to Scotland that the player had not travelled because he was negotiating terms. Given that David had been an Everton player for 10 years and his wife came from a closeknit family up on Merseyside, I even gave our first interview with him the title of 'A TRUE BLUE', with the words 'claret and' scribbled in as an obvious afterthought. It was slightly tongue-in-cheek on my part, although we always feared a repeat of the Mike Marsh situation a few years earlier. And so we assumed that with the Goodison Park outfit in the running to re-sign him, David's return home would be a formality. The news of the Villa deal was a little surprising then, but that was nothing compared to the bombshell of hearing that Unsworth had officially requested a transfer within a week of his move to the Midlands – something he'd not done in nearly a year at Upton Park.

Gregory was disgusted by having his season's plans upset by the player's actions and made all sorts of jokes about David thinking Birmingham was on Merseyside and his wife calling him back for dinner at 1 p.m. each day. You had to respect Unsworth's decision to place the welfare of his family ahead of his personal and professional credibility – the media, in particular, ridiculing him mercilessly throughout the extraordinary episode – but what I couldn't understand was why David's domestic situation hadn't been the first item on the agenda when discussing the move in the first place. 'Given that he's had the best part of a year to think his next move over, it defies belief that he can make such a misjudgement,' I wrote in my monthly column. 'David is presently living in Limboland (not a district of Merseyside the last time I looked), with his next move hanging in the balance.'

Unsworth eventually secured a return to Everton and the relief on West Ham's part was that their sale of the player had been rather less embarrassing. Not that such a claim could be made regarding one of David's replacements on the left side of defence, Javier Margas. The 55-times capped Chilean international was paraded in front of the media at Upton Park on 30 July – alongside new fellow centre-half Neil Ruddock – and one of the obvious questions to put to Peter Storrie was how confident the club were of their very first South American import settling into an East End or Essex environment. With the Unsworth saga still ongoing at the time, Storrie had the perfect reply: 'If somebody can't move 250 miles without having problems, I can't say, "Yes, he's going to settle immediately." But I don't think there will be any problems – Javier is a very intelligent man and he hasn't made this decision lightly. He's taken his time to think about it and we're very confident it's going to work out.' I agreed with Peter's thinking – there are no guarantees when signing *anybody* nowadays (West Ham had already learnt that in 1994 thanks to Joey Beauchamp, who felt homesick after leaving Oxford!) – and, at the end of the day, £2 million wasn't a lot of money to spend on a player who'd just enjoyed a successful World Cup tournament.

The British game was becoming increasingly cosmopolitan and if West Ham were going to be successful they had to play by the same rules as everybody else, recruiting talent from around the globe in order to gain better value for money in the transfer market. The downside from a journalist's point of view was that I was all the more frequently having a foreigner with limited English placed in front of me. I'd got a limited number of words out of Paulo Futre two years earlier and now had to write an introductory piece on Margas. Thankfully, I could take advantage of the presence of Ronen Katzav, Javier's representative, who was able to conduct the translation for both parties. 'He can't speak English properly yet but when he does it will be like having another coach on the field,' he said, as we stepped out on to the Upton Park turf. 'His experience will be a tremendous help to the younger players, especially Rio Ferdinand alongside him.'

Ronen introduced me to Javier and he shook my hand with all the firmness of an army general. 'At every club I have played for I have been the leader at the back,' he said, offering a warm and sincere smile. 'I like to act like a second coach and assume control of what's happening on the field. I am sure I can do that once I have mastered the English language.'

Agent Katzav confirmed: 'It was a big surprise but after just one day here he has started to tell me in Spanish what he understands in English, so he's already learning.' This might have been more impressive had he said Margas had told him in English, but I accepted the point he was trying to make. I was also aware of the South American personnel among the media throng and spoke to Claudio Bustios of TVN Chile. 'West Ham will now have another 50 million supporters,' he said. 'Javier is one of Chile's most important players, so it's crucial that he is successful in England. He is the perfect kind of player to adapt to English football. He's very strong and good in the air and we know those qualities are important in the Premiership. He has a very strong mentality so he will be able to adjust to his new life.'

As we know, of course, things couldn't have gone less to West Ham's pleasing: the signing from Deportivo Universidad Católica endured a nightmarish aerial bombardment in an early game against Wimbledon and looked out of sorts in a heavy defeat at Leeds before succumbing to a bad knee injury and subsequently returning home for treatment and home comforts. He played just three times for West Ham in the 1998–99 season before his self-imposed exile, although he did eventually return in the summer of 1999 to resolve his future. As Peter Storrie had said, 'There are no guarantees . . .'

In my attempts to get a comprehensive story on Margas during that press conference it was easy to forget about the other new arrival, Neil Ruddock from Liverpool. The former Southampton, Tottenham and England 'B' defender was well out of favour at Anfield: he had experienced injury problems and was said to have 'ballooned in size' according to some papers as the deal to bring him to Upton Park was being negotiated. Surprisingly, Neil looked as fit as a fiddle and had slimmed down to such an alarming degree that he was practically invisible as I tried to find him to arrange an interview. Actually, the real reason the 30-year-old was proving so hard to find was that one of the fanzine people had commandeered him and taken him into the Centenary Stand seats for their own private little chat.

Meanwhile, *Clubcall*, Sky TV, myself and various other parties, photographers included, stood around like lemons waiting for Neil to finish chin-wagging. It wasn't just the hanging around that I found frustrating, it was also the fact that the club seemed quite happy to welcome all and sundry with open arms. The arrival of new players provided a huge selling point for the official club magazine and our appeal was obviously being eroded if anybody with a biro in their back pocket could walk in and spend 20 minutes chatting to a new recruit. I felt entitled to write to Peter Storrie to air my views. 'The fanzines exist in direct competition to *Hammers News Magazine* and pay the club no monies whatsoever, yet the doors are seemingly thrown open to them at every opportunity, completely undermining what we are trying to achieve with the official club title,' I wrote. 'I can understand the reasons behind trying to keep the fanzines on the club's side but it needs to be recognised that the current policy is damaging the sales potential of *HNM*. If these people are to be given as much access to players and management as us it leaves me wondering what benefits the official club magazine actually has over its rivals. My experience of travelling around the country for games also suggests to me that very few clubs would show as much hospitality towards those who are making money not just on the back of the club but at the very expense of it. Please understand that my only concern is the continuing success of *HNM*. To exploit our full potential we need to have a certain amount of exclusivity and this cannot happen if unofficial competition is going to be so willingly accommodated by the club.'

I wasn't attacking the fanzines or complaining about their presence at post-match press conferences. Most clubs wouldn't even allow them that but at Upton Park they were even being invited in to meet big money signings. Why? Was the club not interested in their own publication selling as many as possible? Did they not realise the impact of having fanzines on sale outside the ground with their 'exclusive interviews'? Or had they simply not even thought about it? In the past that was possibly the case but with a press officer recently appointed they had no excuse for not giving the matter some thought. Sadly, Peter Storrie was making all the decisions . . .

'I note your comments but I hope you will appreciate it is entirely and utterly the club's decision who they invite into a press conference and as our policy at West Ham has always been to open the doors to all supporters, I cannot say that I agree with your views,' he replied. 'We have unofficial competition, whether we like it or not, directly on our doorstep every game for match programmes. It is a part of life that we just have to put up with. What we have to do is ensure that our official magazine and programme are that much more thought-provoking than these others.'

Of course, the programme was also suffering, which made his response even more difficult to comprehend. I thought his point of view rather naïve. Yes, competition did exist and there's nothing anybody could do about that, but that didn't mean the club had to bend over backwards to help it. Peter's failure to address that point disappointed me greatly. And how could he say it had been his policy to open the door to 'all supporters'? Did that mean that anybody with a West Ham tattoo on their arm could simply turn up for a press conference and talk to somebody like Ian Wright? I suspect not, somehow.

Chapter Twenty-Five

The press conference to announce the signings of Javier Margas and Neil Ruddock wasn't the first of the summer of 1998, of course. That took place on 6 July when the club confirmed the arrival of goalkeeper Shaka Hislop from Newcastle under the Bosman ruling, as much anticipated, plus (at long last) a new sponsorship deal with Dr Martens. The Northampton-based boot manufacturers had agreed a three-year arrangement with the Hammers and their representative at the press conference insisted: 'Maybe there were some preconceptions of an association with Dr Martens for the wrong reasons in the past but we're living in the '90s now and those old stereotypes don't apply.' With Shaka waving around one of the company's products for the photo-session, *HNM* had a ready-made coverline in 'SHAK YOUR BOOTY!'

The most sensational summer recruit came in the shape of the inimitable Ian Wright from Arsenal. A couple of speculative stories had already appeared when I found myself talking to Harry Redknapp and I mentioned the striker's name in passing. 'Yeah, I'd like to think something could happen. He could be our greatest ever signing,' he said, more or less confirming the deal was going through. I knew how to interpret Redknapp's responses and when he answered in such an affirmative way, I knew it was practically done and dusted. That's because managers don't usually like openly discussing their interest in players contracted to other clubs.

Within a few days Wrighty was being paraded in front of the media, having been signed for a fee that was officially undisclosed. Keeping transfer sums confidential is a growing trend and it's anybody's guess as to why that should be. Sometimes it's simply for the sake of convenience, the figures very much dependent on player performance and appearances, while payments are usually staggered over a period of time anyway. Fans generally assume that a £2 million transfer fee is paid in full at the time of the player moving but that's very rarely the case. As agent Rachel Anderson once told me, 'A lot of the figures just exist on paper, because money is coming in and going out at the same time.' The total investment on the part of the club is also difficult to gauge because players' wages, signing-on fees and bonuses have to be taken into account as well. Some clubs might prefer their fans not to be aware how much they've paid or received for a player, while in some respects, as much is going to the player as to the selling club.

Undoubtedly, Wright had been rewarded by Arsenal for his tremendous service, having scored an incredible 185 goals in 288 games since joining them from Crystal Palace for £2.5 million in 1991. Not only were the Gunners prepared to let him secure first-team football elsewhere – something they were not prepared to guarantee themselves – but they allowed him to go for what was considered a nominal sum. This was believed to be around £500,000, although the figure varied. Peter Storrie had declared: 'Print whatever figure you like.' This allowed Ian to continue earning a high salary for the remaining two years of his career.

I first met Wrighty on the club's pre-season visit to Scotland. As I'd done with John Hartson, I'd faxed a note through to the training ground to give him advance warning of my intention to grab some interview time for the following issue of the magazine. As it turned out, however, we arranged our chat in surprising circumstances. Chris Raistrick and myself – along with a string of other lost journos – had spent a good 15 minutes circling Hibernian's Easter Road ground in a vain attempt to gain entry, having been sent from pillar to post by various security staff. 'Getting into your wallet's easier than this,' I said to Raistrick as I stopped to take a snap of him looking glum against a 'no alcohol' sign. Wondering how we were going to last the next 90 minutes, we were eventually led into the ground and thrust through a series of doors, the last of which took us into the players' lounge. We only wanted the press room but, taking advantage of having penetrated this inner sanctum, I went and introduced myself to Wrighty who was sitting in the corner next to Steve Lomas. He hadn't seen my fax ('my wife deals with all that stuff,' he said) but he had no problem talking to me. We duly arranged to meet at the team's hotel the following evening.

Ian spent the Hibs game watching from the sidelines because Harry did not want to risk the 34-year-old after he'd spent the summer recovering from injury. It was all a bit of a farce anyway. After midfielder Scott Mean had given the Hammers a first-half lead, referee Martin Clark decided to level things up by awarding the home side a 75th-minute penalty, supposedly for handball by John Moncur. 'I asked the ref what he gave it for, seeing as the linesman nearby hadn't flagged,' said Harry Redknapp, 'and he told me he hadn't seen anything but because the crowd called for a penalty he assumed he'd missed something and gave it! He seemed like such a nice bloke and admitted he'd probably made a mistake, so I didn't have the heart to have a go at him.' And we thought English referees were bad.

Wrighty finally appeared in the foyer of the team's hotel at around 6 p.m. the next day, after we'd spent an hour or so in the bar with club photographer Steve Bacon, Hammers kit-man Eddie Gillam (both lovely guys) and former West Ham defender Ray Stewart, currently manager of Livingston. He'd come to return somebody's golf clubs and was the life and soul of the party (what a shame his accent was so strong I could hardly understand a word he was saying!). Raistrick had also spent a few minutes in the car park outside talking French to Samassi Abou as I listened in and tried not to laugh as the striker picked bits of fluff off his friend's jacket while chewing away on a piece of gum like a horse munching on lumps of sugar. It reminded me of the alleged comment from one senior figure at the club that Abou 'looked as if he'd been dragged off a beach.'

I shook Ian's hand and was immediately disappointed by his loose greeting. The media have never been his favourite men to share a planet with ('they're parasites,' he once told me) and I, presumably, was no exception. I made polite conversation as we looked for somewhere quiet to position ourselves, mentioning that I'd previously interviewed him for another magazine but that the piece had been heavily cut by former boss Bruce Rioch (who didn't appreciate the striker's comments on the media, with whom he was trying to build a relationship). 'Yeah, didn't get him very far, did it?' he mumbled, as we sat ourselves down.

I love Wrighty, though. He shoots from the lip. He means what he says. He doesn't suffer fools and defends his corner. That deserves respect. 'I'm gonna go and live in America when I retire,' he announced, when I'd won his confidence. 'I'm not gonna stay here. As much as I love playing football and will miss that, I won't miss the unsavoury side of the game – such as the press and the negativity they generate. I can't take it.'

I asked if he'd always had a bad view of the press or whether it was something that had evolved through his years in football. 'That's it, basically. They've been very unfair. When I'm right they slaughter me. When I'm wrong they slaughter me even more. They're just trying to assassinate my character because I'm an easy target. Certain papers more than others.'

I reminded Ian that he still talked to the press – indeed, he'd just agreed a new deal with *The Sun* for a weekly column – but he insisted: 'No, I generally don't speak to them. Some of them come up and say, "How ya doin'?" They know I don't like them but they're just trying to soft-soap me. The press owe it to the people who love football to write about it properly. It's a beautiful game and these writers are making livings out of it by not documenting it right. It's sad because they're not being true to themselves, the sport or people like me. We deserve better.'

I found the conversation fascinating and was delighted to see Ian talk so openly. I was surprised to hear him talk of leaving these shores for the States (the very first time he'd ever unveiled such thoughts) and was pleased that he brought up the subject of the media himself. It would have been easy to wind him up like a clockwork mouse and send him clacking away about the press just by setting the bait – as if dropping a piece of cheese – but on this occasion it wasn't necessary.

Ian speaks passionately about such matters and I think it's good to see players display such a commodity, although his habit of speaking out has often landed him in hot water in the past. While respecting his moves to tackle his problems via counselling, I'd always been highly sceptical because Wrighty was surely far too long in the tooth to suddenly start changing now. 'Some people called it "anger counselling" but it was personal stuff, stuff that goes back to my childhood,' he confided. 'It needed to be talked about, but it was nothing to do with football. If I took away certain parts of my anger, it would take something away from my game. I don't wanna be nasty to referees, I just want them to do their job right,' he added. 'If they get it wrong I let them know about it and I don't think that's out of order. It means a lot to me to win and you've got to hate losing if you're in a professional sport. If people don't like me getting angry, that doesn't bother me. I get booed at every ground I play at but that means that people are afraid of me. That's good.'

Wrighty was particularly conscious of how West Ham supporters had perceived him while he wore the Arsenal shirt (hardly helping matters with three goals on his last three visits to Upton Park). 'I wondered what the reaction from the fans would be, but Harry told me they'd be brilliant if I joined the club,' he said. 'But for all the stick I got from them in the past, it wasn't any worse than I got anywhere else. I've never had any racial abuse at Upton Park. But it used to give me a buzz, because the crowd were so close and hostile. Now I want that kind of support in a positive kind of way.'

Personally, I felt that Ian had overstated the animosity of the East London fans. Yes, he used to give it the big one after scoring against the Hammers – with a display of enthusiasm and effervescence – but we all knew we'd much prefer to have him playing *for* us rather than *against* us, should the opportunity ever arise. Well, in most cases, anyway . . .

'No, mate, I'm not 'appy about it,' declared Rick of Plaistow when I tried to establish the response of the fans to Wrighty's signing in the hour before the Motherwell game the following day (and after Raistrick and I had enjoyed the full delights of what Edinburgh had to offer, ahem!). 'He's over the hill. I thought we'd have got somebody better than Ian Wright. It's a backwards move.' Generally, though, people seemed quite happy with the deal, despite having reservations about Wright's fitness for the entire season. I bumped into Brian Johnston of the North of Scotland Supporters Club – based in Pitmedden (north of Aberdeen!) – and asked him how he came to follow the Hammers. 'With the state of Scottish football nowadays you're better off travelling miles down south to watch some decent football,' he admitted. Needless to say, West Ham failed to beat Motherwell (drawing 1–1), but at least Wrighty made his début, when he came on as a 69th-minute substitute.

Just three days later, Wright was bouncing around like a salmon starved of water in celebration of his two goals at Bristol Rovers in the Billy Clark testimonial. Ignoring the fact that the result was meaningless, Ian's dazzling grin could be seen back in London as he repeatedly threw his arms up into the air in delight at having opened his Hammers account. I considered it a brilliant parody of the sort of things we'd had to witness when victims in the past and even the Rovers fans found it amusing, no doubt grateful to see a true star on their patch of (borrowed) turf.

The other pre-season friendly that mustn't escape a mention (and I can hear Raistrick groaning already) is the game at Bournemouth on 3 August. Stuck in something that resembled a telephone box with birdshit all over the windows, with the skies darkening by the second, it was virtually impossible for the pair of us to tell if a football match was taking place outside at all, let alone who was playing. Well, that's my excuse anyway, having advised Chris that the guy in midfield with the black hair was new signing Marc Keller. 'It's Keller on the ball . . .' 'Keller's gone down to win the Hammers a penalty . . .' 'And Keller has been asked by the referee to leave the field of play after committing one foul too many . . .' he informed the outside world via the *Clubcall* line during various points of the game. Of course, afterwards he was duly obliged to interview the French international when he mentioned the late incident which saw the player being replaced. 'I'm sorry, I do not understand,' replied the confused Keller. Speaking ever so s..l..o..w..l..y, taking into account that the player's English might not be so hot, Chris repeated himself. Still looking mystified, Marc responded: 'Er . . . when I left the pitch? But . . . I wasn't playing! I hurt my leg in the warm-up and Harry thought it best I didn't play.' That was nothing compared to the face Chris pulled as his eyes disappeared into the top of his head and teeth bared themselves. 'Are you blind or what?' laughed Frank Lampard, as he walked past down the corridor.

'I'll have you know this is the low-point of my journalistic career,' spat Raistrick as we left the ground while I made my excuses. Days later, of course, Mean was seen at Orient with half a packet of peroxide on his head. The things some players will do to get themselves recognised!

Chapter Twenty-Six

'I've got some news for you – he's playing tonight!' Rachel Anderson could not have been happier as she revealed that, after nearly 18 months on the sidelines, Julian Dicks was to make his first-team return in the Worthington Cup second-round second-leg match against Northampton Town at Upton Park.

Despite Dicksy making steady progress in a number of friendly and reserve outings, it was still a shock since Harry Redknapp had been quick to insist the player needed more regular involvement in first-team training to be considered ready for action. Yet there we were, on 22 September, with the Terminator set to make a remarkable comeback. The know-it-alls had said it wasn't possible, that Julian's left knee was knackered and that we'd never see him pull on a West Ham shirt for a competitive match again. But the stubborn bastard had other ideas and at 7.45 p.m. that evening, Upton Park gave him a standing ovation that has surely never been more thoroughly deserved. And never has a player shown such courage and commitment in a game, with Dicks giving absolutely everything in a bid to help the team overcome the 2–0 first-leg deficit. As it turned out, Frank Lampard's last-minute strike ultimately counted for little as the Hammers suffered an embarrassing knock-out by the Second-Division strugglers, but for many the night had at least been illuminated by the presence of a genuine star.

'That was one of the greatest performances I've ever seen from a footballer,' declared Redknapp afterwards. 'To go out and perform like that, after everything that's been done to his knee, was miraculous. What we saw out there shows why he is one of the greatest players West Ham have ever had.'

Indeed, based on our impromptu assessment of the greatest ever Hammers teams from the many 'Hammers For Life' columns to be published in *HNM* over the years, we confirmed in our special 50th issue that Dicksy was in fact the club's third most favoured son of all-time, making it on to the rostrum behind Trevor Brooking MBE and Bobby Moore OBE (the latter losing out by one point due to some readers disregarding players not seen in the flesh). By the time I got to speak to Julian he'd achieved another ambition by playing again in the Premiership, in the 1–0 win against Southampton. 'My first game back was the best in terms of performance, but playing against Southampton in the Premiership was the one that mattered,' he told me. 'It was great to prove everybody wrong. Some people wanted me to fall flat on my face but I've made them all look like idiots,' he said, bursting with pride. Julian had even skippered the side against Northampton after Ian Wright had passed over the captain's armband saying, 'You're the captain of the club, this is yours.'

'I just went out to enjoy myself,' he reflected, after confirming his return with an obligatory booking – much to the crowd's delight. 'For all I knew it could have been my last match but my game has always been to get stuck in and if the knee's gonna go, it's gonna go. It might go in a match, in training or even just walking down the street.' Dicksy reserved special praise for Hammers physio John Green. 'He's been superb. I don't think I'd even have made it back the first time had it not been for John. He was with me all the way then and he's been the same this time around.'

I myself had reason to feel grateful to John, who'd been happy to co-operate for the writing of the *Terminator* biography back in 1996 and had given me lots of valuable information as to the nature of Julian's first serious knee injury. Even he must have had grave doubts as to the player's ability to achieve the near-impossible twice but he continued to provide Dicks with total support, despite being called 'everything under the sun' by his patient during the painful recovery process.

Julian was honest enough to concede that things would never quite be the same again. 'I think I'll only ever be 80 per cent fit,' he declared. 'I'll never be 100 per cent fit like I was a few years ago. But as long as I can keep the weight off and play 90 minutes the way I want to, that'll be enough for me. I can only train once or twice a week now and that's the way it will probably be until my contract expires in 18 months time.' He also revealed that he was fully aware of the way the limited bend in his knee was affecting his running. 'Sometimes I can be running and realise the knee doesn't feel the same but I didn't really think about it in my first game back. But I watched about five minutes of the Southampton game on TV when I got home that night and could see that I was running differently. But if that's the only problem then I'm not really worried.'

Other people were, though. With Javier Margas out with cartilage problems and Neil Ruddock suffering from an Achilles injury, Dicksy also played in the 3–0 defeat at Blackburn and the goalless draw at home to league leaders Aston Villa. Despite experiencing swelling in the knee in the days immediately after games, he generally seemed OK – but as days at the office go, 24 October must go down as one of Julian's worst. Played out of position in a left wing-back capacity as part of a 3-5-2 formation at Charlton Athletic, the poor bloke was literally crucified by raiding Addicks John Robinson and Danny Mills as the Hammers crashed to a 4–2 defeat. The press slaughtered him but Dicksy was defiant as he spoke to me during the aftermath. 'I wouldn't say I was too disappointed by my performance because I was playing at left wing-back and I can't play in that position,' he told me. 'I never played there *before* my injury so I'm not going to be any better there now, am I? I'm a left-back or left-sided centre-half and walked away with man-of-the-match performances against Northampton and Southampton when playing in defence.'

I felt a genuine sympathy for Julian. He really *shouldn't* have been so harshly judged when asked to play in an unfamiliar role. Dicksy subsequently knocked on Harry's door to discuss his future deployment, and it was agreed that he'd never be asked to play as a wing-back again. He'd either start in defence or have no involvement at all, as it was also impossible for Julian to come off the bench during games as he needed to warm up with a bath!

The following week the Hammers were up in Newcastle and, thanks in part to Stuart Pearce, who reduced the Magpies to 10 men with a wayward elbow when challenging Trevor Sinclair early on, the Londoners romped to a spectacular 3–0 win. Ian Wright scored twice, bringing his tally to six in his first 13 games, while Sinclair also grabbed a goal to help lift the team six places up the table to eighth. Dicksy, meanwhile, was nowhere to be seen.

'He can't f***ing run!' said Harry when I asked him why Julian had not played as he walked down the touchline towards the St James's Park exit an hour after the game. He'd already told me they'd mutually agreed that Julian would not be exposed in a left wing-back position, but his response came when I pointed out that the team had played in a 4-4-2 formation without wing-backs. Knowing my keen interest in the player, Redknapp led me on to the playing turf to reveal his thoughts in a slightly more discreet place. 'He can't run any more and I had a problem down the left-hand side because [the returned] Ruddock isn't the quickest and I knew that Newcastle would attack with pace through Nolberto Solano and possibly Keith Gillespie. I needed Andy Impey's pace out there to cope with the situation.'

Indeed, Impey – a right-footed player more familiar with playing on the other wing – had been asked to fill in at left-back. This was the ultimate insult as far as Julian and his agent Rachel were concerned. I spoke to Rachel on the Sunday evening after returning from Newcastle and she confirmed that Dicks had not travelled north-east because of the agreement with Harry. 'Er, I've got to tell you this but West Ham didn't play with wing-backs. They played 4-4-2,' I revealed nervously. 'Well, who played at left-back?' she demanded. To say she wasn't happy when I told her a right-winger had been asked to fill the slot is an understatement.

There also appeared to be a misunderstanding as to what had been discussed regarding Julian's future. When I asked Harry about the situation at St James's Park, he'd told me: 'Julian told me he didn't want to sit on the bench and his words to me were, "If I'm not going to play regularly, I may as well pack it in." I told him not to be silly and to stay as part of the squad for the remainder of his contract. But I can't guarantee that he's going to be playing regularly.'

I found myself in a difficult position. If I told Rachel that Harry had actually taken me to one side and said what he had, she'd then be on the phone to the manager asking him what was going on. 'Kirk tells me that you say *blah blah blah* . . .' By the same token, I needed to find out if there was any truth in the theory that Julian had threatened to quit. I therefore said something vague like, 'Somebody said something about Julian maybe retiring,' and she responded by denying any knowledge of Dicks discussing such a possibility with anyone. When I spoke to the player himself, he insisted: 'I didn't put in all that hard work after my knee operation just to call it quits because of not being picked for one game.' However, he wasn't happy at Impey being awarded the place he considered his own. 'I'm the only left-back at the club. I mean no disrespect to Andy but he's a winger. He can't play left-back! But I guess that tells me something, doesn't it?'

Not for the first time, however, Julian's words had a contradictory element. One the one hand he was adamant that he wasn't considering retirement, but on the other he declared: 'If I'm never going to get a game there's no point me being here. I told Harry I'm not the type of person to just sit there and play in the reserves.' Yet he also insisted: 'All I want to do is finish my career at West Ham. And if it's in the reserves it's in the reserves. I'll bide my time for 18 months if I have to. I want to play for the first-team but, to be honest, unless Harry's down to the bare minimum in terms of players, I don't think he'll pick me.'

Dicks had already been aware of that situation, even when picked for the first time against Northampton. 'Frank Lampard called me into his office that morning and asked if I wanted to play that night. I told him the only reason he wanted me to play was that he didn't have a full side and he said I didn't have to play if I didn't want to,' Julian told me as we discussed the situation in a pub just around the corner from the Hammers' HQ after a training session.

It had been quite funny walking into a boozer with Julian at my side. Heads turned, chins dropped and glasses hit the table as we made our way to the bar. Dicksy wasn't drinking alcohol, of course, but he was gasping for refreshment all the same. 'F***ing hell, what are they *doing*?' he whined as the bar staff slowly attended to a bunch of middle-aged ladies ordering their lunch.

'I bet you David Beckham doesn't have to wait like this,' I quipped, waving my tenner around in an effort to cool Julian's rising temper down as much as attracting attention from behind the bar. Which reminds me . . .

Chapter Twenty-Seven

The name of David Beckham had hardly been out of the news following his sending-off against Argentina in the second round of the World Cup finals during the summer. My personal view was that he deserved his sending-off for taking a retaliatory kick at Diego Simone, but that's another story. Still, you can just imagine the fuss people would have made had Julian Dicks been guilty of such an indiscretion and contributed to the country's elimination, can't you?

Not that Julian would have got within a mile of the squad after having publicly declared once again, prior to his injury, that he had no intention of playing for England – he had been told by assistant boss John Gorman that he would need to cut his hair. One closely cropped Hammer who did make it out to France '98, of course, was Rio Ferdinand. Harry Redknapp was disappointed not to see his young defender make an appearance but was delighted that he'd at least had an opportunity to share the experience of a World Cup finals and add to his education. It was a former West Ham centre-half who'd attracted headlines, however, by the time I asked 'H' for his verdict on the tournament. 'We all saw what Bilic did in the Croatia–France game and for me that was a sad sight,' he said, referring to the incident in which Slaven feigned injury and got Laurent Blanc sent off. 'It was yet another case of a man falling down as if hit by a sledgehammer.'

Redknapp was rather more sympathetic towards Beckham, who'd been vilified by many following his own red card. 'I thought he was unlucky to get sent off. I couldn't believe it really,' he told me. I can't say I agreed with Harry and was tempted to say as much in my column when it started to become apparent that a rather hostile reception would await the young midfielder when Manchester United rolled into town for West Ham's opening home game of the season. Suddenly there was an effigy of Beckham hanging from a noose pictured in the press, while the *Star* just happened to be passing the gates of Upton Park when an offensive banner had been hung up. Before we knew it, Hammers fans were being described as the nastiest in the country and Upton Park was being likened to a Roman arena; references, too, were made of David being tossed in to face Goliath. Come the match itself, though, Beckham seemed to handle the predictable abuse quite well although he was in relatively subdued mood, as was United's new £12.5 million signing Dwight Yorke in attack.

By the end of the season, the 0–0 draw with the eventual treble-winners was one of the Hammers' more satisfying home results. Ian Wright had missed the game through injury – although he'd already made his mark by scoring a late winner in the opening game at Sheffield Wednesday the previous week – but he was back by the time the Hammers next played at Upton Park. The match against Wimbledon will go down in history as the first time West Ham have lost a match at home after being three goals ahead. Hartson had got his first of the season in just five minutes and when Wright scored two more within half an hour, what seemed like a rout was well under way. A floodlight failure at that stage would have angered everybody but nobody could have foreseen the amazing events of the remaining 60 minutes of football. Marcus Gayle had pulled one back fairly quickly – the first goal conceded by the Hammers that season – but the points still looked safe as half-time arrived with a 3–1 scoreline. Bizarre as it may sound, the second half had a strange kind of logic in retrospect, in which the Dons acknowledged West Ham's aerial weakness in defence and switched to all-out bombardment. Poor Javier Margas was running around looking for his tin hat as the crosses and long balls rained down from above like bullets. The team had a habit of defending deep at the best of times but, with Eyal Berkovic taken off for Andy Impey, all the initiative was surrendered and it seemed just a matter of time before the inevitable took place, especially once the jitters set in following Wimbledon's second. Gayle scored again to level things in the 77th minute and our misery was complete when Efan Ekoku nodded in the winner. As the cliché goes, it could probably only happen at West Ham. And to make matters worse, table-toppers Liverpool were next to visit just three days later.

For reasons best known to the management team of Gerard Houllier and Roy Evans themselves, the Merseysiders decided to ignore all the evidence provided by the Dons that the Hammers' defence was vulnerable in the air and opted to keep the ball down, leaving big striker Karl-Heinz Riedle on the bench. It was a huge mistake, although Houllier insisted after his side's 2–1 defeat that the game had changed once Hartson put the home side in front after just three minutes. That was more of a key factor, he claimed, rather than any misjudgement on his part. With that kind of logic, is it any wonder that Liverpool finished the season several places behind West Ham?

Chapter Twenty-Eight

If Hammers fans had been fearful of Ian Wright's habit of courting controversy – his goal celebrations against Wimbledon and Southampton seeing him display a shirt in support of Essex firefighters, and hilariously mimicking referee Paul Alcock's collapse after being pushed by Sheffield Wednesday's Paolo Di Canio (in this case with an obliging Neil Ruddock) – it all paled into insignificance alongside the headlines created by John Hartson in the autumn. Or rather his left boot, to be precise.

I'd been informed by phone that some kind of fracas involving Hartson and Eyal Berkovic had taken place in training the day before the home game against Southampton on 28 September. A friend of a friend actually witnessed the incident. I didn't think too much of it at the time because you often get flare-ups and I'd seen enough Hammers sessions to know that most players take them seriously and go into challenges in committed fashion. Hartson has always generally put his weight about, despite what he told me about not training so hard towards the end of the previous season.

Yet within a week the whole thing had become major headline news, as a direct result of Sky's cameras which were present at Chadwell Heath – as they usually are before any televised home game – and captured the amazing scenes on film. Acknowledging that the training ground is generally a private place, Sky resisted any temptation to air the footage but somehow a video tape found its way into the hands of *The Mirror*, who splashed stills all over their back pages (claiming the evidence had been supplied by a fan with a camcorder). Of course, it was later suggested that the pictures had indeed come from a Sky source although nobody stopped to question under what circumstances. Certainly, it's hard to imagine anybody not profiting from some kind of under-the-counter transaction, if that were the case.

The pictures themselves were fairly horrifying, showing Berkovic taken out by a lunge from Hartson before being dragged up off the ground by his assailant. Annoyed by the challenge, Eyal swung a punch at the Welshman's thigh which then provoked his opponent into kicking him in the face with all the venom he could muster. Poor Berkovic recoiled in pain as you imagined teeth, fillings and bits of breakfast flying through the air.

OK, Hartson might argue that the Israeli had shown the first signs of aggression, but one slap on the leg hardly merited a faceful of football boot. But John clearly isn't somebody to mess with and if you show him aggression – however slight – he's not likely to count to 10 and then offer to shake hands, as we've seen several times on the pitch. Rather than cooling the engines, he's more likely to blow and leave you chewing bits of metal (or, in Eyal's case, leather).

Hartson was adamant that his apology had been accepted after ringing Berkovic at home and, even though it had been their intention to fine the big striker for his assault, the club was apparently dissuaded once the Israeli declared the matter closed before disappearing on international duty. But, not for the first time, Eyal changed his tune when back home and the explosion of pictures in *The Mirror* coincided with Berkovic slamming Hartson for his actions and West Ham for their lack of any. 'Hartson called me but I told him it was too late. If my head had been a football it would have flown into the top corner of the net,' he was reported as saying (prompting me to think that it would more likely have gone flying over the bar given the striker's recent performances). 'I am very upset with the West Ham board because they tried to cover up what happened. They did that because Hartson enjoys privileges that others don't. A different player would have been out of the club.'

Hartson's camp – or namely his agent, Jonathan Barnett – hit back by declaring that Berkovic had been 'cowardly and despicable in the way he has acted, accepting John's apology and then going into print slaughtering him'. The key point was whether Eyal did in fact accept Hartson's apology, but John's word would appear to be supported by the club's insistence that Berkovic wanted no further action taken.

With most of the tabloids jumping on the bandwagon to attack the club for not being seen to hit Hartson hard, it was left to Peter Storrie and Harry Redknapp to defend their position. 'We were going to fine Hartson the maximum two weeks wages allowed under FA rules but we didn't because Berkovic asked the manager not to,' confirmed Storrie, no doubt feeling royally stitched up by the midfielder, while Redknapp denied that any favouritism had been shown to certain players. 'No one gets special treatment. John has been fined more than anyone else at the club in the last few couple of years.' Indeed, in the wake of all the fuss – and to try and head off increasing interest from the FA – the club did indeed impose a fine, and the money went to Harry's favoured Leukaemia Busters charity.

The likes of Harry Harris at *The Mirror* complained that West Ham were guilty of trying to cover up the incident, but what did he seriously expect them to do – circulate a press release to announce the bust-up to the entire country? He also insisted that the FA should step in and impose a lengthy ban on Hartson, without considering the precedent that would then be set. Redknapp quite rightly questioned why the game's authorities should get involved. 'What John did was totally out of order, but if the FA don't think there are punches thrown at some training ground every week of the year then they're dreaming,' he said, while Storrie insisted it was an 'internal' matter.

Neither party was happy when the FA subsequently announced that they were charging the player with misconduct, but it did raise an interesting question. I knew they'd want to be seen to be taking action, as a public relations exercise as much as anything else, but how would they react to other training-ground incidents in the future? As no action would have been taken had the pictures not being publicly aired – and Sky soon started showing the footage once stills appeared in the press – could we assume that they'd only act if there was evidence of something taking place? Would a mere photograph be enough to act upon? Or what about stories emerging through word of mouth? And what about the nature of the offence itself? A kick in the head is obviously a nasty business but what about a punch or a mild slap or push? Just where did the FA intend to draw the line? We still don't know the answer to that one, of course, but it wasn't surprising that Storrie should start talking about 'cameras being banned from every training ground in the country' if bust-ups on private land were now to be considered the FA's business rather than just the club's.

Hartson also made himself look like a plonker when he insisted he'd been guilty of nothing more than a late tackle when addressing the incident in his *Recorder* column. Of course, the very day his denial was printed, in response to the rumours that had first started to circulate, the evidence exploded all over the pages of the nationals, much to the embarrassment of his publishers. After some angry words had probably been exchanged, John diplomatically announced his intention to quit the paper. The likelihood, however, is that he told them exactly where they could stuff their regionals.

Quarrels between players – when they become public knowledge – are a nightmare for editors of club magazines because it can be difficult to know how to handle such controversies without upsetting somebody. By the time the next issue of *HNM* was going to press, Hartson had already been charged by the FA so I was able to put the emphasis on West Ham's reaction to that in our news pages, rather than merely repeating what had already been well-documented about the incident itself. Additionally, I felt obliged to address the episode in my 'Ed Mouths Off' column, and chose my words very carefully: 'John will be the first to admit he can be his own worst enemy at times and it's so disappointing to see him inflict damage to his image and reputation in the manner we've seen of late. It's now up to him to confront his personal demons, learn from his negative experiences and work hard to ensure that certain things never happen again. Like I wrote back in August, his future success is in his own hands . . .'

Harry Harris, meanwhile, was a bit too quick out of the traps in announcing Berkovic's imminent departure. 'Eyal Berkovic will be sold within a week,' he declared in an 'exclusive' on 9 October as he spoke of the player threatening to go on strike to secure a move. Obviously, Redknapp and Storrie had to work overtime to bring the pair together and show public reconciliation, but to my knowledge Berkovic never exploited the situation to request a transfer (even rejecting a move to Middlesbrough) although it's possible that certain promises were made for the following summer.

Not all the players were sympathetic towards the Israeli, however. Dicksy admitted to me that Berkovic was hardly the most popular of blokes within the camp and more than one player appeared to feel little pity. That's because John was one the lads, and it's interesting to note that the likes of Neil Ruddock were more interested in leading the Welshman away from the scene of the crime to prevent him from causing more trouble than rushing to Eyal's aid.

As for Hartson, Storrie made his feelings known when he declared that the striker needed 'to stop all this nonsense which has plagued his career of late' (the Welshman had also just been found guilty of causing criminal damage when he elected to use a hanging flower-basket as a football while on the streets of Swansea during a night out). 'He can get to the top but he won't unless he stops to take stock of where he's going,' he added.

Little did he realise it at the time, but within six weeks another dispute would erupt in public and this time it would involve Storrie himself.

Chapter Twenty-Nine

As if it's not embarrassing enough to watch your players engaging in battle, it was even more astonishing to see Harry Redknapp and Peter Storrie locked in a war of words up at Derby County on 22 November. The Hammers had arrived at Pride Park for the Sky televised game with one empty seat on their bus, and the instruction had been issued to Harry from above that Andy Impey should not be considered for selection because of an imminent £1.5 million transfer to Leicester City.

Redknapp was livid that he was being dictated to in such a way, adamant that he wanted to play the wing-back as he'd been a key part of the week's preparations. 'My only concern is trying to win three points,' he said on camera prior to the game, before having a pop at the Hammers' hierarchy. 'I am disappointed at how things have been handled but that's what happens when you get non-football people involved in the game.' It was a clear dig at Storrie, who hit back:

'An offer came in for a player who is not always in the team which we felt was very good and so it was accepted. Every manager in the country knows that if you accept a bid for a player, you can't then go and play him the day before and risk him breaking a leg.' That's not how Harry saw things, however.

'OK, if Impey's got to go, he's got to go, but I was disappointed to be told I couldn't play him. He could have spoken to Leicester the following day as far as I'm concerned.'

For the general media – and indeed Sky – it was highly amusing to see two senior figures within one club bickering between themselves over the circumstances of a player being sold. The irony, of course, was that the fans couldn't have cared less about Impey's departure. Most were just pleased to see the club make a profit (albeit just £250,000) on somebody who'd struggled to impress, although Redknapp had been delighted with the way the player had performed in a number of defensive positions which even Impey admitted he wasn't particularly suited to.

The media love to develop a theme by linking a number of stories together and, with Everton selling striker Duncan Ferguson to Newcastle for £8 million without manager Walter Smith's knowledge, the papers were suddenly talking about the game now being controlled by the men in grey suits – as opposed to tracksuits. They stuck the two situations in the same bag as if they were identical, which was wrong. Smith admitted that he only knew of Ferguson's departure when the player himself told him after the deal was done, while Redknapp's chief complaint was being told he couldn't select somebody who was still a West Ham player. It was more a case of a player being rendered unavailable without his consent rather than being sold without his knowledge. Sadly, few made the distinction.

By this stage I was comfortable in my new position of contributing to the relevant regional titles (*East London Advertiser/Barking & Dagenham Post*) owned by the Independent group (publishers of *HNM*) and this entitled me to become more involved at press conferences. In the past, when purely representing the club magazine, there was no point in me asking questions in front of the rest of the media because everybody else was in a position to use the answers before I could. Now I had a Monday deadline, however, I could ask Harry whatever I wanted although the risk of supplying material for the Sunday papers still existed. Having been commissioned to cover away games only, though, most of the other press personnel were local guys solely interested in the home side (in other words, whoever we were playing). That's not to say they didn't prick up their ears when I asked Redknapp at Derby (after the team had produced their best performance of the season – even without the services of Impey – to win 2–0, with Marc Keller scoring a brilliant goal) if the row could potentially jeopardise his position at West Ham. 'Of course I'm staying at the club,' he insisted, and this became the focal point of my story as I sought to avoid repetition of the debate over Impey's exclusion for the sake of looking ahead to the situation's likely ramifications.

I'd be asking the same question of Harry five months down the line, ironically because of Storrie's departure. But another consequence of this particular rumpus was that some members of the media were quick to make reference to a financial crisis at Upton Park. Storrie had admitted at Pride Park that 'it was agreed with the board that a player would be sold by the end of November to balance the books after investing over £3 million on five new players in the summer', but what he neglected to mention was that David Unsworth had already been offloaded for precisely that amount. Fortunately, nobody seemed to remember that important fact, but that didn't stop the likes of the *Daily Mail*'s David McDonnell speculating that more players would be 'sacrificed to ease West Ham's financial worries'.

Hartson would be the first to go, he said, with the Hammers in deficit in terms of player purchases and sales in recent times. I'd have thought a minus figure would have proved that West Ham were no longer a selling club – expenditure being considered a sign of ambition – but, no, this statistic was interpreted in the most negative fashion possible. Perhaps the funniest thing about the *Sportsmail* 'investigation' was that in attempting to provide a detailed analysis of the club's financial problems, they neglected to include figures relating to gate receipts, the millions received from Sky TV, the money earned through merchandise or the spondoolicks brought in by sponsorship. No, you wouldn't mention the club's four chief sources of revenue, would you?

'I've never read so much garbage,' complained Peter Storrie at the Hammers Forum on 26 November, no doubt irritated by a string of stories that appeared under the same writer's name. These suggested that the club had barred fans from watching training sessions, that Redknapp would be sacked as a result of the team getting knocked out of the FA Cup by Swansea City and that the Hammers boss was feeling the heat. 'Pressure on the pitch and from the bank turns genial West Ham manager into a real bag of nerves,' wrote McDonnell after 'H' told the journalist exactly what he thought when he turned up at Chadwell Heath (how did he get through those locked gates?). 'What was it that so unnerved a man who has spent his life dealing with the pressures of the professional game?' he asked. 'Could we suggest it was dealing with people like him?' I responded in *HNM*.

He was right about Hartson's imminent departure, of course, although the suggestion that any signings would purely be 'papering over the cracks' was absolute rubbish. As if all the business with Berkovic wasn't bad enough, John was still a pale (but rather large) shadow of his former self for most of the season. His goal at Derby – his third of the campaign – had been nicely taken and inspired brief hope that he was finding his feet again. After a self-imposed exile from talking to the press, Hartson agreed to co-operate with the club magazine and we, through his agent, stressed that we were looking to do a nice positive piece in which he could offer a direct apology to Hammers fans. John did just that, and claimed he was back in shape following a week in the French Riviera under the guidance of fitness guru Tiberce Darrou (after Harry thought it wise to get the player out of the spotlight). But I was starting to tire of Hartson's constant assertions that he'd lost the excess flab. The striker had told me he'd been working hard in pre-season training when we met in Scotland and now he was admitting he'd been 'undisciplined' at the beginning of the season – as a result of injury – but had now shed weight again. He seemed to be going in and out like a concertina! Hartson also blamed his poor form on the misconduct charge hanging over his head, but the matter would have been cleared up a whole lot sooner had player and agent not agreed to delay proceedings in order to seek top legal advice. That was fair enough, given it might prove to be something of a test case, but they were also aware that the adjudicators would probably be a touch more lenient once the flames of the media explosion had died down.

By the time West Ham next appeared live on Sky, at Manchester United on 10 January, a huge amount of uncertainty hung in the air. While the rest of the media were preoccupied by speculation surrounding impressive youngsters Rio Ferdinand and Frank Lampard and the fact that a number of clubs were looking at Rio and Spurs were making a £4.3 million bid for Frank, I scented major doubts about the futures of Hartson and Dicks. I'd spoken to Harry that week about John and he'd admitted: 'John's form hasn't been good and he's got to start working harder because that's the only way he's going to rediscover the form he showed last season.' At Old Trafford I asked him about the speculation linking the striker with a move to Wimbledon but he said, 'There was talk of them making an offer but I haven't spoken to anybody about it.' Interestingly, though, Redknapp failed to slap a 'not for sale' tag on the Welshman, as he'd done previously with most players linked with other clubs.

Julian, meanwhile, had been hauled out of his coffin to start the home games against Everton (2–1) and Coventry (2–0) in December, plus the FA Cup third-round tie against Swansea on 6 January, but had not been selected for the subsequent away trips. 'There's no point in me slogging my guts out and playing well if I'm going to be dropped the following week,' he complained, when I rang him to find out what was going on. 'Harry only includes me when he's struggling to put a side out. I'm getting used like a dogsbody. As far as I'm concerned you should pick the players who are doing well, but that's not happening. I should be in the team ahead of some of the others,' he said, obviously referring to Neil Ruddock. 'At the end of the day, there are always other clubs to play for.'

I could understand Dicksy's frustration, although I could never see him joining any other club. He'd always told me he'd see out his career at West Ham and if his relationship with the club finished prematurely he'd simply retire. It was another example of Julian sending out contradictory messages. One of the problems between Harry and Dicks was the player's inability to train like any other squad member. I'd ask 'H' about Julian at regular intervals and he'd respond in much the same way. 'Well, we never see him. He doesn't train and . . . is he still *with* us?' he'd occasionally joke.

'I keep reading that I don't train and that Harry never sees me but that's not true. I go in on Mondays to have treatment on the knee, although if it's swollen up I just do upper body weights. On Tuesdays I go out with the boys, Wednesdays we have off, Thursdays I do my own stuff and I go out training with the rest on Fridays,' Julian told me, trying to put the record straight. Again I found myself playing piggy in the middle when he insisted he was planning on going to see Redknapp to sort his future out. Speaking to Harry immediately after our conversation, I was able to ask him how he'd respond should Dicksy come knocking on his door (without indicating I knew it would happen). 'It would be the same as if any other player came to see me – I'd say, "Sorry, that's the team I've picked, unlucky." I'm not going to guarantee him a place every week. Some weeks he might get picked, some weeks he might not. That's just the way it is,' said Redknapp defiantly.

I'd asked about Julian's whereabouts at Old Trafford and Harry had actually told me that 'his knee was sore and he wasn't fit enough – otherwise he'd have played'. I was sceptical given that Dicks had not made a single trip away from Upton Park since the Charlton débâcle back in October but, surprisingly, he was included in the team that trundled out at Swansea's Vetch Field (and a field it was, too) just three days later. Julian had come to the Hammers' rescue in the initial tie at home – scoring the all-important equaliser with just a few minutes remaining – but could do nothing to prevent his side from suffering an ignominious cup exit in the replay, in which one goal proved enough despite West Ham's dominance. The most pleasing sight of the evening had been that of defender Richard Hall making a surprise appearance, his first since May 1997 and sadly the last of his career, but the most annoying had been Cyril the bloody swan, the Welshmen's mascot.

Birds with beerguts have never done much for me and Cyril hardly endeared himself to the Hammers support by arrogantly strutting his stuff right in front of them as Swansea bagged their winner. The bird-brained creature seemed to have established a close rapport with the local nutters – or nuggets, as Hartson would call them – and spent more time flapping his fists into the air than he did cuddling small children (which is what I thought mascots were supposed to do, rather than wind up the travelling support).

It was perhaps fitting that Hartson's final West Ham performance should be at the ground he paid to enter as a boy. He laboured away but to no real effect and you could have stuck him in a Swansea shirt without him looking out of place. Just two days later John signed for Wimbledon, completing what some would say was a meteoric descent from the marble halls of Highbury to the rented rooms of Selhurst Park. In terms of career building, you'd expect players to make the opposite journey, West Ham being a stepping stone to bigger things at Arsenal, but at least John can show his increasing value in the transfer market (£2.5 million, £3.5 million and £7.5 million) as a defence against such an argument.

By quirk of fate, Hartson found himself making a home début for the Dons against his recent team-mates and he suffered a tortuous 90 minutes, making little impression in the 0–0 draw apart from getting booked for a horrible challenge on Frank Lampard ('you don't expect your mates to do things like that,' complained Frank in his *HNM* diary, which had been running all season) and receiving a barrage of abuse from his former fans. 'Big fat John' and 'Hartson's going bald' were just two of the chants hurled his way, which did nothing to improve his mood. I'd have been tempted to laugh but my main concern was the interview I was hoping John would agree to after the game. I'd commissioned reporter Steve Blowers to have one final chat with the player for *HNM* – in keeping with our usual habit of presenting farewell pieces – but I could see our hopes diminishing with every line of 'Big fat John . . .'

'No way, not after that,' spat Hartson as Steve did his best to persuade him to co-operate in the car park after the match. 'I thought it was harsh; I deserved more than that after all I did for the club,' he added, as my man adhered to the tried and trusted trick of keeping the player talking. In the end, John's insistence as to why he didn't want to be interviewed constituted an appropriate introduction to a feature regardless. I asked Steve to write about the striker's rise and fall and he produced an excellent piece that – with a little help from the admission I'd got out of him the previous summer that he'd given up – perfectly encapsulated the trials and tribulations of his time at Upton Park. 'Only the flame-haired hitman can decide between sliding further down the slippery slope or knuckling down and channelling his energies into rediscovering the firepower that once made the warring Welsh dragon a fearsome challenge for most Premiership defenders,' he wrote, rightly reiterating a point I'd made twice myself during the previous six months. But was John paying attention to anyone?

Dons boss Joe Kinnear had a right old whinge when Hartson was subsequently banned for three matches (and fined an extra £30,000 for his assault on Berkovic), complaining that it was unfair that the south London club should suffer when the crime took place before the player moved. Sorry, Joe, but that's the risk you took. Wimbledon promised to get the player back in shape – and having paid £7.5 million they certainly needed to – and were soon boasting of their striker having lost nearly a stone, which did nothing but confirm how unfit he'd been when leaving West Ham. 'Yeah, I'd gone off the boil,' he admitted at his first press conference after moving. And his measly two goals for his new club in the remainder of the 1998–99 season hardly suggested he was back on it again.

Surprisingly, the Hammers were linked with Hartson again in the close season: Dons supremo Sam Hamman put out a press release stating that Redknapp had acknowledged his mistake in letting the striker go by showing renewed interest and that West Ham could sell all their players and still not have enough cash to persuade him to part. Were those two goals really that good, Sam?

I've no doubt that Harry made a discreet enquiry, since it was strongly suspected that Hartson would be one of the first players to struggle to accept new manager Egil Olsen's strict regime. Redknapp was entitled to have a tentative sniff, thinking he might be able to bring the Welshman back on a cut-price basis, but according to Hamman you're not allowed to consider former players. And if you believe Sam, Hartson's lost another stone (how many can one man lose in one year?). I certainly believe John *will* come good again – he's *got* to because he's running out of time. The 1999–2000 season is a crucial one for him and if he puts his mind to it he's certainly capable of rediscovering some of his old form. The likelihood, though, is that any new-found confidence will once again become complacency and we'll find ourselves back at square one. Enter Harry again, no doubt . . .

Another player on his way in the early part of 1999 was Ludek Miklosko. Having spent three months at Queens Park Rangers on loan, the Czech keeper was hopeful of moving permanently on a free transfer, but a spanner was thrown into the works when West Ham demanded a nominal transfer fee. Cash-strapped Rangers were left looking in biscuit tins for spare change in a desperate bid to raise the cash, but a solution was worked out when Ludo reluctantly agreed to sacrifice certain monies owed to him by the Hammers. 'West Ham said they would only let me go if they could keep most of the money they owed me,' he complained, after completing his move to Shepherd's Bush. 'I was told I could have a free transfer but because it wasn't written down it never happened.'

I felt for Ludo but even gentle giants should know they need to get verbal agreements ratified in writing. I asked Harry if he'd offered to let the veteran go for nothing and he said, 'If there'd have been an agreement, he'd have got his free transfer. The only thing that had been said was that if he was unhappy and wanted to go, we'd allow him to go – but not necessarily on a free transfer. Why should we give him away? Nobody gives West Ham anything! We told QPR we wanted £75,000, which he's worth any day of the week. Then they said, "Oh, we can only give you X amount." But that's *their* problem. In the end, Ludo had to take a cut on the money we owed him so that QPR could afford his wages.'

Harry was reluctant to attack the 37-year-old for his complaints in the press but, just when he thought the negative publicity had died down, one of the Sunday tabloids used some of the comments in the keeper's final *HNM* interview, took them out of context or wrote around them. It was an interview he'd agreed to rather reluctantly, too, feeling in no mood to do anybody associated with West Ham any favours. Anybody reading the story now would have assumed that Ludo had ripped into the club via their official magazine, when that simply wasn't the case. To be honest, I'd already cut a few quotes – to save our own skins as much as anybody else's – but we still allowed Ludo's feeling of discontent to permeate the opening part of the piece.

That was fair enough. After all, he wouldn't be the first to have a bit of a moan in our pages. Even Redknapp was becoming increasingly open with his frustrations, as the Impey episode at Derby proved, although it didn't seem as though he had too much to worry about. The Hammers were ensconced in the top half of the Premiership table and Harry had even picked up the Carling Manager of the Month award in November for the team's run of four wins and a draw (including a 2–1 home win over Spurs that lifted the club to second place). Five successive away defeats – including the cup defeat at Swansea – plus a farcical 4–0 hammering at home to Sheffield Wednesday just days after Hartson departed took some of the wind out of our sails, but Redknapp was already looking rather fed up with things.

I questioned him on his downbeat mood during an interview for the February issue of *HNM* and he responded: 'I tend to say things as they are and maybe I shouldn't do that. I have all the problems every day of trying to get a squad together and when I get a few injuries it's very difficult.

'Sky's Andy Gray said last week he felt we were over-achieving and I agree with him,' added 'H'. 'I've put together a squad of players who mostly weren't regulars at their previous clubs. And when you're in that end of the market, every signing is a gamble. I just get a little bit despondent at times when I can't achieve what I want to.'

It seemed to me that there might be more to Harry's miserable mood at times than met the eye, but I could understand his problems. His job was hard enough, without having his 24-goal hitman of the previous season deciding he didn't really want to play any more. I still don't think people realise how much of a hurdle the Hartson situation placed in front of Redknapp. Sure, £7.5 million was a great sum to receive for a player who'd only scored four times in five months but the upheaval should never have taken place. If John had carried on scoring, people would be talking about him being worth over £10 million and the club could have cashed in at a later date if they'd wanted to. As it was, they had no option but to sell mid-season and Harry, admittedly with cash providing the tools, found himself changing the wheels while the car continued to hurtle round the track.

Chapter Thirty

'AAAAARRRRRRGGGGGHHHHHH!' With the sound of Tarzan screaming outside there came a pounding on the roof of the car. For a split second I had images in my mind of Jaws from the James Bond movies ripping off the ceiling of our vehicle with one hand and scooping us out with the other. Well, nearly.

'We must be quick – I hungry,' said the Italian in the driver's seat as he picked up imaginary bits of pasta and stuffed them into his mouth. 'Yes, it won't take long,' I affirmed, ignoring the presence of Marc-Vivien Foe outside in the training-ground car park as he waited for his lift home.

As Paolo Di Canio started to speak, I found my attention drifting away from his words as I remembered that legendary incident at Hillsborough four months earlier when the temperamental striker – then playing for Sheffield Wednesday, of course – forced his hands through the chest of referee Paul Alcock in the game against Arsenal. With West Ham preparing for the Monday-night clash with Southampton – the weekend, ironically, in which Hartson had some shooting practice with Berkovic's head – I could recall watching Rodney Marsh's reaction in the Sky studios as he saw Di Canio send the official tumbling on his monitor. Two days later, of course, Upton Park was splitting its sides with laughter as Wrighty and Ruddock re-enacted the scenario between themselves while Di Canio was banished to the wilderness with an eventual 11-game ban.

Yet in what seemed like no time at all, I found myself squashed into Paolo's rented car to discuss his re-emergence at West Ham. 'Everybody has an opinion on what I'm like but these people do not know me,' he insisted. 'They think I have an attitude and that I protest too much because I wave my arms about, but that's because I'm Italian and come from another culture.'

Despite a distinct lack of room, he was still waving his arms about. 'The last four months have been a very bad time for me. I have been very unhappy,' he admitted. 'I made a mistake but it won't happen again. I want people to remember Di Canio for his footballing skills – the dribbling, passing and goals – and not for what happened last September.'

TAP! TAP! TAP! I could see Foe waving his arms about to signal his frustration at being kept waiting in the cold. 'Won't be long, don't worry,' I said as I kept his seat warm for him. The back of the car was piled with bags and sportswear and somewhere among it all was a chap who appeared to be a friend of Di Canio's. Paolo's passion for the game was obvious and I could see how his histrionics on the field are often misinterpreted. I found myself warming to his character as I asked about his love of cinema and favourite actors. I bet he likes Al Pacino and Robert De Niro, I thought to myself. 'I like Al Pacino, Robert De Niro . . . and Robin Williams,' he replied, as if he could read my mind. 'I also like Sharon Stone . . . a very sexy girl!' he added, a hint of Latin lust spreading across his face.

BANG! BANG! BANG! It was Fee-Fie-Foe outside again, pacing up and down as the first spits of rain started to bounce off his head. By now he'd become accustomed to my hand signals through the window and a playful two fingers seemed to hold him at bay for another few minutes. Di Canio had been something of a mile-eating maverick during his career, moving from club to club on a regular basis over the years, so I enquired as to how easily he made friends. 'Friend . . . it's a very big word for me. Every player has his own personality but when we all wear the same shirt, I give my body for my team-mates.'

Whether the rest of the Hammers squad particularly wanted his body was another thing, but I knew what he was trying to say. Foe, meanwhile, just wanted to sit next to Paolo's body and I eventually wished my new Italian friend farewell and apologised to the big Cameroon international who looked decidedly unhappy. 'That's OK,' he said, a quick wave of his hand poorly disguising a V-sign in return.

The interview with Di Canio had required a couple of attempts on my part. The press conference to announce the signing of both Paolo and Marc-Vivien had taken place at Upton Park a week earlier but, with so much interest in the Italian returning from exile, it would have been impossible to have a decent conversation at that point. As usual, I sent a fax to Chadwell Heath to introduce myself and wish the 30-year-old good luck, advising him of my intention to meet him there the following Tuesday. On the day in question I waited in the small reception area as the players returned from the training field and approached Paolo as he trudged in with muddy boots in hand. 'I have no time,' he said, 'I have problem with foot.' I insisted I only needed a few minutes (press lie number one) and he told me he'd see me afterwards. After taking his time getting changed, he wandered into the canteen and started making calls on his mobile. Typically, after some 10 or 15 minutes – during which time we could have had our chat – he was dragged away by physio John Green to see the doctor.

'I see you tomorrow, yes?' I said, in broken English that for some reason I thought he'd understand better.

'Yes, yes . . .' he said, dismissively, as he disappeared through the door.

And so I tried again the next day, seriously worried that I'd miss my *HNM* deadline if Paolo was to sneak off unnoticed. But that's often what it's like when you try to get an interview arranged. Players, particularly the foreign ones, very rarely return messages and when you turn up as promised it's hit or miss as to whether they're available. Harry and Frank are always most welcoming at the training ground, though. Lampard goes out of his way to acknowledge you, either shaking your hand or giving you a pat, while 'H' will also say hello and ask who you've come to see. 'You seen Paolo yet? Don't worry, he's still around,' he said, no doubt detecting my concern.

'We do it here?' said Di Canio, when he eventually appeared in the foyer.

'No, let's go somewhere private. Shall we sit in your car?' I asked.

'OK, but I need to give Marc a lift back to hotel for lunch.'

'Don't worry, we won't keep him waiting for long,' I lied.

Chapter Thirty-One

'STOP!!!' Standing with my legs apart and arms in the air I felt as if I was up against an imaginary wall waiting to be frisked from behind, but it's what was in front of me that mattered. The Aston Martin had reversed and started to nudge its way out of the Chadwell Heath gates when I ran to bring the car to a halt. Bringing his bumper to within a few inches of my knees, Wrighty wound his door window down and I looked into the car to see his 11-year-old son Brett sitting alongside him in the passenger seat. 'Er, Ian, we're supposed to be meeting this morning for a *Hammers News Magazine* piece,' I said, disappointed to see him making a quick getaway half an hour before the time agreed with his agent.

'Oh, yeah . . . I forgot. Er, can we do it on the phone?' he asked.

'No, mate. I've hired a car especially to get down here, your office told me you knew I was coming, we've got you on our cover and my deadline's on Monday. We need to do it today,' I insisted, starting to panic.

'Well, what are you doing now?' he said.

'Er, talking to you hopefully. Can we go somewhere and do it?'

With that, he suggested a hotel lounge just off the A127 on his way to the M25 and home. He zoomed off into the Chadwell Heath traffic as I counted the amount of horsepower of my rented car on the fingers of one hand and hung on to the coat tails of his exhaust fumes. Wrighty and son were waiting for me in the car park outside when I finally caught up and I casually remarked that 'I used to have one of those', as we walked away from his Aston. 'Really?' he said, before I reluctantly informed him that journalists earn slightly less than footballers nowadays.

We sat ourselves down and I told Wrighty that I wanted him to talk about more personal issues than simply football, such as his interest in Martin Luther King, for example. Ian had been appearing in the One-2-One mobile-phone ads on TV, in which he nominated the assassinated American civil rights movement leader as the man he'd most like to go back in time to talk to, given the chance. I'd actually bought a book on the man, just so that I didn't appear ignorant if we got involved in an extensive conversation about him, but Wrighty was straight to the point.

'Martin Luther King won the Nobel Peace Prize and was a great man,' he declared. 'He didn't preach segregation, he was simply preaching that we should stand up for our rights as black people and that violence shouldn't be met with violence. He was a peaceful protester and he wanted us to be able to mix with other cultures, be treated on the same intellectual level and be accepted as people. He put into place a philosophy that people can try and follow as a guideline.'

I think Wrighty was genuinely surprised to have a journalist show an interest in his heartfelt beliefs and welcomed the opportunity to talk about such matters. I'd kept a copy of a TV mag that contained a recent interview with Ian in which he admitted he'd lost his way as a person a few years earlier. 'I got involved with some people who weren't right for me, people who cater for your every whim because the name of Ian Wright can open certain doors for them,' he confided. 'All of a sudden I found myself in places and thinking, "What am I doing here?" Things at home were a little rocky and I was going out a lot.'

I pointed out that it's usually youngsters who struggle to deal with fame and fortune, but he countered: 'The more successful I became in football the more attention I got from women. Then a story broke in a newspaper about a certain young lady and when that happens it makes you realise how close you are to losing everything – your wife and your kids – and you have to take a long, hard look at yourself.'

I appreciated Wrighty's intimacy and was warmed by the fact that, despite all the negative experiences he's had with the press, there was still an element of trust there. Not only did he feel comfortable enough to discuss his personal life but he had faith in me to use the information in the correct manner. On a lighter note, I asked Ian about the Chicken Tonight telly ads which showed him doing a chicken dance to promote sizzle-and-stir sauces. 'I'm having a little pop at myself and it shows that I don't take myself too seriously,' he smiled. 'Because I'm a rogey, streetwise kind of guy, a south Londoner with a lot of mouth, it makes people laugh. I can't go anywhere now without people asking if I feel like chicken tonight!'

As we spoke Wrighty's gaze went through the window into the car park outside. 'See that? That's my dream car – a Bentley Continental,' he declared in mid-sentence. I told him I'd have thought he could go out and buy one, but he responded by admitting, 'Yeah, but I don't deserve one yet. I haven't earned the right to drive that car. It's a symbol, something that says, "I've made it!" And I don't think I have made it yet, because I've still got a lot of things to try and achieve.'

I thought this said a lot for the reason Ian continued to show so much frustration when things didn't go his way. Despite all his achievements (becoming Arsenal's record scorer, winning a load of medals and representing his country), he still strove for more. It's as if he'll never be satisfied, because the ambition to keep proving himself on one level or another will always be there (although I didn't for one minute expect Ian to acknowledge that he had anything to prove).

A week later I attended the recording of the first edition of Ian's *Friday Night's All Wright* show at the LWT studios. A very different character was on display this time, a Wrighty carrying a swagger and verve that generally only comes through spending years in front of the camera. 'The producers just want me to be myself,' he'd claimed, but with Ian also confessing to having 'a lot of different sides to my character', he clearly knew which persona the occasion demanded. That's not to say he didn't show nerves or make mistakes – he's far better answering questions than asking them – but you've got to admire his courage.

'Alright, geez?' he said, tapping me on the shoulder as I stood waiting for Paolo Di Canio at the training ground, several months later. 'Listen, I just wanna thank you for that piece you did. Yeah, it was good. I mean it, man.'

Hang on a minute. Something was wrong. This couldn't be Ian Wright, the man who thinks the press are parasites? He doesn't go round thanking journalists. He might tolerate them, but offer them thanks? No way! I was genuinely taken aback and stuttered, 'Oh . . . er . . . thanks very much. Erm, glad you liked it.' It's the first time a player has actually bothered to thank me for an article and I appreciated his gesture very much. All I'd done was remain faithful to the spirit of our conversation, although I could understand that not always being the case with Ian.

It hadn't been the best of seasons for Wrighty so far. As we spoke, he was in the process of recovering from a cartilage operation in January that would eventually sideline him for about four months. Up to that point he'd scored seven goals for the Hammers – and also made a brilliant exit from the England scene with a man-of-the-match performance in the 2–0 friendly win against the Czech Republic – but he was bitterly disappointed to have his campaign interrupted by injury. By the time we were to meet again, more water had passed under the bridge and some of if was dirty.

The game against Leeds United on 1 May will go down in history as the first (and hopefully last!) to see three West Ham players sent off. Wright was the first to be shown the red card (followed by goalkeeper Shaka Hislop and skipper Steve Lomas) by referee Rob Harris after clashing with Ian Harte, but it was more for what happened *after* he left the pitch that created all the headlines. Not that it had been easy getting him off it in the first place. Few seemed to properly see what actually took place down by the Chicken Run touchline in that first-half incident, least of all the cameras and officials, but with Harte playing dead it was decided that Wright had shown enough aggression to merit his second yellow card of the afternoon. Bent over with hands on hips, Wrighty took a few seconds to absorb the reality of the moment and then lost it, throwing himself forward at the startled referee. Fortunately, Lomas and Trevor Sinclair were on hand to drag Ian away but, when he seemed to have calmed down, back he came again. 'F*** off, Wright, you're a nutter. Clear off!' screamed the season-ticket holder next to me, furious with the player's irresponsibility in a game the Hammers desperately needed to win. With more bodies entering the fray, Wright was eventually led away in what must rank as the season's most protracted red-card departure.

But Ian wasn't finished, disappearing down the tunnel and forcing his way into the referee's changing-room to vent his frustration and anger in the most reckless way possible. First he chucked the official's clothing on to the floor, then he lashed out at the television set in the corner before eventually hot-footing it back to the showers. While hardly in the league of The Who's Keith Moon when it came to destructive dementia, there was sufficient damage for the following day's papers to run 'TRASHED!' headlines while the referee's report made its way to the FA.

Six days after the match – which the eight men lost 5–1, by the way – I found myself down at Chadwell Heath, waiting to talk to Julian Dicks. Suddenly Wrighty appeared in the back doorway and he asked how I was doing. I was doing fine, but how was he?

'I feel that I've let the fans down and that's hard to take. I've now got to go away for the summer with that on my mind,' he confided. He'd already used his column in *The Sun* to apologise for his actions and although he certainly regretted his loss of control, his plea for forgiveness was seen by some as a desperate attempt to save his skin while the governing bodies convened to discuss his fate. But I've no doubt that Ian felt deep disappointment at not being able to further contribute to the Hammers' cause: a ban of three or four matches was likely to be on the cards. Just by chatting to Wright I could sense the amalgam of emotions he was experiencing. As well as dissatisfaction – with himself and how things had turned out – he also felt genuine dismay over what, surprisingly, was only the second red card of his career. 'The last thing I expected was to be sent off,' he insisted, feeling as if a real injustice had taken place. 'Harte elbowed me first and I just grabbed him really, just to say, "What are you doing?" To my surprise, he went down as if I'd hit him.' I sympathised with Ian because the decision to book him was made purely on the strength of Harte's overreaction. But when you've had one yellow card, you have to avoid confrontation and Wright should know by now that sometimes you have to turn the other cheek. True, there was an element of aggression in his pursuit of Harte and he was therefore booked for 'acting in an aggressive manner', but the likelihood is that the officials didn't really know of what Wright had been guilty.

'Acting in an aggressive manner? What does *that* mean?' he asked as we stood in the reception area.

'Er, that they think you did something but they're not sure exactly what?' I speculated.

'Yeah, *that's* what it means,' he responded, becoming even more embittered by the whole affair. But few gave Ian the benefit of the doubt, for the simple reason that his career seems to have been one long succession of controversial incidents. Everybody's tired of hearing excuses, pleas of innocence and apologies. I therefore put it to Ian that he really should know how to steer clear of such incidents by now. After all, he was 35 years of age! 'Yeah, people always say, "At your age . . . etc etc," but the passion inside me will always be the same and I can't change that,' he insisted. 'Football means so much to me.'

It's that very intensity, that *mania*, which has dictated Wrighty's fortunes – good and bad – throughout his career. Throw water on the flames and the fire goes out. That's not an excuse for his behaviour, just a simple fact, and the problem has been Ian's inability to manage or control those burning impulses. The question now is what influence these will have on his life beyond football in the years to come.

''

Chapter Thirty-Two

With Ian Wright out for four months, a huge weight of responsibility was placed on the shoulders of new striker Paolo Di Canio in the early part of 1999. Heavy scrutiny was already guaranteed as a result of his altercation with Alcock but, while the media were concerned with the Italian's temperament, the real issue for Hammers fans was his ability to hit the net on a regular enough basis. When push came to shove, could he score enough goals? I was sceptical.

Although he'd registered 15 goals in one season for Celtic and then 17 in Sheffield Wednesday's colours, his record in Italy was rather more modest. During spells with Ternana, Lazio, Juventus, Napoli and Milan, he'd averaged around five or six a year although he was deployed as much as a playmaker as an out-and-out hitman. 'I have played in a lot of different positions because I like to pass the ball and create goals,' he told me, when I asked about his goalscoring record. 'In Italy teams often play with just one main striker and a more creative player behind him. My best qualities are in the last 30 or 40 yards.'

That was all well and good, but West Ham were in desperate need of somebody who could put the ball into the net. Despite the fact he was obviously a much different player from John Hartson, the reality was that he'd arrived as his direct replacement. And his first start at Upton Park hardly inspired confidence, with the side crashing to a second successive 4–0 home defeat (Arsenal following in Sheffield Wednesday's tracks to goal). But it wasn't just Di Canio who had a lot to prove. Cameroon international midfielder Marc-Vivien Foe – a £4.5 million recruit from Lens – had commanded the largest chunk of the Hartson money, while left-back/wing-back Scott Minto was a £1 million purchase from Benfica. The former Charlton and Chelsea man had barely tied his laces up when he was getting slaughtered by the boo-boys, and Arsenal fans were singing 'give the ball to Minto' after a couple of wayward crosses. It was the third time the Hammers had conceded four goals in four outings and the question being asked was how long it was going to take for the team to emerge from this black hole. The 13 February fixture against Nottingham

Forest brought together two of the most nervous teams in the country (with the basement boys having just been slaughtered at home by Manchester United) but goals from Frank Lampard and Ian Pearce secured a tense 2–1 win. A week later a Lampard penalty and a Marc Keller goal direct from a corner guaranteed a share of the spoils at Liverpool, but Harry Redknapp was not a particularly happy chappy afterwards.

'I've never seen a reaction like it after a couple of bad results,' he stormed in the press conference. 'We had a bad month and suddenly the world's coming to an end, I'm no good at my job and the team's useless! People need to understand that we've just brought in three new players and should show a little bit of patience. But now it's a few bad results and bosh!' Marc-Vivien Foe (or Marc-Vivien Slow, as his critics would label him) was another new boy struggling to win friends. 'People were jumping on his back after one or two games. He got slaughtered and it was frightening to read . . . Alright there, Gary?'

Redknapp's late acknowledgement of *OLAS* editor Gary Firmager in the front row of the seats facing him seemed very much like a sly dig, the inference being that negative propaganda had appeared about the players in a recent issue of the fanzine. Certainly, Gary interpreted it that way and immediately defended his position. Harry denied that he was having a go specifically at Gary but moaned about 'people' in general having unrealistic expectations. 'We've avoided the bottom half of the table for nearly two years and now people are expecting us to win championships,' he declared. The pair continued to debate the issue and Harry acceded to Gary's suggestion that football fans can be very fickle at times.

Of course, the Liverpool-based national media interpreted this as a direct attack on the West Ham supporters (partly through assumption, partly for the sake of a good story) and the next day's papers were full of stories of the manager allegedly pointing the finger at his own fans. My view was that Harry was referring more to those with the power of the pen ('it was frightening to read,' he'd said) than those with the power of the penny (who pay to get in) and I stressed that point in my monthly column. But the issue of supporters' expectations was an interesting one. It had been 19 years since the club's last trophy and 13 since the best-ever third place; since then, fans had endured two relegations, enjoyed subsequent promotions and had seen the board invest heavily in the squad in terms of transfer fees and securing players to long-term contracts. 'We're all entitled to harbour dreams and be ambitious in our desires. We all want to win,' I wrote. 'But we have to be realistic at the same time and the club have made no secret of the fact that until the ground redevelopment has been completed, it's going to be a struggle to take on the Arsenals and Manchester Uniteds. It's the long-term picture that counts and on that basis things are certainly on the up. It was only six years ago that the Hammers were trying to get promoted having spent a mere £200,000 on Peter Butler, Mattie Holmes and Mark Robson. I think things have improved somewhat, don't you?'

I also wondered what *The Mail*'s David McDonnell was making of things, especially as he'd claimed that any future signings would merely be 'papering over the cracks' of West Ham's financial crisis, remember. I guess he must have felt rather bemused watching the club spend the entire £7.5 million received from the sale of Hartson, especially as there were now three salaries to pay (to Di Canio, Foe and Minto) instead of one. The only question was whether Redknapp had spent the money wisely. As I've said, I had doubts about Di Canio's goalscoring record while Foe hardly looked like a £4.5 million player. Fans had assumed we were buying a Patrick Vieira type of player, a midfield powerhouse, but we soon came to realise Foe was more of a defensive player who could win the ball on the edge of the box and occasionally ping a nice pass on to the flanks. French football gave him time on the ball to pick his passes out, but the pace of the Premiership might have made it more difficult for him to play his usual game. And the fact that the club accepted Liverpool's £4.5 million bid just a few months later (the deal collapsing when personal terms could not be agreed) suggests that Harry would have been happy to make a modest profit on the player.

Who knows what the future would have held for Redknapp had he made the wrong decisions during that pivotal February period? He insisted at the time that the new players should have time to settle and become fully integrated and, slowly but surely, he was proved right. After slumping to ninth after the humiliation at home to Arsenal, the Hammers lost just two of their next 11 games – typically, to strugglers Southampton and Charlton.

The Saints match was a ludicrous affair: the team wasted an incredible 15 clear-cut chances to score and fell to one deflected shot by striker Kachloul. 'We threw three points away today,' confessed Harry after watching his side's domination come to nothing. I had the audacity to suggest that one of the problems may have been that our two frontmen on the day – Di Canio and Trevor Sinclair – were hardly out-and-out goalscorers, often drifting deep and wide to collect the ball and send in crosses for others to get on the end of. Redknapp's brow started to furrow and before he said anything I added, '. . . especially with Di Canio taking corners.'

'Di Canio taking corners? What's Di Canio taking corners got to do with anything?' he retorted. Suddenly I found myself discussing Harry's tactics in front of the rest of the press.

'Er . . . well, if one of your strikers is taking the corners, that means there's one less player with predatory instincts in the box,' I offered.

'No, Neil Ruddock can head a ball, can't he?' said 'H'. Before I'd weighed up all the evidence to come to any firm conclusion on that one, Redknapp admitted, 'But I know what you mean, Sinclair and Di Canio do tend to drift out on to the flanks at times.' Exactly. Both players had worked their socks off but because they've both got instincts to create as well as finish moves off, they're not necessarily going to be inside the six-yard box when you need them to be. But that's just where Di Canio found himself to score his first goal for West Ham when they took on Blackburn Rovers on 27 February. The 2–0 win dumped Rovers into the bottom three but it was still difficult to envisage them going down. The Lancashire club had finished above the Hammers the previous summer and spent a net figure of £27 million on players under their two managers (Roy Hodgson and Brian Kidd) that season. West Ham's balance sheet showed a net expenditure of £1 million, yet look how things ultimately turned out.

Rovers were relegated while Harry guided his troops to fifth, despite some bizarrely erratic results in the closing stages. Paul Kitson scored the only goal at Stamford Bridge on 13 March to give championship-chasing Chelsea the blues, after which Gianluca Vialli was asked if he was disappointed by his team's recent failure to find the net. 'No, it doesn't disappoint me . . .' said the Italian, 'it just f***ing pisses me off!' Shortly afterwards, Ian Wright returned to the old enemy Tottenham and promptly scored his ninth and last goal of the season to set up a 2–1 win in which John Moncur was sent off for a rash tackle on José Domínguez. Moncs duly gave the visiting Hammers fans a two-fisted salute as if to say, 'I did it for you, boys!'

If we'd have been told that West Ham would score just 4 of the 16 goals to be witnessed in the team's remaining three games of the campaign, a top five place would have seemed an impossibility. Yet despite the 5–1 hammering by Leeds (in which referee Rob Harris heavily influenced the outcome) and the pathetic 6–0 thumping by Everton the following week, the 4–0 win over clueless Middlesbrough on the final day was enough to secure fifth place – the club's second-highest placing EVER!

Chapter Thirty-Three

The completion of the double over Tottenham at White Hart Lane in April was one of the highlights of the 1998–99 season, but Harry Redknapp was in subdued mood after the match. 'It's been a sad week what with the announcement that Peter Storrie is leaving the club,' he admitted. 'Only chairman Terence Brown would know the reasons behind the move, although I think Peter has seen it coming for a while.'

Indeed he had. In fact, so had quite a few people. Rumours about Storrie's long-term future at the club had been circulating for some time, especially after he gave up the position of managing director to become chief executive/director of football at the end of 1997. Peter maintained that this allowed him to concentrate more on issues directly related to football, while allowing more financial issues to be presided over by new director Paul Aldridge. Yet whispers suggested that he could be on his way long before the club issued the following statement in April. 'Following a board decision to restructure the management side of the club, by mutual agreement Director of Football Peter Storrie will leave the club after nine years' dedicated service.'

It may have been 'mutually' agreed that he would leave, but Peter certainly didn't want to go. And neither did Redknapp want him to go. 'The chairman called me in and I told him that I was disappointed and couldn't see any reason for it. We've never been in better shape,' said Harry. 'Peter has worked his socks off and played a major part in setting up the youth academies, but he told me he felt that perhaps it was partly due to the fact that he supports me so much.'

Redknapp and Storrie certainly worked in tandem, especially when dealing with the buying and selling of players, but it was clear that Brown wanted to initiate major changes in the way the club operates. Even though Graham Mackrell was due to arrive from Sheffield Wednesday as company secretary, it was natural to assume he'd be expected to work more independently of Harry (even though the pair had previously spent time together at Bournemouth). Although Peter expressed his disillusionment in the press shortly after the news became public, it's likely that his terms of departure would have involved some kind of secrecy agreement, preventing him from disclosing anything about his business activities or circumstances of departure.

The fans may have been surprised and perhaps a touch disappointed that the public face of the West Ham board was going, but not everyone was. 'I couldn't care less,' said Julian Dicks when we spoke shortly after the announcement. 'The only reason Harry hasn't gone with him is because the team's been winning,' he added. Dicksy had little regard for Storrie, especially for the way he'd been treated by the club during his years of injury. Even physio John Green admitted to me: 'Julian basically went from being club captain to a leper. That was the attitude in the club towards him.' There was no love lost between the pair and nothing has happened since to improve Dicksy's view of the man.

The general media jumped to rash conclusions over the news, naïvely assuming that the public rift with Harry over the sale of Andy Impey had been a contributory factor. 'H', very much a supporter of Peter, dismissed those suggestions as 'scandalous' and even went so far as to say the mood within the camp was such that the players had dedicated their win over Tottenham to Storrie. That was perhaps a bit hard to believe, but at least Redknapp was making it clear whose side he was on. At the press conference after that game I asked Harry how this development would affect his relationship with the club and he insisted that the politics would not divert him from his course. 'I just take things as they come now,' he sighed. 'All I try to do is build a good football team and I can sleep at night knowing I have done that.'

In many ways that response summed up Redknapp's mood and attitude in the second half of the season. All he could do was his best, given the circumstances, and if that wasn't good enough, the blame couldn't be laid at his door. He was entitled to feel frustrated at working on a limited budget while trying to meet ever-growing expectations, and I constantly heard him complaining about the shallowness of his squad. He was being asked to compete with the likes of Manchester United, Chelsea, Arsenal, Liverpool and Newcastle, who could all go out and spend millions on new players as and when they wished, yet he was having to wheel and deal like a second-hand car dealer – bringing in three players for the price of one (as he did with the sale of Hartson) – in order to replenish the squad.

But that had always been the case and nothing had changed in that respect. Nonetheless I could understand him feeling envious (or even slightly resentful) of the cheque-book Charlies such as Ruud Gullit and Gianluca Vialli, for example, who, on the strength of world-class reputations as players as opposed to a proven pedigree in management, were in a position to make huge demands in terms of financial support. It just wasn't a level playing field and maybe Harry was tiring of the uphill struggle.

But I also detected an air of resignation about Redknapp during this period, as if to suggest his time at West Ham may be coming to an end. I heard one piece of gossip a year earlier which indicated that his contract may not be renewed and I was even tempted to offer a bet to a friend that Harry would not be in charge at the beginning of the 1999–2000 season. I'm glad we didn't shake hands on it, because it was confirmed in the summer of 1999 that 'H' had signed a new three-year deal with the club. The negotiations would have taken place during the season and they'd have been protracted, I imagine with the key issue being that of salary. Redknapp had spoken to me on more than one occasion about the growing disparity in earnings between players and bosses and was clearly concerned about what was happening in that respect. 'What the players are earning compared to managers is ridiculous,' he complained to me as far back as June 1997. 'Even the kids are earning more than their bosses at some clubs. It's gone crazy.'

With the Bosman ruling having an increasing influence on the financial structure of the game, it was only going to get worse, of course. I anticipated the true effects of the ruling that very month (before it applied to domestic transfers), writing in my column: 'The balance of power has shifted and clubs are going to be held to ransom. Imagine this scenario, if you will: Player X has a good couple of seasons. His contract has only a year or two to run so, with agent alongside him to hit the buttons on his calculator, he strides manfully into his chairman's office and demands a huge salary increase. "I want my money doubled . . . no, tell you what, make it trebled. And you can extend my contract by two years. And if I don't get what I want, I'll be off and you won't get a single penny for me. That could cost you over £10 million." The club, realising they could see one of their prize assets walk out of the door, quickly realise it's far better business in the long run to pay huge wages, enjoy the benefit of the player's services for a few more years and then recoup the cash from a big sale. Hence Player X gets his new contract and the "good news" is announced.'

That's the climate West Ham United are operating in. Harry once told me: 'All the power now is with the players – and that's bad. The spiralling wages alone have made my job so much more difficult. And are they really worth these salaries? I don't think so.'

Immense credit must be given to the club for recognising the threats of

Bosman and responding quickly. The directors very rarely get credit for their work but can you imagine what scenes would take place at Upton Park if a player like Rio Ferdinand was lost for nothing? At least we can say we've taken advantage of the Bosman ruling by recruiting the likes of Shaka Hislop and Marc Keller on free transfers. And so it was no surprise when we read that Ferdinand and Frank Lampard had agreed new terms yet again in the summer of 1999. Yes, the club is being placed under huge financial pressure but since the players are tied to lengthy contracts, the investment is protected. When the time is right for the club – or when the demands of the players cannot be met – both will leave for huge sums.

Harry's ace card, apart from building a winning side and taking the club into the top five in May '99 – is his ability to work efficiently in the transfer market and make money for the club in that way. Money may have been lost on the likes of Raducioiu, Dumitrescu and Boogers, but he recouped that in one fell swoop when he sold Bilic to Everton. He doubled his money on Hartson. He trebled his money on Berkovic when he eventually left to join Celtic. He sold Lazaridis to Birmingham for *five* times the £300,000 paid to West Adelaide. Yet throughout the turnover of personnel, he's improved the Hammers' fortunes on the field of play. Chairman Terry Brown has acknowledged Redknapp's worth in that respect by agreeing a package that effectively doubled the manager's earnings. Again, it's an investment that will prove to be worthwhile.

The 1998–99 season also saw the publication of Harry's autobiography, imaginatively titled, er, *My Autobiography*. It's a lively read, as I acknowledged in my *HNM* review: 'That Harry Redknapp's a pain. Kept me in the pub all night, he did. Actually, before you conjure up visions of 'H' and yours truly enjoying a lengthy binge and quaffing huge quantities of alcohol together, I should confirm that it was Redknapp's book – rather than the man in person – whose company proved so entertaining on the night in question. Any chance of paying my bar bill, Harry?' I wrote.

The stories of greater interest to me were those which exposed Redknapp's determination to see a deal through, even if devious means were required. He told of how he'd once put together a syndicate to raise £20,000 to fund the purchase of striker Colin Clarke for Bournemouth when the club failed initially to come up with the cash, while he persuaded Weymouth manager Stuart Morgan to sell him centre-half Shaun Teale for £50,000 (when Reading had apparently offered double) by offering Morgan a coaching position with the Cherries. Is it any wonder that some directors don't like managers negotiating transfers?

Publishers Collins Willow threw a lunch-time launch party for the book in London on 2 November and, as well as attracting all the usual media men (who are never far from a free drink), Harry was supported by plenty of family and friends in addition to a few players (including Frank Lampard and Neil Ruddock). I remember meeting Redknapp's dad, Harry senior – a great old character – and thinking he looked exactly as you'd expect his son to in 25 years' time. Spray the hair white and off you go.

By the end of the afternoon, only the usual suspects remained and I can (just about) remember sitting around a table with Harry, his father, Frank Lampard Snr, former Chelsea star Alan Hudson, Neil Ruddock and various scribblers who've contributed to *HNM* over the years. A group of us later retired to a nearby pub (so much for Ruddock not drinking!) and I spent half an hour in the company of Harry's great friend Hudson, who'd spent some considerable time recovering from serious injury after being run over by a car. He'd had his pelvis crushed and spent time in a coma, but thankfully he had pulled through and was doing his best to lead a normal life again. The trauma of the last year could not be disguised, though, and it was like talking to the shell of a man who'd literally had the stuffing knocked out of him. I felt great sympathy for him but was honoured to share a drink and wish him well.

When I interviewed Redknapp about his autobiography, I asked him about the gulf between the earnings of players and managers and he reiterated the points made forcefully in the book. 'I've had players who were nowhere near getting into the first team earning more money than me. I don't think that's right,' he said. 'I'm not saying we should earn as much as the best players but certainly as much as the average earners.'

With Harry the highest-placed English manager in the Premiership table at the end of the 1998–99 season, who's to say he's not worthy of his new contract? Peter Storrie, meanwhile, surprised a few people by taking a senior position with Southend United. I'd have thought the ambitious Storrie would have sought a position with another large club but maybe the attraction of having greater power was enough to lure him into the Third Division. Peter had initially been the one to rubber stamp the deal for *HNM* with Independent Magazines (UK) Ltd but, when his responsibilities changed, the company found itself negotiating with different personnel when the time came to address our contract situation. It was the beginning of the end.

Chapter Thirty-Four

Some official club magazines exist purely for propaganda purposes and can be thoroughly disposable but, to West Ham's credit, having made an agreement for Independent Magazines (UK) Ltd to produce *Hammers News Magazine* on their behalf, they were happy to leave us to our own devices. Some might consider this negligence on their part, expecting the club to control the content or influence the feel of the magazine, but I was always grateful for the freedom that allowed us.

Nobody can ever say *HNM* was short of substance. As each month unfolded, we always tackled the topical issues in an authoritative way and had empathy (and often sympathy) with the supporters. That's because its editorial staff and contributors have always been West Ham fans themselves. I like to think we displayed an integrity and passion that readers could relate to as the magazine evolved in character and personality through my near-five years of editorship.

Throughout it all we got little feedback from the club and I took that to indicate they were happy with the product. We'd included controversial interviews with the likes of Paul Ince and Frank McAvennie, provided a platform for players to make their plea for a first-team place and allowed the fans every opportunity to have their say (via our 'Vox Pop', 'Pub Talk' and 'Hammers For Life' pages) without a single word of complaint from Upton Park, so obviously we weren't going far wrong. Sales had virtually doubled since my arrival as editor and readers seemed to like our objective and balanced approach along with the odd splash of humour.

One observation I did receive from the club in the summer of 1998 was there were 'too many fans' in the magazine. 'Supporters want to read about players, not fans,' I was told.

'They're not reading about fans, they're reading about fans talking about players – there's a difference,' I claimed. I took the opportunity to stress that by allowing the supporters to have a profile, we achieved two key objectives in our quest to maximise the magazine's potential. Firstly, it helped us to offer a genuine alternative to the matchday programme (which is more corporate in its feel and very information led) by producing something with a different character. Secondly, the inclusion of fans gave us credibility with the readership – not only could individuals express their views but it also illustrated that we were in tune with the mood of the support. I wasn't too sure my points had been accepted, though. I was also disappointed that my attempts to arrange a meeting with the club during the 1998–99 season to discuss the content and character of *HNM* proved fruitless.

It was subsequently confirmed in the summer of 1999 that West Ham had decided to place the contract for the publication of *HNM* elsewhere. That was their prerogative, although I was obviously disenchanted. I felt we'd done a good job but it had rarely been acknowledged. Whether the club's motivation was finance-based or an indication of their desire for a new type of editorial product was unclear. It may have been that their new arrangement looked potentially more profitable, while the club may even have considered the option of taking the title 'in-house' (effectively producing it themselves). The comment from one club official that 'printing is easy' hardly showed a deep appreciation of what publishing is about or what is required to create a magazine. Certain personnel were also surprised to learn that a national consumer title available through retail outlets – in marked contrast to a product such as the programme which is simply sold at the ground – only usually sells around 60 per cent of the amount produced (the print-run figure). That's one of the fundamental rules of publishing and the secret is to estimate the right quantity to place on the shelves to maximise sales potential while reducing the amount of wastage.

I wouldn't expect the club to be aware of this information and I'm certainly not blaming them for any lack of publishing expertise. After all, their business is football and that's why the magazine was contracted to a publishing house in the first place. I just hope that decisions haven't been made without the necessary appreciation of certain facts of publishing life.

I'm sure the club were also looking for the magazine to take on a new identity. We'd probably taken the title as far as we could in its particular direction and I'd have been more than happy to initiate a complete change of course. I'd have welcomed the chance to produce a magazine with a more sophisticated feel if only the club had indicated they wanted something different. Sadly, I was never given the opportunity to offer any new ideas or alternative proposals; I only heard when it was far too late that the magazine should 'reflect the new corporate image of the club'.

Certainly, some of the things we'd done in the past may not have been to chairman Terry Brown's liking. I got the vibe that our 'Pub Talk' pages

– in which we got a group of supporters around a table of beers to discuss all things claret and blue – occasionally ruffled a few feathers: one issue in particular had a photograph of one of the participants taking a leak in the toilet. The picture only showed the guy's back and was just above a photo of Shaka Hislop unravelling a load of bog roll from his netting. We supplied appropriate captions to link the two pictures but it appears that not everybody shared our sense of humour.

Another 'Pub Talk' even upset a few of our readers. It was proposed by one of my contributors that we make a departure one month by accepting an invitation to talk to the wives and girlfriends of a group of blokes who'd previously appeared in the magazine. I must admit the final piece wasn't quite what I envisaged but it still made for an entertaining, although disposable, four pages. Before I knew it, I had a lady on the phone complaining that we'd single-handedly set the women's liberation movement back 10 years! 'We've portrayed the girls as bimbos,' she protested.

'No, some people may view it that way but that's not our fault,' I replied. She gradually got more and more hysterical until she was screaming:

'YOU . . . HAVE . . . NO . . . IDEA . . . HOW . . . UPSET . . . I . . . AM!!!!!'

'Er, I think I might have a slight idea,' I said, holding the phone a good three feet from my damaged right lughole.

A couple of other light-hearted features may also have upset the Hammers hierarchy, but nothing was ever said and we were only exploiting a freedom the club were happy for us to have. Some of the lack of feedback could be attributed to the fact that nobody at the club was designated to preside over our activities or act in a liaisonal capacity, but I felt later that I'd perhaps been made a scapegoat for the club's negligence and lack of interest.

Editing a club magazine is not the easiest job in the world. You're trying to gain credibility from an often cynical group of supporters, develop relationships with the playing and management staff, while at the same time providing the club with the product they'll be content with. It's easy to be pulled in a number of different directions and keeping all the people happy all the time is easier said than done. Sure, I'd have made the odd error of judgement – in five years it would be nigh on impossible not to – but in the main I think we handled most situations correctly.

We'd seen Harry Redknapp take over from Billy Bonds in controversial circumstances, the Boogers embarrassment, Rio Ferdinand's drink-driving headlines, John Hartson lose his head with Eyal Berkovic (who almost lost his) and Harry publicly complain about 'non-football people' interfering in team affairs. Unlike some club magazines, which would have brushed these issues under the carpet, we addressed them all and I like to think we did so in a sensible and intelligent manner. Unfortunately, it appears that some people took much of what we did for granted.

Chapter Thirty-Five

The final issue of *HNM* under my editorship coincided with the end of the 1998–99 season and, with Ian Wright allowing me an exclusive interview following the nightmare of the Leeds United match, we couldn't have gone out on a more controversial note. In retrospect it seems like the 'aggro issue': as there's a bust-up of one sort or another on virtually every page! There are pictures of Wrighty being restrained after getting red carded, John Moncur being led off the field after being sent off at Tottenham, Moncur swinging a punch at Steven Carr in the same match, Lomas appearing to biff German midfielder Steffen Freund moments later, fans venting their fury during the Leeds match and Razor Ruddock showing typical fight as he reflected on his acquittal after being charged with threatening behaviour (on the night of the players' Christmas bash).

It was also a final opportunity to catch up with Julian Dicks and find out what the future held in store. He hadn't been seen on duty since the 4–0 home defeat by Arsenal in February and word was that we'd probably not see him in action again. I could see this being a 'Goodnight from us . . . and it's goodnight from him!' style of piece. We sat ourselves down in the players' canteen down at Chadwell Heath and the first thing Dicksy did was confirm the bad news regarding his left leg. 'The shin's slipped,' he said, as I winced at the thought. 'I trained too hard with the weights and that's ruled me out for the last few months. Now it's a case of seeing how things go in the summer.'

The injury was the key factor as to whether Julian saw out the remaining year on his contract. Certainly, if he was unlikely to find an acceptable level of fitness again, his retirement would be the inevitable outcome. Otherwise he'd hope to see out his final season at West Ham, although he admitted he was '99 per cent' certain he'd not get too many opportunities to play, whatever his condition. 'I don't want to retire yet,' he said, revealing that he wouldn't be forced into calling it a day just to ease the club's wage bill. West Ham had yet to suggest any sort of deal, but he was adamant that his contract would have to be paid up in full before he walked away. From the club's point of view, the only real advantage to paying Julian off would be to save money and they'd therefore need to persuade the player to agree to a compromise. I couldn't see that happening myself, unless the injury made the decision for him.

Dicks was in reasonably good spirits and was delighted to have succeeded in making the most unlikely of comebacks that season. 'I can't say it's worked out as well as I thought it would, but I took a chance and it paid off. If you include reserve games I've probably made about 20 appearances since coming back and that's not bad considering that I was told by everybody I wouldn't kick a ball again.'

Yet he confessed to becoming disillusioned with the sport to some extent. 'The standard of refereeing has got worse and I think football is going downhill,' he conceded. 'I think I would be better off out of it, to tell you the truth, but I'd like to have left the sport in a better way than this. I'd like to have played until the summer of 2000 but it doesn't look as if I'll be able to.'

And so it was. Official Hammers media announced just a few months later that Julian was to retire from professional football. I was surprised not to have heard the news directly from his agent and suspected that the club had effectively made the decision for him. 'West Ham wanted to get rid of me, full stop,' confirmed Dicksy when I rang him on 9 August, just one day after his 31st birthday. 'The club wanted me off the wage bill and I knew Harry wasn't going to play me anymore – even though my knee and shin are giving me no problems now – so it was a case of trying to come to an agreement.'

But as we spoke, it emerged that an agreement had yet to be reached and Julian certainly hadn't announced his retirement himself. 'Today I'm still contracted to West Ham,' he said. 'But I went into training a couple of Mondays ago and it was clear they didn't even want me there.'

Rachel Anderson alleges that that was because, under the terms of her man's transfer from Liverpool in 1994, a further sum of money would be owed to the Merseyside club if Julian was still with West Ham at this point in time. It's her view that it was for that very reason that Harry announced Julian's imminent retirement as early as May 1999, and why club media had been used to convey the message prematurely.

Julian had clearly resigned himself to the inevitable, however. 'I had a chat with my wife Kay and didn't think there was any point in going into work to slog my guts out for no reason,' he told me. 'I know I'm contradicting what I said a few months ago about sitting at the club for a year, but at the end of the day we should come to an agreement which is good for me and saves West Ham a few quid as well.'

The agreement package was expected to represent what Julian would have earned in his remaining 12 months less bonuses related to the team's success (whether he was in the side or not). 'By rights, he should have his contract paid up in full,' added Anderson, who also confirmed there was a big dispute over tax liability.

Said Julian: 'Six months' money is tax free but at this point in time I'm still waiting to hear if the money on top is going to be taxable. I said to the club, "There's no way I'm paying the tax on it!" And they said, "There's no way we're paying it." So we'll have to see what happens.' Julian confirmed that he'd been offered a testimonial game but according to his agent, 'West Ham claimed he wouldn't automatically get one. They definitely used it as leverage to get their way.'

It's no wonder that Dicksy echoed Wrighty's sentiments exactly when he added: 'I'll miss the football a lot but I won't miss all the other aspects of it. I've had eight or nine operations on my knee now and if you'd told me when I had my first operation that I'd have that many and would be 31 when my career ended, I'd have been happy. To tell you the truth, I think I could still play. I wouldn't play for a league side, I'd rather play semi-pro football just for the fun of it. I've had so many years of shit I just don't need the hassle any more.

'At least I can concentrate on my golf now, which is the most important thing for me. I'd say that was the major thing that allowed me to change my mind about sticking around.'

Dicksy is indeed setting his sights firmly on a professional golfing career and if he shows the same type of commitment we saw from him in a Hammers shirt, he should go a fair way (if you'll excuse the pun). Also on the agenda – to follow up my *Terminator* biography – is an autobiography, the very mention of which has Julian licking his lips in anticipation. 'It's going to be a bit special and there's a few people I'm gonna take down with me, don't you worry,' he told me. 'Not players, because they've been as good as gold, but there are a few others I'll be giving plenty of stick to.' Place your orders in the club shop now, folks . . .

The Dicksy issue was just one of many the club had to attend to during what amounted to its shortest close season ever. The team had finished fifth in May to secure the second-highest league placing in its history, but somehow missed out on automatic qualification for a UEFA Cup spot. Thanks to the top clubs also winning cup competitions in 1998, the seventh position which was good enough the previous year, was not good enough this time around: only the top four were guaranteed European places. To be honest, I was never really in any doubt about that. With UEFA expanding the Champions League to appease those giants considering the formation of a European Super League, it was always a case of the top three clubs qualifying for that and there being three UEFA Cup places – one for fourth place and the other two from the cups.

Many assumed that places would move down the league if cups were won by teams near the top. That's a logical scenario but we'd already seen in 1998 that the place via the FA Cup had to go to a team from that competition (Newcastle going into the Cup-Winners' Cup as losing finalists to Arsenal). What confused the issue for some was that three of the last four teams in the 1999 FA Cup competition were already likely to qualify via their achievements elsewhere. Newcastle were guaranteed a place in Europe this time around for simply reaching the semi-finals. Harry Redknapp was one of many who slammed the system and, to be fair to him, he had a point. Had Newcastle been in the top three as well, what would the governing bodies have done – have a play-off involving the losing quarter-finalists? No, of course not.

There was also an argument for places moving down when Manchester United won the Champions League, as they'd qualified twice (once as holders, once for winning the Premiership). But no, UEFA simply allowed Chelsea to skip one of the qualifying rounds as the bonus for an English club winning Europe's top competition. West Ham had already declared their intention to enter the Intertoto Cup going into the final month of the season (despite much confusion as to when the tournament started and how many games would need to be played) and to their credit they gained the fifth position needed to claim their place.

My feeling was that the club had gone as far as it could in terms of threatening at the top of the Premiership. The fact is that Manchester United, Arsenal and Chelsea are in a financial league of their own and even though the Hammers finished above Liverpool and Newcastle, both clubs have the financial clout to quickly overtake us. Everybody was saying good things about Leeds in fourth position, so a finish in the top six at the end of the 1999–2000 season would be a fantastic achievement. Top eight is far more realistic, West Ham hoping to stay ahead of the likes of Aston Villa, Tottenham and Middlesbrough.

That would be tough enough anyway, but Redknapp had the added problem of holding onto his best players. Rio Ferdinand and Frank Lampard may have agreed new deals, but the loss of the influential Eyal Berkovic – which most saw as inevitable – to Celtic in a £5.75 million move is bound to have an effect on the long-term creativity of the side. Young Joe Cole was introduced slowly during the early part of 1999 but it's asking a lot of the talented teenager to impose himself immediately. Winger Stan Lazaridis also left, to Birmingham, while Ian Wright was expected to have a diminished role in his final season (even going to Nottingham Forest on an initially temporary basis).

The big summer signing for the Hammers was striker Paulo Wanchope. The gangly Costa Rican was brought in for a sensible £3.5 million from Derby and took little time to make his mark. With Paolo Di Canio and Paul Kitson also figuring, at least there are options up front. The problems, however, were up the other end of the pitch. I anticipated as much at the end of the previous season, asking Harry about his plans after the match at Leicester on 10 April. 'Oh, I knew somebody was going to bring his name up!' quipped Harry when I mentioned Javier Margas. The Chilean had twice disappeared to South America, claiming injury and homesickness, and could not be contacted, despite sudden announcements that he was intending to retire. 'He said he was going to finish with international football but he hasn't told us he's retiring yet,' said Redknapp. Of course, not only did Margas represent his country in the Copa America tournament that summer but he eventually returned to England, despite having had his wages stopped by the club. Some were of the view that he'd only reappeared to try and arrange some kind of settlement, despite his insistence that he was ready to play, but Harry's preferred option was to sell the player.

The Leicester game also saw Redknapp discuss the retirement announcement of Richard Hall, who'd finally succumbed to the inevitable after a three-year fight for fitness. 'It's a great shame,' he said, admitting he was going to have to search for defensive reinforcements with Dicks, Margas and Hall out of the picture. To the surprise of many, top of Harry's list was our good old friend Slaven Bilic. The Croat had had a nightmare couple of seasons at Everton, being red-carded three times in his first year and barely playing at all in the second because of injury. Even though one bloke I knew was talking of handing back his season ticket if Bilic returned to West Ham, I think the general populace would have accepted the situation – especially as something like a bargain £500,000 fee had been agreed. It would almost have been like Slaven admitting he'd made a mistake and, given that the club would have been making a £4 million profit, I don't think too many would have complained if he'd reproduced his form of old. Sadly, for him at least, he failed the club's medical and returned to Merseyside to ponder an uncertain future. Right-back Rob Jones was brought in on trial after being released by Liverpool and actually started one Intertoto Cup game, although yet another operation put paid to any immediate deal.

The tale of woe continued. Neil Ruddock pulled up with a hamstring problem during one of the Intertoto Cup games and was immediately ruled out for the beginning of the Premiership season. Fellow centre-half Ian Pearce had broken a leg at the tail-end of the previous campaign but returned to replace the injured Ruddock. His good fortune was short-lived, however, as he was carried off in the opening league game against Spurs after clashing with new team-mate Stuart Pearce, signed on a free transfer from Newcastle just days beforehand. It was later confirmed that Pearce One would miss the entire season. Oh, does it pour at times . . .

Ironically, to boost his defensive numbers, Harry signed 31-year-old Croatian international Igor Stimac, who immediately declared: 'Don't worry, I can advise West Ham fans that John Hartson will not score against me this season.' Isn't it funny how things turn out in football?

The Intertoto Cup competition at least allowed the Hammers to hit the ground running in the opening league match against Tottenham. Having played competitive football for nearly a month, I think it certainly gave them an edge when the serious stuff began. Having said that, there was no indication that the club weren't taking the Intertoto Cup matches seriously – not if the Upton Park pricing policy was anything to go by. I'd have thought the least the club could have done, having increased some season tickets by nearly £100, was to include these home games as either part of the ticket or on a reduced-price basis. But no, not only did everybody have to pay but the club decided to award the games 'category A' prices. Some season-ticket holders therefore had to pay £31 for their regular seat to watch the opening game against FC Jokerit on 17 July.

Not surprisingly, the fans hardly flocked to the ticket office to make their advance reservations and, by 12 July, chairman Terence Brown was starting to worry. Consequently, he sent out a letter to all supporters confirming what players would make up the team (since when did Harry start choosing his line-up a week in advance?). The problem for the fans hadn't been the likely team, it had been the price of admission. The club's misjudgement was reflected in the fact that a paltry 11,908 turned up to watch Paul Kitson score the only goal of the first leg against the Finnish outfit, as the Hammers' early superiority diminished in the afternoon heat. It was adjudged to have been down to a lack of fitness (the players had only just returned for pre-season training) but I felt the players needed time to mentally tune in as well.

Far more entertaining was the Jokerit coach, Pasi Rautiainen, in the press conference afterwards. 'Yes, we are halfway through our league season and so we have been playing while West Ham have been drinking beer. I could tell in the second half they were f***ing knackered! Did I say something funny? But, no, I do not think we will go through, otherwise we will all need doping tests! This competition is just about attracting interest in our players. When somebody makes a good offer, I carry our man to the airport!'

We travelled to Helsinki for the second leg and even though there were worrying signs of the team missing the imagination of Berkovic as they fell behind to a first-half goal, Frank Lampard scored from a short free kick late on to secure a 2–1 aggregate win and save our blushes. Di Canio looked as if he was in real trouble by waving his arms about when he went down and being carried off injured, but he looked at me as if I was asking a stupid question when I enquired afterwards as to whether his leg was badly hurt. 'It's OK, really,' he insisted, leaving me wondering what all the histrionics were about.

Lampard was on target again (from a full 35 yards!) in the next match at home to Dutch outfit Heerenveen, but this time a meagre 7,485 bothered to offer their support where maximum admission prices were charged once again. I'd have thought the Jokerit game would have prompted a re-think – not only would they have made more money through having twice as many people paying less per ticket, but a packed house would have generated the atmosphere needed to help the players lift the tempo. Fans would have been entitled to think the club had scored an own goal because the poor atmosphere hardly improved the team's chances of making progress: another slender 1–0 first-leg lead had to be settled for. But new signing Paulo Wanchope *Watson* – as the Dutch press office decided to name him for reasons best known to themselves – had the 'elementary' task of scoring the only goal in Heerenveen to send the Hammers through to the final against French league leaders Metz. Thankfully, the club acknowledged the lessons of the previous two rounds and drastically reduced admission prices, being rewarded with a capacity crowd. Sadly, a goal from French striker Louis Saha and a missed penalty by Frank Lampard seemed to signal the end of the European road yet, against all the odds, the Hammers triumphed 3–1 in France two weeks later to qualify for the UEFA Cup for the first time in the club's history.

The Intertoto Cup had been much-maligned since its inception in the early '90s but in reality the competition should simply be viewed as the preliminary rounds of the UEFA Cup. There's no difference, at the end of the day. If you keep winning you keep playing. At least the Hammers had got three trips into Europe by the end of August and, for the fans, that's exactly what it's all about.

Despite suffering the disappointment of losing the magazine editorship – which had been a real labour of love over the past five years – I was delighted to have the opportunity to travel with my friends on these

European excursions. I'm still a fan, after all, although I will admit to seriously questioning my loyalty at the time of leaving *HNM*. Fans support their club through thick and thin but who are they really investing their faith in? It's certainly not the directors. Most of them nowadays are businessmen with no real interest in the sport itself. They get it in the neck when they put the ticket prices up and rarely give the manager enough to spend in the transfer market. They come and go without half of us taking a blind bit of notice.

It's not the management or playing staff either. The turnover in football is greater than ever and there's little loyalty shown to the fans in return. The club crest or badge is used to signify what we are devoted to, but what does it really represent? At least fans at Upton Park can claim some kind of allegiance to a particular footballing philosophy, although there's no guarantee the product will provide what it says on the tin. And while we feel at home within the Boleyn Ground, plenty of other clubs have moved to new stadiums without losing their support.

Ultimately, it's the clansmanship that we experience with our fellow faithful – but that would feel the same if we were supporting that 'orrible lot from N17. See, there I go, getting embroiled in petty, and some would say childish, rivalries. There's a good argument for claiming that to succumb to the attraction of football is to volunteer for a permanently arrested state of development. It certainly makes you cry at times.

But unless I'm told my presence isn't required, I'm sure I'll keep going back to Upton Park. It's been a privilege and a pleasure to have worked with West Ham United and there are some very genuine people involved with the club. Standing in the Heerenveen corridor outside the Hammers' dressing-room after the game on 4 August, there was the familiar sight of photographer Steve Bacon helping kit-man Eddie Gillam with the team's gear. Goalkeeping coach Les Sealey was rounding the boys up, Frank Lampard Snr was still friendliness personified to all the usual faces on the periphery, such as mine, and Harry Redknapp was holding court in the corner, discussing all things West Ham with the press. There's an indefinable spirit there and, while that remains, we'll continue to be lured by its magic. Incredibly, some people still ask me who I support. The answer, of course, is always the same: whoever's playing Spurs today . . .